Elizabeth R. Hayes
The Pragmatics of Perception and Cognition
in MT Jeremiah 1:1–6:30

Beihefte zur Zeitschrift für die alttestamentliche Wissenschaft

Herausgegeben von
John Barton · Reinhard G. Kratz
Choon-Leong Seow · Markus Witte

Band 380

Walter de Gruyter · Berlin · New York

Elizabeth R. Hayes

The Pragmatics of Perception and Cognition in MT Jeremiah 1:1–6:30

A Cognitive Linguistics Approach

W
DE
G

Walter de Gruyter · Berlin · New York

∞ Printed on acid-free paper which falls within the guidelines of the ANSI
to ensure permanence and durability.

ISBN 978-3-11-020229-8
ISSN 0934-2575

Library of Congress Cataloging-in-Publication Data

Hayes, Elizabeth R. (Elizabeth Russell), 1952–
    The pragmatics of perseption and cognition in MT Jeremiah 1:1–6:30 :
a cognitive linguistics approach / Elizabeth R. Hayes.
        p. cm. – (Beihefte zur Zeitschrift für die alttestamentliche Wissenschaft ;
Bd. 380)
    Includes bibliographical references and index.
    ISBN 978-3-11-020229-8 (23 × 15,5 cm, clothbound : alk. paper)
    1. Bible. O. T. Jeremiah I, 1–VI, 30 – Criticism, textual.   2. Bible. O. T.
Jeremiah I, 1–VI, 30 – Language, style.   3. Bible. O. T. Jeremiah I, 1–VI, 30
– Grammar.   4. Cognitive grammar.   I. Title.
    BS1525.52.H39   2008
    224'.2066–dc22

                                                                    2008026315

Bibliographic information published by the Deutsche Nationalbibliothek

The Deutsche Nationalbibliothek lists this publication in the Deutsche Nationalbibliografie;
detailed bibliographic data are available in the Internet at http://dnb.d-nb.de.

Preface

This volume began as doctoral thesis, written at Oxford University. Prof. H.G.M. Williamson, my thesis supervisor, provided patient encouragement, wise counsel and an unsurpassed eye for detail. His sense of timing is impeccable, and I have grown to respect the phrase '...just one or two little things'. I am more than grateful for his generosity and support.

The Theology Faculty in Oxford offered many opportunities for academic development. Professor John Barton fostered connections through the Oxford-Bonn theological exchange and the Oxford-Leiden exchange. Writing papers and attending these events have been formative experiences, and the friendships that have grown in the process are priceless.

The input of three other mentors has been important, as well. Dr. Darrell Hobson, professor of OT, nurtured a love of Biblical Hebrew and respect for academic integrity during my undergraduate years at Northwest University, Kirkland, WA. Dr. Pamela Scalise and Dr. Charles Scalise of Fuller Seminary have been unceasingly supportive, and their time and attention during my student and graduate assistant days has been highly prized.

Presenting a first paper at the Northwest section of the Society of Biblical Literature opened the door for this research project. Ehud ben Zvi provided gentle encouragement, which has fostered both academic progress and collegial contacts, The SBL Linguistics and Biblical Hebrew section has been a source of valuable information for this volume. Particular thanks go to Cynthia Miller, who was willing to engage in an extended e-mail dialogue.

Several linguists have taken time to answer questions and share information. Among these are: Eep Talstra, whose guided tour through his BH computational linguistics project at Free University, Amsterdam added depth to this thesis, Ron Langacker, from UC San Diego, who engaged in a very helpful e-mail dialogue regarding cognitive grammar, and Gilles Fauconnier, whose work in the area of cognitive science provides substantial undergirding for the ideas in this volume. Thanks also to Eve Sweetser for critiquing the earlier manuscript. Finally, I am most grateful to Dr. David Cram of Jesus College, Oxford, who read an early chapter draft and offered many helpful comments.

Special thanks are due to Oxford friends, including Helen Kraus, Patricia Terrell and Betsy Livingstone. I am grateful to long-time Seattle friend Carrell Quinn and to my new friend Linda Swanberg, whose son Shane inspires me to run the race with confidence.

I would like to thank the editors of the series *Beihefte zur Zeitschrift für die alttestmentliche Wissenschaft*, Prof. John Barton, Prof. Reinhard G. Kratz, Prof. Choon-Leong Seow and Prof. Markus Witte, for accepting this volume for publication. The transformation from thesis to volume has been an adventure, indeed. Thank you also to Albrecht Döhnert for helping this volume to find a home at de Gruyter.

It is a delight to acknowledge the efforts of two excellent friends, who proof-read the manuscript and provided valuable comments: Diana Atkinson and Beth Elness-Hanson. Your kindness and generosity are treasured, indeed. A special thank you goes to Ryan Hayes for re-checking the final proofs. Additionally, Sabina Dabrowski of de Gruyter has provided timely advice and encouragement during the editing process. All remaining infelicities in the text are mine alone.

Endless thanks go to my husband, Glenn, our children, Becky, Jeremy, Ryan, Robin, and their loves: Jay, Narina, and Aaron. Their antics never cease to amaze and their love is the light of my heart. For all of their goodness and patience, I dedicate this book to my family.

Table of Contents

Table of Figures

Abbreviations

ASTI	*Annual of the Scandinavian Theological Institute*
BHRG	Biblical Hebrew Reference Grammar
BO	*Bibliotheca Orientalis*
BZAW	Beihefte zur Zeitschrift für die alttestamentliche Wissenschaft
CBQ	*Catholic Biblical Quarterly*
CL	*Cognitive Linguistics*
ETL	*Ephemerides Theologicae Lovaniensis*
GKC	Gesenius' Hebrew Grammar
HTR	*Harvard Theological Review*
HCL	*Hebrew Computational Linguistics*
HS	*Hebrew Studies*
ICC	International Critical Commentary
JM	Grammar of Biblical Hebrew
JA	*Journal Asiatique*
JBL	*Journal of Biblical Literature*
JBLMS	Journal of Biblical Literature Monograph Series
JL	*Journal of Linguistics*
JNSL	*Journal of Northwest Semitic Languages*
JP	*Journal of Pragmatics*
JSS	*Journal of Semitic Studies*
JTTL	*Journal of Translation and Text Linguistics*
OS	*Oudtestamentische Studiën*
SBL	Society of Biblical Literature
SLCS	Studies in Language Companion Series
VT	*Vetus Testamentum*
VT Sup	Vetus Testamentum Supplement Series
WBC	Word Biblical Commentary
ZAH	*Zeitschrift für Althebraistik*
ZAW	*Zeitschrift für die Alttestamentliche Wissenschaft*
ZP	*Zeitschrift für Phonetik*

Clause Tag Conventions

Wayyiqtol-S	waw-consecutive imperfect with explicit subject
Wayyiqtol-0	waw-consecutive imperfect without explicit subject
W-*Qatal*	waw-consecutive perfect
Yiqtol	imperfect
Qatal	perfect
Impv	imperative
Qotel	participle (only tagged when used verbally)
Qetol	infinitive construct
Qatol	infinitive absolute
NmCl	nominal clause
PrepP	prepositional phrase
W	waw
X	sentence constituent occurring prior to the verb, other than:
S	subject
O	object

Due to space constraints the clause tag column only contains tags for clause constituents that contribute to focus. Consequently, clauses are tagged for verbal forms and for constituents that occur prior to the verb. (There may be occasional exceptions.)

Mental Spaces Conventions (MSC)

Base initial space in a mental spaces cognitive construction

M   generic mental space, (added superscript indicates character)

C   Character's Perspective – marked for primary characters

> C^1 – The LORD
> C^2 – Jeremiah
> C^3 – Jerusalem

P   Perception space: Character's Perspective
      (based upon terms of perception and cognition)

N   Narrative space or domain: Narrator's Reality
      (based upon narrative text-type; narrative starting from wayyiqtol)

      N1: anonymous narrator
      N^2: Jeremiah as narrator
      N^3: Jeremiah as narrator of embedded space that includes the
      Complex Speaker and Jerusalem as interlocutors.

Q   Quotation space or domain: Character's Reality
      (based upon discursive text-type; direct speech starting from quotation)

D   Discursive space or domain: Character's Reality
      (based upon discursive text-type; starting from yiqtol in narrative text)

Subspaces are generated recursively, and include spaces opened by terms and constructions from the semantic fields of deixis, speech and perception, epistemic and deontic modality, hypotheticals, and interrogatives, among others

1. Text Dynamics: An Integrative Approach

The Hatter opened his eyes on hearing this; but all he said was
"Why is a raven like a writing desk?"

~ Lewis Carroll[1]

During the second half of the twentieth century, biblical studies began to witness the rise and confluence of two elements as seemingly disparate as Carroll's raven and writing desk. The first has been a movement away from diachronically oriented historical-critical inquiries and toward synchronically oriented linguistic and literary interpretations of biblical texts.[2] The second has been the rapid and pervasive advance of technology, specifically within the area of computers and text processing, which has contributed to formal, structural and distributional analyses of biblical text. While these movements are artistic on the one hand, and scientific on the other, are they indeed ravens and writing desks?

At minimum, these movements have prompted fresh approaches to biblical text and its relationships with its originators and readers.[3] Text

---

1   Originally, no answer was expected for this riddle, although Carroll did devise one as an afterthought. Lewis Carroll and Hugh Haughton, *Alice's Adventures in Wonderland*, Centenary ed., Penguin Classics (London: Penguin, 1998), 311, n. 314.

2   The beginnings of this movement were seen with the application of the New Criticism, originally utilised for the study of English literary texts, to the study of biblical texts. For a short history see J. Cheryl Exum and David J. A. Clines, *The New Literary Criticism and the Hebrew Bible*, JSOT Sup 143 (Sheffield: JSOT Press, 1993), 11-26. For application of the literary approach to BH text see Robert Alter and Frank Kermode, *The Literary Guide to the Bible* (Cambridge, Mass: Belknap Press of Harvard University Press, 1987); Adele Berlin, *Poetics and Interpretation of Biblical Narrative*, Bible and Literature Series, 9 (Sheffield: Almond Press, 1983); Meir Sternberg, *The Poetics of Biblical Narrative: Ideological Literature and the Drama of Reading*, Indiana Studies in Biblical Literature (Bloomington, Ind: Indiana University Press, 1987). For the interrelationship between interpretive approaches and theology see John Barton, *Reading the Old Testament: Method in Biblical Study* (London: Darton Longman & Todd, 1984); S. E. Gillingham, *One Bible, Many Voices: Different Approaches to Biblical Studies* (London: SPCK, 1998); Robert Morgan and John Barton, *Biblical Interpretation* (Oxford: Oxford University Press, 1988).

3   The debate between synchronic and diachronic approaches to the text of the Hebrew Bible is explored in J. C. de Moor, ed., *Synchronic or Diachronic? A Debate on Method in Old Testament Exegesis*, Oudtestamentische Studiën 34 (Leiden: Brill, 1995). Van der Wal proposes a synchronic reading of MT Jeremiah in A. J. O. van der Wal, "Toward

dynamics (TD) is such an approach. TD is a cognitively oriented, linguistics-based approach to biblical text that is characterised by its panchronic and integrative nature.[4] As such, this approach seeks to combine insights gained from analyses of the biblical text at the syntactic, semantic and pragmatic levels with information derived from historical and cultural studies, focusing upon "blocks of material that are larger than the sentence."[5] This exploration into the dynamics of biblical text gives special attention to features that contribute to text segmentation and textual unity, as well as to the manner in which these features affect meaning construction.[6]

The term *dynamics* in the heuristic term TD refers to the nature of the text as a means of human communication, which is an active, fluid and dynamic process. From this perspective, the text is not a mere artefact, but rather it acts as a focal link between present-day readers and hearers and the originators of the text. While the contexts and cultures of the author/speaker and various groups of hearers/readers are seemingly quite disparate when an ancient text is involved, the cognitive processes involved in human communication provide many points of connection between the originator of the ancient text and its readers. Additionally, the high incidence of reported speech that is attributed to characters within prophetic text highlights the nature of the human communicative process. To a certain extent, such passages yield to conversational analysis and the concepts that are integral to speech act theory. However, speech act theory alone is insufficient to deal with the narrative portions of the text. The TD approach draws from three cognitive theories in order to account for the variety of information in the text: cognitive science and cognitive linguistics provide the theoretical underpinnings, and cognitive grammar enriches the findings of Biblical Hebrew grammarians.

Three presuppositions are fundamental to the TD approach. First, the text is the focal point of inquiry. Secondly, the text is the product of

---

a Synchronic Analysis of the Masoretic Text of the Book of Jeremiah," in *Reading the Book of Jeremiah: A Search for Coherence*, ed. Martin Kessler (Winona Lake, Ind: Eisenbrauns, 2004), 13-23.

4   The term *panchronic* is used to describe a method that is conscious of both the diachronic and synchronic aspects of biblical text and seeks to incorporate historical insights within the exploration of a text. See John A. Cook, "The Hebrew Verb: A Grammaticalization Approach," *ZAH* 14 (2001), 117-144.

5   Walter Ray Bodine, *Discourse Analysis of Biblical Literature: What It Is and What It Offers*, Semeia Studies (Atlanta: Scholars Press, 1995), 1.

6   Meaning construction is a process that writer and reader share. For the writer, this occurs as part of the creative process, while for the reader, meaning construction is cued by product of the creative process, the text.

a dynamic relationship between language users and language. Finally, the process of text analysis and interpretation involves a similar, dynamic relationship between language users and language. The text, then, stands as a focal link between the language, context and culture of the text producer(s) and the languages, contexts and cultures of a wide array of text consumers.[7] Thus, while this method is not intended to solve historical-critical quandaries, it does seek to relate the text both to its original audience and to its modern audiences as well.

Because these presuppositions are broad, the cognitive sciences notion of *conceptual blending* has been chosen as the integrative principle behind a TD approach. Conceptual blending is a cognitive mechanism by which conceptual information from various input spaces is projected into a space that is called the blend.[8] Conceptual blending is at the root of a wide array of cognitive processes, and thus, is available for multiple aspects of text analysis and integration, such as mapping the syntax-semantics interface; establishing textual boundaries and connections; incorporating extra-textual knowledge with textual information; and providing a basis for understanding metaphor. Additionally, insights from cognitive linguistics and cognitive grammar enrich a TD approach when used to re-examine grammatical categories and terminology from a cognitive perspective.[9]

However, before introducing the TD method and the analysis of Jeremiah 1.1-6.30, a short accounting of recent linguistic, literary and technological research is in order. This will be followed by an introduction to the theory and methodology utilised by a TD approach, and by a short discussion regarding the strengths and limitations of the approach.

---

7   In other words, the text acts as a material anchor for complex projections. Gilles Fauconnier and Mark Turner, *The Way We Think: Conceptual Blending and the Mind's Hidden Complexities* (New York: Basic Books, 2002), 211.

8   As Fauconnier suggests, there may be "many different and sometimes clashing inputs into a single blended space." Ibid., 329.

9   Ronald W. Langacker, *Foundations of Cognitive Grammar* (Bloomington, Ind: Indiana University Linguistics Club, 1983); idem, *Foundations of Cognitive Grammar*, vol. 1 (Stanford: SUP, 1987); idem, *Concept, Image, and Symbol: The Cognitive Basis of Grammar*, 2nd ed., Cognitive Linguistics Research; 1 (Berlin: Mouton de Gruyter, 2002).

A. Linguistic, Literary and Technological Approaches to BH Text

Recent linguistic, literary and technological research demonstrates significant theoretical and methodological shifts. The following sections detail the contributions of several scholars in each of these areas.

1. Theoretical Shift: The Sentence and Beyond

Scholars such as Robert Longacre, Peter Cotterell, Max Turner, Cynthia Miller, Kirk Lowery and Adele Berlin are representative of those who have explored BH at levels above the sentence and who have incorporated insights from other areas of linguistics, such as pragmatics, into their description and analyses of texts.[10]

Robert Longacre's discourse analysis approach to biblical text was influenced by F. I. Andersen, who was the first to bring together Pike's tagmeme theory and BH text.[11] Beginning with the assertion that "… language is language only in context", Longacre clarifies a programme for work in the area of discourse analysis (text linguistics).[12] His list of tasks requiring a discourse analysis approach over and against a sentence grammar approach includes features such as, "… definitivization

---

10   Berlin, *A. Berlin, Poetics*; Adele Berlin, *The Dynamics of Biblical Parallelism* (Bloomington, Ind: Indiana University Press, 1985); Peter Cotterell and Max Turner, *Linguistics and Biblical Interpretation* (London: SPCK, 1989); Jean-Marc Heimerdinger, *Topic, Focus and Foreground in Ancient Hebrew Narratives*, JSOT Sup 295 (Sheffield: Sheffield Academic Press, 1999); Robert E. Longacre, *Joseph: A Story of Divine Providence: A Text Theoretical and Textlinguistic Analysis of Genesis 37 and 39-48* (Winona Lake, Ind: Eisenbrauns, 1989); Kirk Lowery, "Theoretical Foundations of Hebrew Discourse Grammar," in *Discourse Analysis of Biblical Literature: What It Is and What It Offers*, ed. Walter Ray Bodine (Atlanta: Scholar's Press, 1995), 103-130; Cynthia L. Miller, *The Representation of Speech in Biblical Hebrew Narrative: A Linguistic Analysis*, HSM (Winona Lake, Ind: Eisenbrauns, 2003).

11   Francis I. Andersen, *The Hebrew Verbless Clause in the Pentateuch*, JBLMS 14 (Nashville: Published for the Society of Biblical Literature by Abingdon Press, 1970). Both of these scholars follow a functional approach to BH text, as opposed to a formalist, theoretically motivated approach such as the Chomskyan, generative approach. C. H. J. van der Merwe, "Some Recent Trends in Biblical Hebrew Linguistics: A Few Pointers Towards a More Comprehensive Model of Language Use," *HS* 44 (2003), 7-24 (17).

12   Robert E. Longacre, *The Grammar of Discourse*, Topics in Language and Linguistics (New York: Plenum, 1983).

and the use of deictics; verb tense, aspect, and mode; word order phenomena; sequence signals and conjunctions."[13]

Three aspects of Longacre's work are pertinent to the discussion of the TD approach to BH. First, Longacre's model functions at the discourse level.[14] Secondly, Longacre's model is hierarchically structured. The largest unit is a macrostructure. The macrostructure may be macro-segmented and micro-segmented by various text-internal features such as verbal forms, or by thematic content. Finally, the focus of his work has been in the area of narrative discourse. His descriptive model includes discussion of text-type categories such as narrative, procedural, hortatory and expository, with the later addition of predictive-procedural and hortatory-judicial. The later additions reflect his desire to explore a text-type other than narrative.[15]

Peter Cotterell and Max Turner incorporate insights from the study of linguistics to the process of biblical interpretation. They define the term discourse as "any coherent stretch of language."[16] Coherence involves topic continuity, grammatical structure and meaning. Cotterell and Turner claim that understanding discourse as a communication event necessarily involves not only syntax and semantics but pragmatics as well. They present a set of six components that are features of a discourse: the set of descriptions referred to; the set of propositions included; the set of actual sentences used; the set of thematic nets; the net of time reference; and the reference-relation diagram.[17] Each of these categories is relevant for the TD approach.[18]

---

13 Bodine notes that these items reflect problem areas in Hebrew studies. Bodine, *Discourse Analysis*, 11. The list also includes pronominalisation; the use of locative and temporal expressions; the use of adverbial clauses; variations in reported speech; and variation in the length of syntactical units. Longacre, *Grammar*, xv.

14 See Robert E. Longacre, "The Paragraph as a Grammatical Unit," in *Syntax and Semantics*, ed. Talmy Givon (New York: Academic Press, 1979), 115-134. See also Robert De Beaugrande and Wolfgang U. Dressler, *Introduction to Text Linguistics*, Longman Linguistics Library 26 (London: Longman, 1981); Joseph Evans Grimes, *The Thread of Discourse*, Janua Linguarum. Series Minor; 207 (The Hague: Mouton, 1975).

15 Robert E. Longacre, "Building for the Worship of God: Exodus 25:1-30," in *Discourse Analysis of Biblical Literature: What It Is and What It Offers*, ed. W. R. Bodine, Semeia Studies (Atlanta: Scholars Press, 1995), 21-49.

16 Cotterell and Turner, *Linguistics*, 230.

17 Cotterell and Turner are quoting from C. F. Rieser, "On the Development of Text Grammar," in *Current Trends in Text Linguistics*, ed. Wolfgang U. Dressler (Berlin: de Gruyter, 1978), 13. In turn, Rieser is quoting J. S. Petofi, "Studies in Text Grammar," in *Studies in Text Grammar*, eds J. S. Petofi and H. Rieser (Dordrecht: Reidel, 1973).

18 The set of descriptions intersects with the information structure category *topic*, the set of propositions intersects with the information structure category *focus*, the set of actual sentences represents the pragmatic aspect, the set of thematic nets correlates

Cotterell and Turner encourage interpreters to move beyond the level of the sentence and they create an understanding of text that is not genre-limited. In addition, they stress the necessity of incorporating pragmatics, or language in use, with syntax and semantics in textual processing and propose a set of features for assessing textual cohesion.

The work of Adele Berlin includes detailed studies of both narrative and poetic texts. Although Berlin claims, "I am not a linguist nor a disciple of linguists,"[19] her approach to biblical parallelism reflects the understanding of one who is cognisant of structuralist, psycholinguistic and text linguistic approaches, as well as with the poetic theory of Roman Jakobson as well.[20]

Berlin explains the concept of biblical parallelism by elaborating upon Jakobson's statement, "The poetic function projects the principle of equivalence from the axis of selection into the axis of combination."[21] In other words, parallelism moves equivalence from the realm of the selection (paradigmatic) to the realm of the created sentence (syntagmatic).[22] In addition to parallelism at the line level, this type of relationship may be discerned at levels smaller than the line (words, phrases and sounds), and conversely, may be discerned within larger segments of the text.[23] When the understanding of parallelism is enlarged in this way, new possibilities for grasping the text arise.[24]

Berlin makes a second contribution to the understanding of parallelism, which also has to do with the concept of poetic function. Since the days of Bishop Lowth, there has been a tendency to associate parallelism with poetry.[25] Berlin explores Kugel's thesis that there is not a

---

with the concept of *semantic domain* and the net of time reference correlates with the category of *temporal deixis*. The reference-relation diagram is a species of mental spaces mapping. These issues are introduced in the following chapter.

19   Berlin, *Dynamics*, ix.

20   Roman Jakobson, "Linguistics and Poetics," in *Style and Language*, ed. Thomas Albert Sebeok (Bloomington: 1960), 350-377; idem, "Poetry of Grammar and Grammar of Poetry," *Lingua* 21 (1968), 597-609.

21   Jakobson, "Linguistics and Poetics," 358.

22   Berlin, *Dynamics*, 7.

23   An example of this is the repetition of the roots קוֹל and שׁמע as an *inclusio* in Jeremiah 3.21 and 3.25. The two occurrences are in different syntactical constructions, yet form an interesting set of bookends for the section.

24   For example, see van der Wal, "Toward a Synchronic Analysis of the Masoretic Text of the Book of Jeremiah."

25   However, it is worthwhile to remember that Lowth's observations regarding parallelism are the product of his study of prophetic literature. In Lecture 19, Lowth states, "In order the more clearly to evince this point, I shall endeavour to illustrate the Hebrew parallelism according to its different species, first by examples taken from those books commonly allowed to be poetical, and afterwards by correspondent examples taken from the prophets." Robert Lowth, *Lectures on the Sacred Poetry*

strict bifurcation between prose and poetry in BH, but rather a continuum exists that moves from prose to elevated style.[26] She goes on to
explain that elevated style comprises both terseness and parallelism,
and that the presence of poetry is discerned by observing text for the
predominance of these two factors. For Berlin, parallelism functions as
the "constructive principle on which a poem is built."[27] Berlin's insights
into the nature of parallelism are helpful when approaching prophetic
text, which contains a variety of different constructive principles.[28]

Finally, Berlin presents an overview of scholarship that links linguistics with BH parallelism.[29] She notes that syntactic analysis is the
unifying factor for these studies, and that this analysis may take place
at either a surface structure or a deep structure level.[30] Berlin's examination of parallelism contributes to the TD approach in several ways.
First, she opens the door for the discovery of parallelism within units of
text both smaller and larger than the sentence. This stretches the possibility of discovering thematic links within a large span of text due to
the presence of parallel structures. Second, she clarifies the nature of
poetic function by including both terseness and parallelism and adds to
these the concept of predominance as a diagnostic criterion. Finally, she

---

of the Hebrews, vol. 1 (London: Routledge/Thoemmes Press, 1995), 34. Watson is
equally comprehensive in his approach. See Wilfred G. E. Watson, Classical Hebrew
Poetry: A Guide to Its Techniques, 2nd ed., JSOT Sup 26 (Sheffield: JSOT Press, 1986);
idem, Traditional Techniques in Classical Hebrew Verse, JSOT Sup 170 (Sheffield: Sheffield Academic Press, 1994).

26   Berlin, Dynamics, 5.

27   Ibid., 6.

28   In addition, these insights are important to the Jeremiah text, as they offer an option
to the strict prose-poetry bifurcation within source-critical arguments, by which
some have sought to isolate the ipsissima verba of Jeremiah. See "Poetry and Prose,"
in Jack R. Lundbom, Jeremiah 1-20, The Anchor Bible, vol. 21A, (New York: Doubleday, 1999), 63-67. For further discussion, see William L. Holladay, "Prototype and
Copies: A New Approach to the Poetry-Prose Problem in the Book of Jeremiah," JBL
79, 351-367. For a technical discussion regarding the differences between prose and
poetry in BH see Johannes Cornelis de Moor and Wilfred G. E. Watson, Verse in Ancient near Eastern Prose, Alter Orient und Altes Testament (Neukirchen-Vluyn: Verlag
Butzon und Bercker, 1993), x-xvii.

29   In this regard, see Stephen A. Geller, Parallelism in Early Biblical Poetry, Harvard
Semitic Monographs, No. 20 (Missoula: Scholars Press, 1979); idem, "The Dynamics
of Parallel Verse," HTR 75 (1982), 35-56; idem, "Through Windows and Mirrors into
the Hebrew Bible: History, Literature and Language in the Study of Text," in A Sense
of Text (Winona Lake, Ind: Eisenbrauns, 1982), 3-40; Edward L. Greenstein, "How
Does Parallelism Mean?" in A Sense of Text (Winona Lake, Ind.: Eisenbrauns, 1982),
41-70; Dennis Pardee, Ugaritic and Hebrew Poetic Parallelism: A Trial Cut ('Nt I and
Proverbs 2), VT Sup 39 (Leiden: Brill, 1988); Dennis Pardee and S. David Sperling,
Handbook of Ancient Hebrew Letters: A Study Edition, Sources for Biblical Study; No. 15
(Chico, CA: Scholars Press, 1982).

30   Berlin, Dynamics, 19.

notes that linguistic studies of parallelism have engaged in syntactic studies at both the deep and surface levels of the text. These points allow poetry to be analysed using some of the same criteria as prose, which opens the way to a more unified description and analysis of a multi-genred text such as Jeremiah.

Cynthia Miller has undertaken a linguistic analysis of reported speech in BH narrative. Her primary focus is the application of the theory and method of modern linguistics "…to a description and analysis of the various syntactic devices for reporting speech in Biblical Hebrew narrative." Miller then explains the distribution and significance of these devices by making reference to their place "…within the enclosing narrative."[31] Thus, while not using an overt text linguistics approach, Miller nonetheless examines text at a level beyond the sentence.

Miller discusses the pragmatics involved when one context of speaking reports another context of speaking, thus introducing the idea that all reported speech is metapragmatic. This insight is particularly relevant to prophetic text such as Jeremiah, because reported speech is a prominent feature of these texts.

Finally, a word must be said regarding the thoroughgoing nature of Miller's research. In the course of her research, Miller analysed over 4,500 tokens of reported speech in Genesis-II Kings.[32] Her work demonstrates a tendency to go beyond the sentence, to incorporate insights not only from syntax and semantics, but from pragmatics as well, and to approach the interpretive task with scientific rigour. However, the term *computer* is conspicuously absent from Miller's description and analysis.

2.   Methodological Shift: Computers and Biblical Hebrew Text

During the last twenty-five years, the computer has taken over the role of the writing desk for many scholars. From simple searching to complex linguistic study, the computer opens a wide range of possibilities for study and analysis. Eep Talstra, C.H. van der Merwe, John H. Sailhamer, and A. E. den exter Blokland are some of the of the scholars who have made significant contributions to the development of tech-

---

31   Miller, *Representation*, 4.
32   Ibid., 19.

nology as a means of furthering linguistic research into the complexities of BH.[33]

In his article, "Recent Trends in the Linguistic Description of Old Hebrew," van der Merwe provides a survey of three trends in the field of linguistics and Old Hebrew (OH), the first of which is "...the computerized compilation of taxonomies of linguistic constructions – with special reference to the role of the linguistic frameworks that are used in the databases."[34] He then goes on to provide a synopsis of the working theories of several scholars, including W. Richter, W. Eckhardt, W. Gross, E. Talstra, L. J. De Regt and K. Lowery. As van der Merwe observes, Richter's work has been foundational in providing a theoretical framework regarding morphology and syntax of OH, while it has been the task of the others to make use of that framework by developing computer programmes for analysis of OH text. He then contrasts Talstra's theory with that of Lowery, noting that Talstra's theory involves a "...strict surface level structuralist approach," while Lowery adopts a functional approach that allows for the intersection of syntax, semantics and pragmatics.[35]

In practical terms, this contrast is significant for the TD approach. On the one hand, Talstra's clause hierarchy notational system provides a comprehensive system for tracking a close analysis of the surface structure of BH texts, which is beneficial in that it accounts for the greatest amount of distributional data. On the other hand, Lowery's theory also includes the functional aspects of semantics and pragmatics for the analysis of text, which moves the discussion towards language

---

33　A. T. den exter Blokland, *In Search of Text Syntax: Towards a Syntactic Text-Segmentation Model for Biblical Hebrew* (Amsterdam: VU Press, 1995); Ferenc Postma, E. Talstra and M. Vervenne, *Exodus: Materials in Automatic Text Processing*, Instrumenta Biblica 1 (Amsterdam: VU Boekhandl, 1983), 19; John Sailhamer, "A Database Approach to the Analysis of Hebrew Narrative," *MAARAV* 5-6 (1990), 319-335; E. Talstra, "Text Grammar and the Hebrew Bible I: Elements of a Theory," *BO* 35 (1978), 169-174; idem, "Text Grammar and the Hebrew Bible II: Syntax and Semantics," *BO* 39 (1982), 26-38; idem, "Toward a Distributional Definition of Clauses in Biblical Hebrew," *ETL* 63 (1987), 95-105; idem, "Text Grammar and Biblical Hebrew: The Viewpoint of Wolfgang Schneider," *JTTL* 5 (1992), 296-297; C. H. J. van der Merwe, "Recent Trends in the Description of Old Hebrew," *JNSL* 15 (1989), 217-241. Also of interest are C. Hardmeier and E. Talstra, "Sprachgestalt und Sinngehalt: Wege zu neuen Instrumenten der Computergestützen Textwahrnehmung," *ZAW* 101 (1989), 408-428; Emmanuel Tov, "Computer Assisted Research of the Greek and Hebrew Bible," in *Computer Assisted Analysis of Biblical Hebrew Text*, ed. E. Talstra (Amsterdam: VU Press, 1989), 87-118.

34　van der Merwe, "Some Recent Trends," 217.

35　Ibid., 229.

as a means of human communication.[36] Because of this, the TD approach begins with a close tracking of the text by a notational system similar to Talstra's and includes an analysis of semantic and pragmatic aspects of the text as well.[37]

The work of A. F. den exter Blokland illustrates both the capabilities and the complexities generated by a computational analysis of BH text. Utilising a computer analysis, den exter Blokland sets forth a hierarchical description of I Kings 1 and 2. His method is a bottom-up processing of the text, in which he joins clauses in a manner determined by various surface structure characteristics, such as verb forms and reference tracking.[38] This is an eleven-step process, resulting in an eleven-stage hierarchy of segmentation. He demonstrates that it is possible to turn this analysis on its head, and reading the results from the top down, he applies this reversible method to a comparison with an analysis by Longacre.[39] This method is a thorough syntactic description of the text at hand, and den exter Blockland's compilation of features, which tend to join units of text at given levels in the hierarchy, bears attention for a TD approach.

Computer assisted analysis provides a significant tool for some of the analytical tasks required by a TD approach to BH prophetic text. It is particularly useful for examining the text at levels higher than the sentence, while giving attention to surface level features such as morphology and syntax. A thorough description and analysis at this level provides the basis for examining semantic features, which in turn play into pragmatic features, such as poetic function.

Technology for the morphological analysis of BH is widely available.[40] However, the complexities of clause and sentence level syntactic analysis require a sizeable database and the ability to access and manipulate the data by means of programming languages.[41] At the time of

---

36   Thanks are due to Kirk Lowery, who provided the present author with a copy of "Jona 1 – Clause Hierarchy According to Eep Talstra", (Werkgroep Informatica, Vrije Universiteit, Amsterdam), as well as many helpful remarks.

37   Thanks are due to Eep Talstra, who has generously provided database information, and a personal explanation of the computational linguistics project at VU, Amsterdam.

38   Blokland, *Search*, 152-154.

39   His critique of Longacre is rather harsh, and perhaps unjustified, given the differences in approach. Ibid., 293.

40   For example, the Logos Library System includes a morphologically tagged version of the *Biblia Hebraica*. *Logos Library System* (Logos Research Systems, Inc.), 1997. Other widely available programmes are Bible Works and Bible Windows.

41   The history of computing and the history of computer-assisted analysis of Biblical Hebrew texts are intertwined. Currently it is possible to perform many complex functions with personal computers, networks and the Internet. These are recent de-

this writing, the release of the *Stuttgart Electronic Study Bible* has expanded the horizons by making word, phrase and clause information accessible to Libronix users. Although the current search engine is unable to exploit all data, this a significant step forward.[42]

B. Text Dynamics: Theory and Method

As previously mentioned, TD is a cognitively-oriented, linguistics-based approach to Biblical Hebrew text, which is characterised by its panchronic and integrative nature. Three presuppositions are basic for the TD approach: the text is the focal point of inquiry; the text is the product of the dynamic relationship between language users and language; and the reading process involves a similar, dynamic relationship between language users and language. From a cognitive perspective, the text stands is a material anchor between the text producer(s) and the text consumer(s).

1. The Scope of the Task

Narrative text has been the primary field of study for the top-down discourse analyst, the bottom-up computational linguist and the determined distributional analyst as well.[43] Notably, prophetic literature

---

velopments. The shift from large mainframe computers, replete with their massive air-conditioned rooms, to desk top computers with similar capabilities is reflected in E. Talstra, *Computer Assisted Analysis of Biblical Texts: Papers Read at the Workshop on the Occasion of the Tenth Anniversary of the Werkgroep Informatica, Faculty of Theology, Vrije Universiteit, Amsterdam, November 5-6, 1987*, Applicatio 7 (Amsterdam: Free University Press, 1989). Progress from desk top to Internet capability, including the decision to utilize a data base approach in conjunction with an SGML/HTML Web compatible format, is documented with regard to the formation of the Database Project, see J. Hoftjitzer, "The History of the Database Project," in *Studies in Ancient Hebrew Semantics* (Louvain: Peeters, 1985), 65-85.

42   Talstra states, "Of course, access to the options available in the data can only be realised by a search engine that is able to exploit in an effective way all the textual features present. Creating a database is one thing, using it is something else." E. Talstra, "Text Segmentation and Linguistic Levels," (2003), 1-40 (34).

43   Narrative studies predominate in recent linguistic research. For example, see Robert D. Bergen, *Biblical Hebrew and Discourse Linguistics* (Dallas: Summer Institute of Linguistics, 1994); Walter Ray Bodine, *Linguistics and Biblical Hebrew* (Winona Lake, Ind: Eisenbrauns, 1992); Bodine, *Discourse Analysis*; Cynthia L. Miller, *The Verbless Clause in Biblical Hebrew: Linguistic Approaches*, Linguistic Studies in Ancient West Semitic (Winona Lake, Ind.: Eisenbrauns, 1999). A recent addition to this list is Sebastiaan J.

is among the unploughed fields for each of these approaches. Two features of prophetic literature contribute to this situation: the text comprises many genres, including prose, poetry and elevated speech; and prophetic literature is highly discursive: reported speech and direct address are prominent features of the text.[44] Thus, delimiting a coherent and comprehensive frame of reference for the linguistic analysis and description of prophetic texts poses a significant challenge.

Some recent linguistic studies of BH text concentrate on single genres: discourse analytic approaches, such as Longacre's, prove useful for the description and analysis of narrative text; the studies of Watson, Kugel and Berlin provide insight into poetic texts and metaphor studies such as Doyle's assist in discerning abstract meaning.[45] However, little has been written regarding a holistic analysis of prophetic text.[46] Additionally, we lack a coherent method for integrating research results from multiple perspectives.

Nonetheless, utilising an integrative approach to text analysis is important, as the results of any single theory are bound by its strengths and weaknesses.[47] For example, two particular problems arise when structural approaches are paired with prophetic text. The first problem has to do with the Hebrew verbal system. Some structural approaches rely heavily upon the role of verbal forms as structural cues. Such reliance upon verbal forms is insufficient, primarily because there is no consensus regarding the nature of the verbal system since the BH tense versus aspect debate is ongoing.[48] Additionally, little has been written regarding the linguistic role of the *binyan* system, which is complex and

---

Floor, "From Information Structure, Topic, and Focus, to Theme in Biblical Hebrew Narrative." (DLit, University of Stellenbosch, 2004).

44   Although narrative studies predominate, a small number of BH poetry studies have been undertaken from a linguistics perspective. See Randall Buth, "Topic and Focus in Hebrew Poetry: Psalm 51," in *Language in Context: Essays for Robert E. Longacre*, eds Shin Ja Joo Hwang and William R. Merrifield (Arlington: Summer Institute of Linguistics and the University of Texas at Arlington, 1992), 83-96. For a discussion of prose, poetry and elevated speech in BH, see James L. Kugel, *The Idea of Biblical Poetry: Parallelism and Its History* (New Haven: Yale University Press, 1981), 77.

45   Brian Doyle, *The Apocalypse of Isaiah Metaphorically Speaking: A Study of the Use, Function, and Significance of Metaphors in Isaiah 24-27* (Leuven: Peeters, 2000).

46   However, see Martin Kessler, *Reading the Book of Jeremiah: A Search for Coherence* (Winona Lake, Ind: Eisenbrauns, 2004); Ernst R. Wendland, *The Discourse Analysis of Hebrew Prophetic Literature*, Mellen Biblical Press Series, vol. 40, (Lewiston, New York: Mellen Biblical Press, 1994).

47   van der Merwe, "Some Recent Trends," 18.

48   Inroads have been made into the Hebrew verbal system. See, for example, Tal Goldfajn, *Word Order and Time in Biblical Hebrew Narrative*, Oxford Theological Monographs (Oxford: Oxford University Press, 1998), Cook, "Grammaticalization." However, the issue is far from resolved.

affects many aspects of meaning construction.[49] The second problem has to do with the one form/one function notion behind some structural approaches, which is limiting for narrative text and places undue constraints upon elevated speech and prophetic parallelism. Indeed, it is possible that one linguistic form might signal several functions, or multiple linguistic forms might represent a single function.[50]

Thus, the task of delimiting a coherent and comprehensive approach to BH prophetic text is two-fold: first, it is necessary to establish suitable links between the language, context and cultures of the original text producers and those of the present text consumers; secondly, it is necessary to thoroughly explore all aspects of the text itself. Since language use is the product of human conceptualisation, insights from the areas of cognitive science, cognitive linguistics and cognitive grammar have an important place in delimiting a coherent and comprehensive frame of reference for interpreting BH text.[51] The TD approach incorporates these ideas in two ways: first, by elucidating the reconceptualisation of the interrelationship between author, text and reader; and secondly, in the text analytic method itself.

---

49   See, however, E. J. van Wolde, "Linguistic Motivation and Biblical Exegesis," in *Narrative Syntax and the Hebrew Bible*, ed. E. J. van Wolde, Biblical Interpretation Series, V. 29 (Leiden: Brill, 1997), 21-50. Nili Mandelblit, "The Grammatical Marking of Conceptual Integration: From Syntax to Morphology," *CL* 11 (2000), 197-241.

50   Mandelblit, in her conceptual blending analysis of the Modern Hebrew verbal system, has observed that the syntactic form of the sentence and the morphological form of the verb (its *binyan*) combine in two distinct ways. Two sentences with the same syntactic forms, but with two different morphological forms, will have the same basic event structure with different cross-space mappings, while different syntactic forms with the same morphological form will exhibit a different event structure, but with the same cross-space mapping. The issue of cross-space mapping has to do with the underlying motion construction specified by the *binyan*. For instance, although sentences with *niphal* verbs have a subject, they are essentially agentless, as the one performing the action is not encoded in the verb form. A similar situation exists with imperative forms, in which action is requested by a non-subject entity whose identity must be contextually assessed.

51   The present author became aware of the cognitive approaches through Martin Follingstad's work. Coincidentally, van der Merwe encountered the work of S.S.A. Marmaridou, whose research programme has many points of contact with the theoretical underpinnings of this effort to articulate a text dynamic approach to BH text, including the view of language as dynamic rather than static and the importance of embodied experience for meaning construction. Carl Martin Follingstad, "Deictic Viewpoint in Biblical Hebrew Text: A Syntagmatic and Paradigmatic Analysis of the Particle Ki." (Doctoral Thesis, Vrije Universiteit te Amsterdam 2001, SIL International, 2001); Sophia S. A. Marmaridou, *Pragmatic Meaning and Cognition*, Pragmatics & Beyond; New Ser. 72 (Amsterdam: J. Benjamins Publishing, 2000).

2. Author, Text and Reader

Like any text, the text of Jeremiah appears to be a static entity. This perception is reinforced by the limitations of BH, which has been preserved as a formally articulated language only for worship. Because of this, there are no speakers to create fresh examples. The data available for formulating grammatical conclusions is limited to the corpus at hand. Even so, the text itself is the product of real language users, communicating in real contexts and under the influence of real cultural influences and constraints.[52] There is a communicative dynamism surrounding the text, which is best explored by including the human element in the interpretation process.

The first task involved in delimiting the TD approach is reconceptualising the relationship that holds between the author (from hereon, *originator*), the text and the reader.[53] A model from cognitive grammar has been selected for this task. This model, described as the *canonical viewing arrangement*, is dependent upon known features of perception and is represented in the following diagram.[54]

---

52 This is why it is not safe or prudent to jettison historical-critical study.

53 In this analysis the term *originator* replaces the term *author* and acts as a cover term for the group of people who have contributed to the final form of the text, including the original author and any subsequent redactors or editors.

54 In terms of cognitive grammar, a viewing arrangement may be described as *canonical*, in which case the viewer is distinct from the object of perception, the object of perception is sharply delimited, and the viewer's attention is directed outward. In this viewing arrangement, the viewer construes the perceived object with "...maximal objectivity and construes himself with maximal subjectivity." Ronald W. Langacker, "Deixis and Subjectivity," in Grounding: The Epistemic Footing of Deixis and Reference, ed. Frank Brisard (Berlin: Mouton de Gruyter, 2002), 1-28 (15).

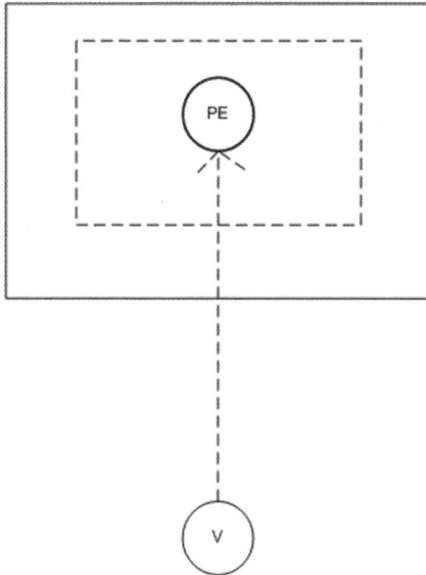

Figure 1.1 Langacker's Canonical Viewing Arrangement

The canonical viewing arrangement is based upon visual perception. It consists of the following components: V represents the viewer; the box represents the visual field; the dashed rectangle indicates the locus of viewing attention, which is also referred to as the onstage region; PE represents the perceived entity; and the dashed arrow represents the perceptual relationship that holds between the perceiving individual and the entity being perceived.

In his discussion of subjectivity, Langacker utilises this diagram to explain the "… inherent asymmetry between the roles of subject and object of perception." When the role of the viewer as the *subject* of perception and that of the perceived entity as the *object* of perception are maximally asymmetrical, they exhibit the following three characteristics: V and P are wholly distinct; P is sharply delimited; and V's attention is directed outward, so that he does not perceive himself in any way.[55] Additionally, Langacker notes that it is possible to discuss abstract conceptualisations, such as the meanings of linguistic expressions within a speech situation using a similar diagram.

---

55 Langacker, "Deixis and Subjectivity,"15.

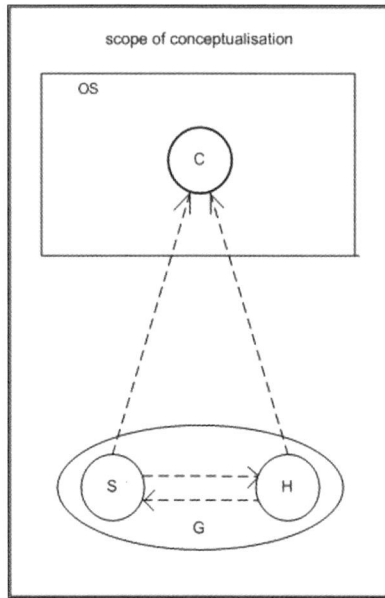

Figure 1.2 Langacker's Viewing Arrangement for Speech Situations

In this case, the scope of conceptualisation includes the speaker and hearer, the ground of the speech event and the shared conceptualisation of the communication. This situation is represented in the diagram as follows: the speaker and hearer are the relevant conceptualisers (corresponding to V in figure 1). The interrelationship between the speaker and hearer is represented by the horizontal dashed lines. The speaker and hearer are *off stage* – they are maximally subjective, but nonetheless present. Their shared conceptualisation, C, is *on stage* as the focus of attention; it is maximally objective. The outer box represents the overall scope of the expression, and the inner rectangle represents the immediate scope of the expression.[56] This diagram represents a prototypical speech situation, in which the speaker and hearer have immediate access to one another and to elements within the ground of the speech situation, such as time and space. In other words, the deictic centres represented by the speaker and the hearer share the same ground.[57]

---

56 Ronald W. Langacker, "Context, Cognition, and Semantics: A Unified Dynamic Approach," in *Job 28: Cognition in Context*, ed. E. J. van Wolde (Leiden: Brill, 2003), 179-230 (183).
57 For Langacker, the term ground includes the speech event, its participants and its immediate circumstances. Langacker, "Deixis and Subjectivity," 7.

The dotted lines that join the speaker and hearer to the object of perception represent *shared gaze*. In a face-to-face communication situation, shared gaze is an important communication cue. Bailenson states:

> Aside from verbal channels, non-verbal channels available during face-to-face communication include gaze from head posture and eye direction, arm gestures, body posture, and facial expressions (as well as non-verbal aspects of language such as variations in intonation and voice quality).[58]

Text level deictic terms are one means available to the author for encouraging shared gaze (see 2.B.2 below).

From a TD perspective, it is possible to reconceptualise the relationship between the text, the originators of the text and the readers of the text using an expanded version of the previous diagram.

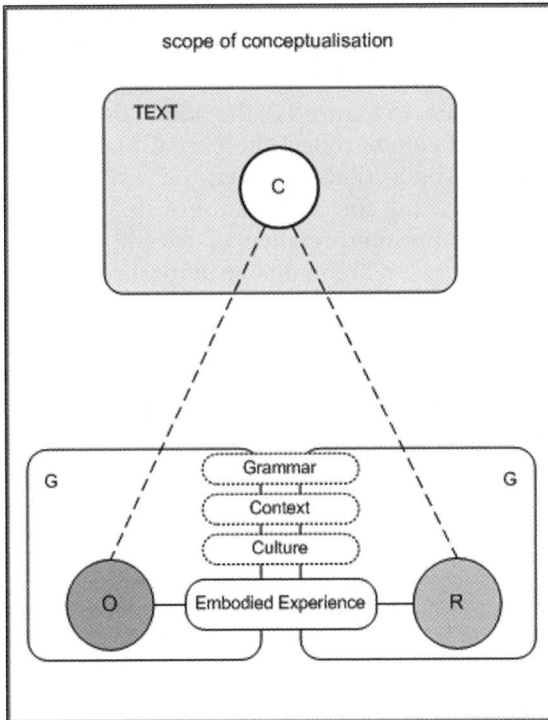

Figure 1.3 Re-conceptualisation of the Relationship between Author, Text and Reader

---

58   Jeremy N. Bailenson, Andrew C. Beall and Jim Blascovich, *Gaze and Task Performance in Shared Virtual Environments* (2002, accessed); available from http://www.stanford.edu/~bailenso/papers/VCA%20Gaze.pdf.

In this diagram, the outer box delineates the scope of the conceptualisation. This encompasses the following aspects: the locus of viewing attention, or the onstage region, represents the text; C indicates the focus frame, or the conceptualisation of the portion of text under consideration at a given moment; O is a cover term for the original author and all subsequent editorial hands; R is a cover term for all readers; G indicates the ground that holds for the relevant conceptualiser. Once again, the conceptualisers are off stage. They are maximally subjective but present. Importantly, the degree of subjectivity would change if one of the interlocutors were to become the subject of the communication event.

In contrast to the diagram Figure 1.2, which represents a prototypical speech event with speaker and hearer sharing a common ground, the diagram in Figure 1.3 highlights the disjunction that exists for the originators and readers of an ancient text. In this case, the speech event is non-prototypical, with the communication participants separated by space, time and culture. In Figure 1.3, the dotted lines around the terms *grammar*, *context* and *culture* reflect the partial manner in which these categories establish connections between the text originators and the readers, thus emphasising the importance of linguistic, historical and cultural studies for the interpretation of ancient text. The solid line around *embodied experience* highlights an important analogical connection between originator and reader.[59] This connection is proposed based upon the idea that humans possess similar neural networks, which may be modelled by *connectionist networks*, and that such networks are characteristic of embodied human experience.[60]

---

59   Although this volume is based upon recent research in the area of cognitive grammar and linguistics, there is a sense in which the reconceptualisation presented in Figure 1.3 provides a new wineskin for the old wine of the historical-critical method. John Collins argues that the principle of analogy is foundational for the historical-critical approach, stating, "To understand the ancient context of a text requires some sympathetic analogy between ancient and modern situations. Indeed, one of the assumptions of historical criticism is that texts are human products and that human nature has not changed beyond recognition over the centuries". Thus, both the emphasis upon analogy based upon human experience and the maintenance of the distinction between subjectivity and objectivity expressed in the re-conceptualisation render this volume more modern than post-modern. John J. Collins, *The Bible after Babel* (Grand Rapids, Michigan: Eerdmans, 2005), 5.

60   Marmaridou states, "...connectionism views the brain as a network characterised by causal processes by which units of intricate systems excite and inhibit each other and thus dynamically adapt to their environments. One of the major features that has attracted cognitive scientists to network models is that, being neurally inspired, they seem more compatible than symbolic models with what we know of nervous systems." Marmaridou: 48.

The diagram in Figure 1.4 demonstrates that the inclusion of information generated by the *embodied experience* factor is effective in narrowing the gap between the perception of the originator and that of the reader.[61]

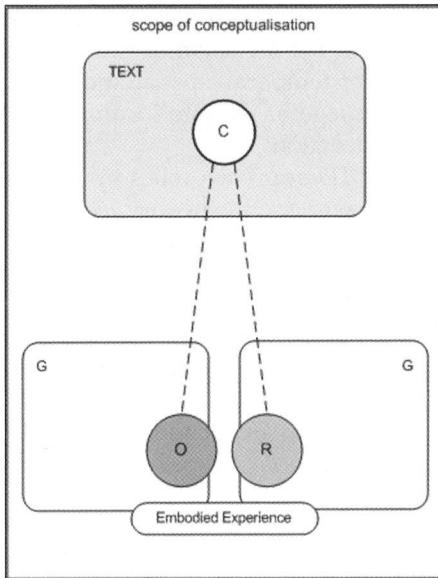

Figure 1.4 Viewing Arrangement Based upon Embodied Experience

The TD re-conceptualisation draws attention to cognitive processes that are inherent in the embodied human experience shared by text originator, speaker, hearer and reader alike. It opens the way for incorporating prototype structures, image schematic structures, conceptual metaphor, idealised cognitive models and Mental Spaces Theory (MST) into the interpretation of ancient text, in so far as it may be demonstrated that these categories have universal characteristics.

This re-conceptualisation also paves the way for a shift in the metaphor that is used to describe human communication. Typically, communication is described in terms of the *conduit metaphor*, a conceptual metaphor based upon the *path schema*.[62] In this model, words and

---

61 This also holds for the speaker and hearer in Figure 1.2. They share the ground of the speech event and the embodied experience as well.

62 Mark Johnson, *The Body in the Mind: The Bodily Basis of Meaning, Imagination, and Reason* (Chicago: UCP, 1987), 26.

grammatical structures are said to contain meaning. The speaker is said to *pack* and *send* this information to the hearer, who then *unpacks* the meaning. This model is only partially compatible with the prototypical speech situation in Figure 1.2, where the speaker and hearer share a situation of speaking in which temporal, spatial and cultural elements of the situation are available to both parties. Significantly, the conduit model fails to account for the inclusion of extra-linguistic information, such as the awareness of temporal, spatial and cultural aspects of the situation, the body language of the interlocutors, and how these contribute to meaning construction.

For this reason, the TD approach relies upon a network model. In this model, both the speaker and the hearer, *qua* conceptualisers, participate in the construction of a shared cognitive network.[63] The speaker/author has in mind an event that he or she wishes to share with the hearer/reader. The speaker selects words and grammatical constructions and uses these as tools to prompt the hearer to open, structure and link mental spaces, forming a network of spaces as discourse unfolds. As the spoken or written word is encountered by the hearer or reader, linguistic information is blended with both generic (image schematic) and specific (temporal, spatial and cultural) background information in the process of meaning construction. This model is compatible with Figure 1.3.

The second task involved in delimiting the TD approach is designing a comprehensive text analysis that is compatible with the re-conceptualisation just discussed. The theory and method for the TD text analysis will be introduced in the following section.

3.   Text as a Material Anchor

The second task involved in delimiting the TD approach is to create a comprehensive text analysis. A model from cognitive science has been selected for this task. From a cognitive science perspective, the text of Jeremiah represents a *material anchor for complex projections*.[64] In other words, the physically available text acts as an anchor, or focal link, for conceptual processing.[65] For the reader, this processing includes creat-

---

63   This model is based upon Fauconnier's MST.

64   Fauconnier and Turner, *The Way We Think*, 202.

65   The term *focal link* belongs to the re-conceptualisation schema developed by the present author and is compatible with the diagrams in the previous section. Fauconnier's *material anchor* is used in much the same way, with the advantage of including actual physical properties of the entity involved.

ing adequate links between the language, context and culture of the text producers and those of the present-day text consumers. A description of this process begins with the analysis and description of the syntax, semantics and pragmatics of the text. Understanding the text, or material anchor, is the first priority. [66]

Once again, a feature of computerised information processing acts as a source domain for understanding the TD approach.[67] In this case, it is the *layer* feature that is used in many computer applications, from text and image management to musical arrangement, architecture and design. Texts, musical scores and cathedrals are all examples of material anchors for conceptual processing. A musical score acts as a material anchor for the cognitive processing of music. A composer uses a notation system to create an anchor for the combinations of pitches, rhythms and tones that he or she imagines. Other musicians are able to follow the combination of instructions that the score contains, giving rise to an actual performance of the music. The score is not the music, but rather a highly compressed record of cues, a record which is compressed by the composer and subsequently decompressed by the musician. A cathedral is a material anchor which represents the intersection between the physical world and the divine. It is firmly situated spatially, as opposed to the ephemeral deity, so when individuals travel to the cathedral, they are approaching a stationary spot where the presence of the deity is located. To enter into the cathedral is to encounter the unseen, but now localised deity.[68]

Composers, cathedral architects and authors create material anchors, while musicians, the faithful and text analysts make use of them. Although composing, designing and authoring do not seem to resemble playing symphonies, attending worship or analysing texts, all of these activities are processed via conceptual blending. The composer combines novel groupings of pitches, rhythms and tones with notations in a score; the architect combines imagined space and material; and the author combines new conceptions, syntactic forms and marks on a page (or tablet, or scroll, or pot, or plinth). The musician combines notations with voice or instrument, creating music. The faithful ones move to-

---

66 This analysis moves in the same synchronic-diachronic order as proposed by Talstra in his analysis of Deuteronomy 9 and 10. E. Talstra, "Deuteronomy 9 and 10: Synchronic and Diachronic Observations," in *Synchronic or Diachronic: A Debate on Method in Old Testament Exegesis*, ed. J.C. de Moor (Leiden: Brill, 1995), 187-210.

67 Source and target domains are used in the discussion of cognitive metaphor, which will be taken up in chapter 4.II.C. See Zoltan Kövecses, *Metaphor: A Practical Introduction* (New York and Oxford: OUP, 2002); George Lakoff and Mark Johnson, *Metaphors We Live By* (Chicago; London: University of Chicago Press, 1980).

68 Fauconnier and Turner, *The Way We Think*, 206.

ward the deity, conceptually merging material space with *non-space*. The reader, or text analyst, encounters the text via the reading process, creating an elaborate conceptual structure which replicates the author's conceptions on many points.

The similarities involved in these seemingly disparate conceptual blends may be illustrated by examining the computer technology that supports the creative process, specifically the layering feature that is at the heart of the computer programmes used for design and composition.[69] These programmes utilise a series of layers to build up a unified file, be it a three dimensional drawing or a complete musical score. The 21st-century cathedral architect will begin by creating a layer representing the most permanent feature, such as the floor plan of a building, and then add successive layers representing built-in features, large design features, and follow these with layers representing the placement of less permanent features, such as furniture. Finally, the layers may be combined and viewed as a whole. At this point, with a three-axis programme, the designer is able to view the virtual space dynamically: the computer will allow a walk-through of the imagined space. Although there are drawbacks involved in not actually being there, the results are more vivid than traditional blueprints, allowing for a comprehensive decision-making process for the project. Likewise, a composer or arranger might digitally master a musical score by creating separate layers for each vocal part or each instrument, which the programme then combines to form a unified score. A synthesizer is able to play the score to the composer, who is able to make on-line adjustments. Once again, there are certain drawbacks. A synthesizer is a disappointing (compressed) substitute for a live orchestra. While it can replicate the pitch patterns represented by the musical score, a synthesizer is unable to recreate the emergent nature of the embodied experience, which is the live performance. It is far more satisfying to participate in the concert hall event, with skilled musicians playing before a receptive audience. Nonetheless, the composer or arranger has a tool that helps the creative process. A completed text is similar to a musical score in that it represents multiple parameters for meaning construction, such as syntax, semantics and pragmatics. If the text is viewed as a composite series of layers, the text analyst is able to create a principled analysis by mapping one set of features at a time, then combining the mappings to view the text in a holistic, dynamic manner.[70] By moving

---

69 Many thanks are due to Rebecca Brown of Rebecca Brown Design, who graciously explained the inner workings of design programmes.

70 Importantly, there is not necessarily a one-to-one correspondence between observed structures at the syntactic, semantic and pragmatic levels.

in a most permanent to least permanent direction, the text analyst is able to account for text features on a continuum from the most concrete to the least concrete, then to "hear" the layers as a unified composition. It is posited that various text features function at different levels, and that the process of meaning construction involves both the layers and the whole.

Similarly, the proposed TD process is integrative, in that it comprises the serial description, analysis and conceptual blending of three main layers: syntax, semantics and pragmatics.[71] Syntax represents the most concrete aspect of the text, while semantics is slightly less concrete, but available, and pragmatics is the least concrete.[72] The analysis will be enhanced by the reader's encyclopaedic knowledge of the world, and by extra-textual understandings, such as those developed through historical-critical and anthropological inquiries.

The TD procedure consists of the following stages:

1. Synchronic analysis: syntax and semantics;

2. information structure: topic and focus;

3. cognitive structuring: the network model and metaphor; and

4. conceptual blending: incorporating extra-textual information.

Stage 1 is a comprehensive mapping of the syntactic features of Jeremiah 1.1-6.30 and an accounting of the basic formal relationships that hold for these features. This stage involves a "bottom-up" analysis, based upon the model utilised by the Werkgroup Informatica, Vrije Universiteit, the Netherlands. The text is presented in a clause analysis format, as in the short example below.

---

71 Curiously, this blending operation occurs in everyday speech, although native speakers generally are unaware of anything except the final communication. Translating for non-native speakers highlights the complexities that are 'hidden' in everyday communication.

72 For an introduction to issues involved in the study of pragmatics, including deixis and speech-act theory, see D. A. Cruse, *Pragmatics* (Oxford: OUP, 2000); Jacob L. Mey, *Pragmatics: An Introduction*, 2d ed. (Oxford: Blackwell, 2001).

Clause Layout	Jer
וַיֹּאמֶר יְהוָה אֵלַי בִּימֵי יֹאשִׁיָּהוּ הַמֶּלֶךְ	3.6a
הֲרָאִיתָ	b
אֲשֶׁר עָשְׂתָה מְשֻׁבָה יִשְׂרָאֵל	c
הֹלְכָה הִיא עַל־כָּל־הַר גָּבֹהַּ וְאֶל־תַּחַת כָּל־עֵץ רַעֲנָן	d
וַתִּזְנִי־שָׁם	e

Jer	Type	Clause Tag	PNG	Focus	MSC
3.6a	N	*Wayyiqtol-X*	3sg M	PRED	Base
b	NQ	*X-Qatal*	2sg M	*Inter*	SB for M[1]
c	NQP	*X-Qatal*	3sgF	ARGU	M[1] *Focus*
d	NQP	*Qotel*	sgF	PRED	
e	NQPN	*Wayyiqtol-0*	3sgF	PRED	

Figure 1.5 Clause Analysis for Jeremiah 3.6

The analysed text is presented in the top box, with one clause per line and includes both *kethiv* and *qere* readings when relevant. The syntax analysis involves the three left-most columns in the lower box. These columns contain the following information: the first column contains the clause identifier; the second contains the discourse type (N: narrative, D: discursive, Q: quote, P: perception); the third contains the shorthand verb form. The formal syntactic patterns discovered by this process are made available for further analysis. Information regarding constituent order is given in column 5 and information regarding mental spaces construction is given in column 6. Constituent order is an important indicator of focus type in discussions of information structure, and is a characteristic formal feature in certain types of parallelism. The presence or absence of the subject gives information for maintaining reference in the text and is valuable for discerning typological information. Finally, fronted particles are valuable clues for the structure of the text. The syntax analysis is a highly compressed, black-and-white record of formal textual features and has much in common with the floor plan of a building or the notation of a musical score. It is synchronic in nature, encompassing the whole text, without commenting upon the diachronic development of syntactic forms represented. This stage also involves tracking semantic features that indicate basic relationships that hold between clause constituents. Semantic features represent the merger between syntactic form, lexical choice and meaning construction. This includes column three and the following columns. In this example, the fifth column contains the person, number and gender of the verb. The sixth column contains information structure detail and the seventh contains notations regarding conceptual structuring.

By way of an example, the syntactic notation *Wayyiqtol-S* might represent either the phrase, *Now the Word of the Lord came,* as in 1.4a, or *And the banner was raised,* depending upon lexical choices, i.e. the definiteness of the noun or noun phrase and the *binyan* of the verb. Similar constructions without markers of definiteness would yield the phrases *Now a word came,* or *And a banner was raised.*

New information is available at this point. The question may be posed as to why a certain term or combination of terms is used as opposed to another term or combination of terms. Additionally, the issue of meaning change over time may be addressed and insights gained from analyses such as Cook's study of verbal forms.[73] The combination of word order and the presence of verbs of speaking or perception play into the MST concept of *space-builders,* which provides important cues for meaning construction. Word choices from a single semantic domain play a part in the construction of certain types of parallelism. Synchronic observations might combine with diachronic observations regarding lexemes or verbal forms.

Stage 2 is an information structure analysis. This analysis has to do with language as a form of human communication, or *the use of language in context.* Prior to this discussion, sentences in the text have been analysed at level 1. Comments may now be made about the information structure of the sentences, which includes both the author's lexical and syntactic choices for prompting meaning construction and modelling the mapping of decompressed conceptual blends cued by the text.

---

73 Cook, "Grammaticalization."

Information structure, according to Knud Lambrecht, is the relationship between linguistic forms and the mental states of speakers and hearers.[74] Information structure is concerned with how information is transmitted between the speaker and hearer (author-reader). This is reflected in the formal properties which the speaker (author) deploys in his or her communication strategy and how these reflect the speaker's assumptions regarding the encyclopaedic knowledge of the world that is shared with his or her hearer (reader). It is also reflected in how the shared knowledge is expanded upon by the addition of new discourse information.

Lambrecht discusses information structure under four categories: (i) pragmatic presupposition and pragmatic assertion; (ii) identifiability and activation; (iii) topic and (iv) focus. The first category, pragmatic presupposition and pragmatic assertion, is of primary importance for understanding the relationship between linguistic forms and the mental states of speakers and hearers. For example, the present author assumes that those reading this chapter are familiar with terms such as MT and Jeremiah, thus these terms are considered to be shared information and do not require definitions or even full spellings.[75] On the other hand, definitions are offered for certain words and concepts. This demonstrates the present author's assumption that the linguistic terms used to describe information structure may not be shared knowledge at this point in the communication process. As the author's goal is to increase the amount of shared knowledge of the world, these terms have been given special formal treatment. This example reflects the interrelationship between pragmatic presupposition and pragmatic assertion, or "…the speaker's assumptions about the hearer's state of knowledge and awareness at the time of an utterance."[76] The remaining three categories will be taken up in the following chapters.

Stage 3 is an assessment of the cognitive structure that is cued by textual features. This assessment is based on Mental Spaces Theory

---

74   Information structure is "… that component of sentence grammar in which propositions as conceptual representations of states of affairs are paired with lexicogrammatical structures in accordance with the mental states of interlocutors who use and interpret these structures as units of information in given discourse contexts." Knud Lambrecht, *Information Structure and Sentence Form: Topic, Focus, and the Mental Representations of Discourse Referents*, Cambridge Studies in Linguistics; 71 (Cambridge: Cambridge University Press, 1994), 5.

75   This assumption may or may not reflect the *truth*, depending upon who is engaged in reading this section. While members of the OT scholarly community would have no trouble with either *MT* or *Jeremiah*, it is likely that a group of cognitive linguists would benefit from a full spelling for *Masoretic Text* and some information regarding its background.

76   Lambrecht, *Information Structure*, xiii.

(MST). This theory describes and explains how "…as we think and talk, mental spaces are set up, structured, and linked under pressure from grammar, context, and culture. The effect is to create a network of spaces through which we move as discourse unfolds. Because each space stems from another space (its 'parent'), and because a parent can have many offspring, the space network will be a two-dimensional lattice."[77]

According to Fauconnier, MST is concerned with "…the interaction between grammar and cognitive structure: in particular, on the principled relationship between mental space structures and syntax and semantics."[78] Like information structure, MST is interested in examining the relationship between text (formal grammar) and the cognitive constructions which text evokes. As cognitive constructions, Fauconnier's *mental spaces* bear a strong resemblance to Lambrecht's *mental representations*. In addition, because MST also examines the relationships that are established between spaces due to cognitive connections, this theory may provide additional understanding regarding the interrelationship between sections of text and the text as a whole.

4. Text Dynamics: Problems and Possibilities

The goal of the TD approach is to gain an integrated understanding of BH prophetic text, a process that is doubly complicated. The first complication is the composite nature of the material. The second is applying the variety of in-depth and focused research results from recent distributional and structural approaches to stretches of text that are larger than the sentence, in this case Jeremiah 1.1-6.30. In order to accomplish the task of bringing all aspects together in a coherent and comprehensive manner, the cognitive sciences notion of conceptual blending will act as the unifying principle for the TD approach.

At first glance, this approach may appear to be nothing more than an extended close reading of the biblical text. With its emphasis upon a comprehensive syntax analysis and a corresponding semantic analysis, this approach does resemble such a reading, albeit in an enriched form. However, a TD approach moves beyond a close reading, due to its emphasis upon the contribution made by cognitive processing.

From a TD perspective, the symbols that combine to form the text are not viewed as beads on a string, with one-to-one correspondence to entities or processes. Rather, they represent prompts for meaning con-

---

77 G. Fauconnier and E. Sweetser, *Spaces, Worlds, and Grammar* (Chicago: UCP, 1996), 11.
78 Ibid.

struction. This allows for the possibility that one form might act as a
prompt for more than one function or that one function might be
prompted by more than one form. Additionally, meaning construction
is viewed as a dynamic process, whereby meaning accrues as text is
processed. Word order and information from various semantic domains combine in the author's conceptual construction, which in turn
act as prompts for the reader or text analyst in his or her process of
meaning construction.

Recent research into individual features of BH text, such as Miller's
study of reported speech and Follingstad's study of the particle כִּי, provide information regarding features which have an impact upon meaning construction at the syntactic, semantic, and/or pragmatic levels. By
utilising the series of analyses in conjunction with the cognitive
sciences notion of conceptual blending, the TD approach provides a
coherent and comprehensive method for incorporating the results of
such studies in the interpretive process.

2. The Sentence and Beyond: Introduction to the Text Dynamics Approach

Very dangerous things, theories!

~ Dorothy Sayers[1]

The aim of this chapter is to outline the primary features of the TD approach, demonstrating that this approach offers a comprehensive method for understanding the text of the Hebrew Bible. This approach has several strengths. It provides a fresh look at an ancient text; it allows for an examination of the conceptual understandings of the originator of the text and it provides a principled way to integrate information from a variety of linguistic and technical studies. This approach is effective for an array of interpretive tasks. [2] However, since it has been designed specifically to handle some complexities unique to prophetic literature, this chapter will concentrate upon a short example taken from Jeremiah 3.6-10.

---

1 Dorothy L. Sayers, *The Unpleasantness at the Bellona Club* (London: Ernest Benn, 1928; reprint, London: Stoddard and Houghton, 1968), 30.

2 The TD approach has proved useful for investigating quotations and allusions in the NT, demonstrating that the conceptual component of this approach is effective across genres. See E. R. Hayes, "The Influence of Ezekiel 37 on 2 Corinthians 6:14-7:1," in *The Book of Ezekiel and Its Influence*, eds Johannes Tromp and H. J. De Jonge (Hampshire: Ashgate, 2007), 115-118.

A. Theory and Method

1.   Author, Text and Reader: A Re-conceptualisation

Re-conceptualising the relationship between originator, text and reader is essential to the TD approach, as this assists in understanding the role of the text as a physically available focal link and as an anchor for complex cognitive projections. It is possible to re-conceptualise the relationship between the originator, the text of Jeremiah 3.6-3.11 and the present reader as follows:

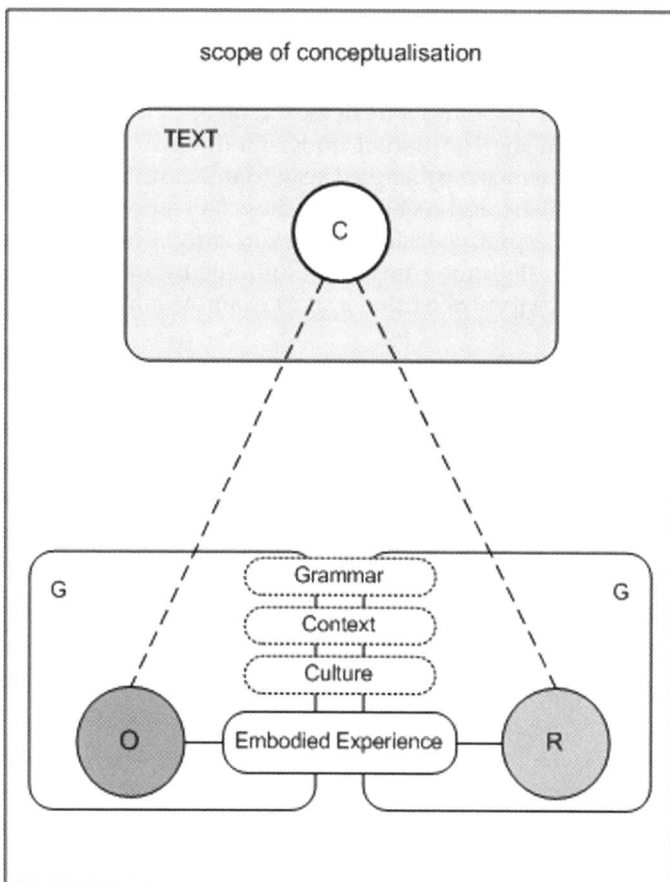

Figure 2.1   Originator, Text and Reader in Jeremiah 3.6-3.11

For this chapter, Jeremiah 3.6-3.11 occupies the text-space, which is the locus of viewing attention or onstage region. Within this region, C indicates the portion of text under consideration at a given moment, and thus is the dynamic portion of the diagram. At the lower left, the O indicates the original author and all subsequent editorial hands. At the lower right, R is a cover term for all readers, including the present author and readers of this chapter. The chapter is the ground for the present writer and reader.

Information regarding both the originator and the historical and cultural framework of the text is available from at least two sources: the encyclopaedic background knowledge of the reader(s) and external sources. This is an important differentiation. Encyclopaedic background knowledge is located in the mind of the reader, modelled here in a subjective position, and is immediately available for reactivation and conceptual blending. However, external historical and cultural material is located outside of the conceptualization diagram. Accessing external material requires bringing such material to the onstage, objective position in a separate conceptual event. After the external information has been processed and is retained as encyclopaedic background knowledge, it becomes internally accessible and subjectively available when engaging in further study.[3]

Traditional exegetical methods address this issue by isolating historical, cultural, textual analyses and inquiries regarding the identity of the author/originator, effectively creating a distinct, objective viewing arrangement for each. The TD approach takes this one step further by redefining the relative position of the originator and reader during the reading process. In the TD analysis *both* are off stage, where they are present but maximally subjective.[4] This allows for the exploration of the very strong connection that exists between author and reader based upon embodied experience. Finally, the TD model explicates the conceptual blending process, which allows for a principled integration of information from various sources. This model has implications for the reading process and for interpretation.

---

3 In reality, the process is recursive: encyclopaedic background knowledge is supplemented by study of external sources. This information becomes part of the encyclopaedic background knowledge and so on. Each recursion involves further conceptual blending.

4 It is possible for this configuration to be altered, particularly if the author/originator/narrator or narrator as character is included as a first or second person reference in the text, at which point he or she is simultaneously objectively onstage and subjectively present as viewer. This is an issue of cross-space identity. See chapter 5, section B.5.

2. The Reading Process

The reading process isolates a single text as the locus of viewing attention. Yet the single text is itself a complex object, and as a result, so is the reading process. When considering such complexity, Talstra notes:

> Human readers usually perform grammatical analysis and textual interpretation in one run… recognition of patterns of the concatenation of words, the segmentation into clause constituents and the process of interpretation all are performed in the same process of reading. However, when using a computer to identify patterns of concatenation and segmentation and also to assign them labels of grammatical functions, one has to separate the various routines in order to make clear how exactly the flow of information is established in the process of reading.[5]

Acknowledging this is the case, the TD approach uses a five-fold analysis to model conceptualization that underlies the reading process. This model is, in effect, a layered blending template.[6] According to the computer programme analogy described in Chapter 1, each analytical stage resembles a layer in a computer programme: from floor plan (syntax analysis) to permanent features (semantics); from virtual decorating (pragmatics) to a virtual walk-through (cognitive modelling). Information accrues as each layer is integrated via conceptual blending. In this way conceptual blending contributes to the mental space network, which acts as a cognitive substrate for reasoning and is an underlying feature of the reading process.

3. Explaining the Network Model

TD is a cognitive approach. It draws from cognitive linguistics, cognitive grammar and cognitive science in order to create an adequate frame of reference for the description and analysis of BH text.[7] For cog-

---

5   Talstra, "Text Segmentation and Linguistic Levels," 11.
6   This term is used by Edwin Hutchins to describe the conceptual blending process involved in the *method of loci*, a memory aid which is used by associating the material to be remembered with locations along a familiar path or within a familiar structure. Remembering the material then becomes a matter of mentally traversing the familiar path, which cues the respective associations. Fauconnier and Turner, *The Way We Think*, 208.
7   For cognitive linguistics see William Croft and D. A. Cruse, *Cognitive Linguistics*, Cambridge Textbooks in Linguistics (Cambridge: Cambridge University Press, 2004); M. Haspelmath and others, eds., *Language Typology and Language Universals: An International Handbook* (Berlin: Walter de Gruyter, 2001); David Lee, *Cognitive Linguistics: An Introduction* (Melbourne and Oxford: OUP, 2001). For cognitive grammar see Langacker, *Foundations of Cognitive Grammar*; idem, *Foundations of Cognitive*

nitive grammar *semantics is conceptualization*. In this view, linguistic units are comprised of words and phrases which act as prompts for on-line, cognitive level meaning construction.[8] This view of meaning construction is compatible with cognitive sciences *network model*, presented by Fauconnier, who states:

> Mental spaces are small conceptual packets constructed as we think and talk for purposes of local understanding and action... Mental spaces are very partial. They contain elements and are structured by frames. They are interconnected and can be modified as thought and discourse unfold.[9]

Given this description, it seems entirely possible to understand a mental space network as an emergent three-dimensional creation, similar to the interconnected and occasionally encapsulated structure which occurs when hot water encounters liquid detergent or when a child blows bubbles in milk.[10]

With regard to cognitive processing at the biological level, Fauconnier states:

> In terms of processing, elements in mental spaces correspond to activated neuronal assemblies and linking between elements corresponds to some kind of neurobiological binding. On this view, mental spaces operate in working memory, but are built up partly by activating structures available from long-term memory. Mental spaces are interconnected in working memory, can be modified as thought and discourse unfold, and can be used generally to model dynamic mappings in thought and language.[11]

The network model posits that a mental spaces network begins with a *base space*, a space which represents the mutually known world of the interlocutors.[12] The base space is where a situation is set up. Thereafter,

---

Grammar; Ronald W. Langacker, *Grammar and Conceptualization*, Cognitive Linguistics Research 14 (Berlin: Mouton de Gruyter, 1999); Langacker, *Concept, Image, and Symbol: The Cognitive Basis of Grammar*. For cognitive science see Fauconnier and Sweetser, *Spaces, Worlds, and Grammar*; Gilles Fauconnier, *Mental Spaces: Aspects of Meaning Construction in Natural Language* (Cambridge: Cambridge University Press, 1994); idem, *Mappings in Thought and Language* (Cambridge: Cambridge University Press, 1997); Fauconnier and Turner, *The Way We Think*; Ray Jackendoff, *Languages of the Mind* (Cambridge, Mass: MIT, 1999); Lee, *Cognitive Linguistics: An Introduction*; John R. Taylor, *Cognitive Grammar*, Oxford Textbooks in Linguistics (Oxford; New York: Oxford University Press, 2002).

8   The term *on-line* is used here to describe meaning construction as a process that occurs in the mind of the conceptualizer and is prompted by both linguistic and non-linguistic cues.

9   Fauconnier and Turner, *The Way We Think*, 40.

10   In the early stages of research, the present writer entertained this thought as a likely extension of the two-dimensional lattice. Coincidentally, Fauconnier has introduced a bubble chamber metaphor in his later writing. Ibid., 321.

11   Ibid., 102.

12   Fauconnier, *Mappings*, 38-39.

it remains accessible for meaning construction from other derivative spaces. As discourse progresses, new spaces are opened, structured and linked. *Space-builders* are terms which act as cues for establishing new mental spaces or which refer back to previously opened mental spaces.[13] New spaces are linked to the base space, and the network is extended as these new spaces are incorporated. At any given point in time, one space will be the *focus space* in the developing discourse. The focus space is where new information accrues (corresponding to the onstage region in Figure 1.1). It is accessed from the current *viewpoint* space (corresponding to the viewer/reader in Figure 1.1).

Once established, mental spaces are internally structured by frames and cognitive models.[14] A mental space is said to be *framed* when "...elements and relations are organized as a package that we already know about."[15] A frame is a recognisable organisation of elements and relations which is present in long-term memory and may be recruited into the mental spaces network at the working memory level. A frame may include information based upon scales: *how quickly, how much, how large*; it may possess force dynamic structure: *tapping a key, slapping a back, hitting a wall*; there may be image schemas involved: *containment, path* or *direction*; and vital relations, such as *change, identity, time* and space may be expressed.[16] These features are likely to appear in various combinations within a single frame, prompting Fauconnier to note: "There is a massive interplay among scales, force dynamic patterns, image schemas, and vital relations, all of which are ubiquitously available in human conceptual structure and cognition."[17]

A frame may exhibit various degrees of complexity. A frame might be quite specific, such as the frame represented by a boxing match, which would include a boxing ring, two opponents, a referee, a particular type of force dynamics and so on. A frame might be more generic, such as a fighting frame, which would include opponents and force dynamics. Finally, a frame might be more generic yet, such as a competition frame, which would include competitors but leave the force dynamics unspecified. Additionally, mental spaces might exhibit an even more finely-grained typology which includes various details, such as

---

13   Fauconnier, *Mental Spaces*, 17.

14   Fauconnier, *Mappings*, 39.

15   Fauconnier and Turner, *The Way We Think*, 104.

16   Additional vital relations include: cause-effect, part-whole, representation, role, analogy, dis-analogy, property, similarity, category, intentionality and uniqueness. Ibid., 93.

17   Ibid., 104.

the colour of the boxing ring, the shoe size of the fighter, the time of day and so on.[18]

Frames and cognitive models represent two linguistic construal operations, or conceptualization processes involved in human communication. Additionally, mental spaces, or conceptual packets, may be structured internally by deixis, metaphor, metonymy and other vital relations such as cause and effect.[19] The present study highlights image schemas as elements that are shared by the text originator and the reader. Additionally, there is an emphasis upon information structure and deixis, as these processes contribute to establishing perspective. Image schemata are described below, and perspective will be discussed in the section to follow.

4.   Image Schemata

Image schemata are one way that human beings retain generic background knowledge of the world, incorporating it with linguistic structures and more complex cultural background knowledge in the process of meaning construction. The generic nature of image schemata within human experience provides an important link between the author/originator of an ancient text and the variety of readers of the text. Regarding image schemata, which also operate at *level C*, Mark Johnson notes:

> … image schemata and their transformations constitute a distinct level of cognitive operations, which is different from both concrete rich images (mental pictures), on the one hand, and abstract, finitary propositional representations on the other.[20]

> … they operate at one level of generality and abstraction above concrete, rich images. A schema consists of a small number of parts and relations, by virtue of which it can structure indefinitely many perceptions, images, and events. In sum, image schemata operate at a level of mental organization

---

18   Paul Werth uses the boxing ring analogy in his analysis. A consistent use of this finely grained typology is one detail that distinguishes Werth's discourse worlds, text worlds and sub-worlds from Fauconnier's mental spaces. Paul Werth, "How to Build a World (in a Lot Less Than Six Days, Using Only What's in Your Head)," in *New Essays on Deixis: Discourse, Narrative, Literature,* ed. Keith Green (Amsterdam: Rodopi, 1995), 49-80.

19   Croft and Cruse argue, "If linguistic construal operations are truly cognitive, then they should be related to or identical with, general cognitive processes that are postulated by psychologists." Croft and Cruse, *Cognitive Linguistics,* 45.

20   Johnson, *The Body in the Mind: The Bodily Basis of Meaning, Imagination, and Reason,* 27.

that falls between abstract propositional structures, on the one side, and particular concrete images on the other.[21]

Additionally, for Johnson, image schemata are derived from and help to order embodied human experiences. He proposes:

> In order for us to have meaningful, connected experiences that we can comprehend and reason about, there must be a pattern and order to our actions, perceptions, and conceptions. *A schema is a recurrent pattern, shape, and regularity in, or of, these ongoing ordering activities.* These patterns emerge as meaningful structures for us chiefly at the level of our bodily movements through space, our manipulation of objects, and our perceptual interactions.[22]

Generic image schemas are subject to transformation by the conceptualiser. Lakoff observes that the conceptualiser is able to perform various transformations upon basic image schemata by manipulating abstract structure in mental space. Johnson highlights four possible transformations:

a. path-focus to endpoint-focus;

b. multiplex to mass;

c. following a trajectory; and

d. superimposition.[23]

Thus, a generic image schema, such as the path schema, may be manipulated in the mind of the conceptualiser to produce motion along the path that begins at one point and ends at another. The vanishing of the Cheshire Cat, *beginning with the end of his tail and ending with the grin,* is a whimsical, rich image based upon the path schema and manipulated by the path-focus to endpoint-focus transformation. This process is accompanied by a twist in the usual figure-ground configuration, in which the figure is highlighted against the ground. In this case, the figure is systematically erased from the ground until only the grin remains. By leaving the grin, Carroll plays upon expectations, this time by a manipulation of the centre-periphery schema. This generic schema springs from the embodied human experience, in which bodies have a core, and they have extremities. It has been observed that the core contains the vital elements of life and is required, while it is possible to get on with missing extremities. Carroll reverses the internal logic of the centre-periphery schema by leaving the peripheral and removing the

---

21   Ibid., 29.
22   Ibid.
23   Ibid., 26.

centre.[24] Image schemata are one way that embodied human experience may be said to be shared across cultures and across time; thus examining the text from this perspective provides a significant point of contact.

B. Prophetic Text and Perspective

Perspective, which includes viewpoint, deixis and subjectivity-objectivity, provides much relevant information for understanding prophetic text. Linguistic construal operations such as viewpoint and deixis originate from embodied experience and provide means for understanding non-spatial abstractions as well.[25] A brief description of viewpoint and deixis, as well as perspective in non-spatial domains follows.

1. Viewpoint

The discussion of cognitive viewpoint is particularly important for the TD analysis of Jeremiah 1.1-6.30. Cognitive viewpoint, according to Langacker, is a "focal adjustment."[26] Langacker differentiates between *vantage point* and *orientation*. For example, construal of the statement *Timmy is in front of the tree* depends upon the physical vantage point of the speaker as well as the relative positions of Timmy and the tree. Of the three coordinates used in assessing the situation, the tree is the most stable. The observer and Timmy are both movable. Thus when Timmy is located between the observer and the tree, he is said to be in *front* of the tree. Alternatively, if the observer and Timmy are located at opposite sides of the tree, the statement *Timmy is in back of the tree* is more accurate. *Orientation* is determined by verticality, the understanding of which is derived from a person's canonical, ordinarily upright position, which results in the cognitive differentiation of *above* and *below*.[27]

---

24   A case might be made for the universality of image schemata, based upon the worldwide popularity of *Alice's Adventures*. Carroll's masterful manipulation of image schemata is attractive, if not slightly disturbing.

25   For a cognitive linguistics view of deixis, see the essays in Frank Brisard, *Grounding: The Epistemic Footing of Deixis and Reference*, Cognitive Linguistics Research; 21 (Berlin: M. de Gruyter, 2002).

26   Langacker, *Foundations of Cognitive Grammar*, 40-45.

27   Croft and Cruse, *Cognitive Linguistics*, 59.

Significantly, when the term *viewpoint space* is used to describe part of a mental space construction, it is used in a much more schematic way. Thus, in his landmark study of the particle כִּי, Follingstad rightly differentiates between *viewpoint*, which is a cognitive concept, and literary *point of view*. In other words, *viewpoint*, when applied to a mental spaces configuration, is a cognitive level function, while literary *point of view* is a manifestation of the viewpoint function by an entity in a specific discourse. From a TD perspective, the speaker/author uses literary *point of view* as a cue for meaning construction on the part of the hearer/reader.[28] Thus it is a specific instantiation, or manifestation, of the more schematic cognitive *viewpoint*.[29] The author/originator employs literary *point of view* to create perspective in the text. Thus, the author/originator might assign the O (originator) role to him- or herself, as in a letter; to a narrator or to anonymous third person; or to any one of a number of characters in the text. The narrator, or generic third person speaker, is the default choice. The narrator has the widest access to pragmatic information regarding the ground of the event described and the characters involved. The narrator, as speaker, is able to report the speech and thoughts of the characters (both directly and indirectly), and to assign access to the character's *situatedness in the world*. This includes not only spatio-temporal information, but information regarding his or her state of knowledge and consciousness (epistemic information) and will, wishes and desires (deontic information). Thus, when a character speaks or evaluates a situation, access to information is constrained to the character's perspective. Most importantly, the reader is accompanied by a variety of "companions" as the literary point of view shifts in the text. However, cognitive structuring is not limited to literary point of view, and subsidiary mental spaces might accrue within the scope of a single instance of literary point of view, i.e. when a character reports a thought that includes a shift in ground.

---

28   Inevitably, the author's use of this cue will be conditioned by grammar, context and culture. The reader's encounter with the cue will also be conditioned by grammar, context and culture.

29   Fauconnier states, "Language, as we know it, is a superficial manifestation of hidden, highly abstract, cognitive constructions... Mental spaces are the domains that discourse builds up to provide a cognitive substrate for reasoning and interfacing with the world." Fauconnier, *Mappings*, 34.

2.   Deixis

Deixis is defined as:

> ...the characteristic function of linguistic expressions that relate to the personal, spatial, and temporal aspects of utterances depending upon the given utterance situation.[30]

Thus, deixis provides perspective that is anchored in some way to a speaker in a given situation of speaking. A situation of speaking might be prototypical, as represented by a face-to-face conversation, or non-prototypical, as represented by a written text. Text is non-prototypical due to its *meta-representational* character. A second layer of complexity arises in that written text often contains reported speech acts occurring between characters. For this reason, deictic terms and constructions act at a minimum of two distinct levels when a text is involved. First, there are text-level, or *meta-linguistic* deictic terms and phrases which an author uses to guide his or her reader through the text. These are often used as space-builders. Secondly, there are *real world* terms that act as cues for cognitive structuring of situations and predications involving characters within the text. These terms and constructions are also used in face-to-face communication situations, and are examples of deixis as a structuring device.

3.   Deixis and Biblical Hebrew

Konrad Ehlich has made a significant contribution towards understanding deictic terms in Biblical Hebrew. Ehlich expands upon the work of Bühler in distinguishing between deictic function and anaphoric function. He states:

> The deictic procedure is a linguistic instrument for achieving focusing of the hearer's attention towards a specific item which is part of the respective deictic space (*deiktischer Raum*). The deictic procedure is performed by means of deictic expressions.[31]

> The anaphoric procedure is a linguistic instrument for having the hearer continue (sustain) a previously established focus towards a specific item on

---

30 Hadumon Bussman, *Routledge Dictionary of Language and Linguistics* (London: Routledge, 1996), 117.

31 Konrad Ehlich, "Anaphora and Deixis: Same, Similar, or Different?" in *Speech, Place, and Action*, eds R. J. Jarvella and Wolfgang Klein (Chichester: Wiley, 1982), 315-338 (325). Another important contribution to the discussion of deixis is Karl Bühler, "The Deictic Field of Language and Deictic Words," in *Speech, Place, and Action: Studies in Deixis and Related Topics*, eds R. J. Jarvella and W. Klein (Chichester: John Wiley and Sons, 1982), 9-30.

which he had oriented his attention earlier. The anaphoric procedure is performed by means of anaphoric expressions.[32]

Ehlich's distinction between the pointing function of deictic terms and the attention sustaining function of anaphoric terms is significant from a cognitive point of view. Deictic terms are likely to be involved in activating new discourse entities (sentence focus) or calling attention to previously introduced entities (argument focus). In other words, deictic terms act as space-builders, whereas anaphoric terms are likely to be used as structuring devices.

The following chart contains a selection of BH terms and constructions which cue both deictic and anaphoric functions. It is noteworthy that these terms and constructions represent a number of semantic domains, including prepositions (spatial), pronouns (person), adverbs (time and space), particles (text), and conjunctions (text). The terms are separated into three categories: *real world* terms that are used in face-to-face communication; *linguistic world* terms that are used by the originator to assist the reader through the text; and *relation words*, which are used to establish the relationship between elements in a sentence, in which perspective is determined by the elements.

---

32   Ehlich, "Anaphora and Deixis: Same, Similar, or Different?" 330.

Biblical Hebrew Deictic Terms		
"Relation Words" *Relationswörter*[33] *Author, Narrator or Character Perspective in Text*	ב ל כ מן על אל בין אצל בעד נגד אחר סביבות עד אשר מאז עד־בלתי בטר מעם מתחת תרם	
"Real World" Terms Personal, Spatial and Temporal *Character Perspective in Text*		
1st and 2nd person pronouns *Speech Act*	אנכי אני אנחנו את אתה את אתם	"I" 1/s "we" 1/p "you" f/s; f/p "you" m/s; m/p
Demonstrative Pronouns: *Deictic Function*[34]	זה זאת אלה הוה היא הן המא הנה	"this"; "these" "he"; "she" "they"
Locative Adverbs: *Deictic Function*	הנה פה הלם שם שמה משם	
Temporal Adverbs: *Deictic Function*	עתה ועתה היום אז אזי מהר טרם אטמול שלשום תמול עדן עדנה כבר	
"Linguistic World" Terms *Discourse and Text Author's Perspective*		
Text Deictics	ויהי והיה ועתה	
Sentence Deictics	הנה והנה הן הא	
Discourse Markers	ה ככה לכן על־כן כזכ	

4. Perspective and Non-spatial Domains

Viewpoint, deixis and image schemata are spatially based phenomena. However, these perspective-inducing terms and constructions are

---

33 Harald Schweizer, Metaphorische Grammatik: Wege zur Integration von Grammatik und *Textinterpretation in der Exegese* (St. Ottilien: EOS-Verlag, 1981), 236-237.
34 Konrad Ehlich, *Verwendungen der Deixis Beim Sprachlichen Handeln: Linguistisch Philologische Untersuchungen zum Hebräischen Deiktischen System* (Frankfurt am Main and Las Vegas: P. Lang, 1979).

available for structuring non-spatial domains as well. As Croft and Cruse note:

> Perspective, especially deixis, is perhaps the most obvious and most commented upon of the construal operations. Particularly for spatial descriptions, perspective is essential and its dependence on the relative position of the speaker is well known. But perspective is also found in nonspatial domains: we have a perspective based on our knowledge, belief, and attitudes as well as our spatiotemporal location.[35]

Perspective based upon knowledge, belief and attitudes forms the basis for a specific category of space building terms and constructions. This group of space-builders, which includes terms from the semantic fields of perception and cognition, are particularly prominent in prophetic literature, hence they are key to the concerns of this volume.[36] The space-builder that initiates a new space is the first indication of the manner in which a space is to be construed by the conceptualiser. Temporal references, such as *in 1925*, indicate a time space; locative references, such as *on the planet Mars*, indicate a locative space; references to schematic information, such as *in the game of chess*, refer to a domain space. Verbs of speaking, such as *…and God said…* at Jeremiah 3.6a, indicate a quotation space; verbs of perception, such as *…and I saw…* at Jeremiah 3.8a, indicate an intake of information space.[37] Perspective based upon knowledge, belief and attitude is indicated by the use of a mental state predicate, such as *think, believe, doubt, know, suppose* and *guess*.[38] Thus, these terms set up propositional attitude spaces, spaces that are closely associated with the individual or entity involved, as are the propositional content quotation spaces and intake of information spaces.

---

35 Croft and Cruse, *Cognitive Linguistics*, 58.

36 These are the *verba sentiendi* and *verba sciendi*, terms such as see, hear, know, understand, remember, forget and consider. These terms take an experiencer as grammatical subject and often take complement clauses as grammatical object.

37 The scalar nature of this category is well represented in the Jeremiah 3.6-11 example in Chapter 2, where אמר indicates both speech and thought and ראה indicates both visual perception and observation.

38 Nuyts describes epistemic modality as a semantic domain and proposes a list of mental state predicates which overlaps with one group of space building terms. This implies that the remaining groups of space-builders, such as time reference, spatial reference and social reference, are represented in language by groups of words and terms from specific semantic domains, which may vary widely in their grammatical composition (i.e. prepositions involved in spatial description, temporal adverbs and verb tense involved in temporal description and personal pronouns involved in social description). Significantly, a variety of grammatical forms act as cues for the cognitive space-builder function. Thus, the correspondence between grammatical form and cognitive function is not one to one, but rather many to one, and is based upon the interface between syntax and semantics.

A propositional attitude space has affinities with the concept of epistemic modality, or "a speaker's evaluation of the likelihood of a state
of affairs, as expressed in language."[39] As in spatial and temporal references, perspective is indexed by the position of speaker as centre, albeit
in a more abstract manner than the normal deictic centre. Nuyts takes
an experientialist view, stating:

> Evaluating the likelihood of a state of affairs is not just a (modal) linguistic
> category. It relates directly to the way we perceive, memorize and act in the
> physical and social world we live in ...our capacity to reflect on our know-
> ledge and our reasoning with it...our capacity to metarepresent.[40]

Nuyts speaks in concert with Marmaridou, who argues for an experientialist approach to deixis, and with Croft and Cruse, who associate
perspective with "the philosophical notion of our *situatedness in the
world* in a particular location – where location must be construed broad-
ly to include temporal, epistemic, and cultural context as well as spatial
location."[41] The TD approach adopts this experientialist perspective, as
it provides a comprehensive basis for determining the ground of a situation of speaking, both as it relates to the speaker/author and to the
representation of situations of speaking from the embedded perspective of various characters. [42]

Because of its emphasis upon cognitive structuring, the TD approach is useful for confronting two interrelated questions that loom
large for exegetes, translators and students of BH text. First, what constellation of linguistic features serves to delimit a section of text for
interpretation? Secondly, what linguistic and cognitive factors structure
and interconnect various sections of the text? The network model is
able to account for cognitive structuring that is indicated by both sentences and longer segments of text.[43] A primary goal of the TD approach is to examine texts for grammatical cues that act as space-
builders and space connectors, as well as for elements that structure
and interconnect spaces. Thus, a comprehensive synchronic text level
analysis both precedes and informs historical and cultural study. It is

---

39   Jan Nuyts, *Epistemic Modality, Language, and Conceptualization* (Amsterdam: John
     Benjamins, 2001), xv.

40   Ibid.

41   Croft and Cruse, *Cognitive Linguistics*, 58; Marmaridou, *Pragmatic Meaning and Cogni-
     tion*.

42   The experientialist approach is also evident in conceptual metaphor studies, such as
     those by Lakoff and Johnson. This issue will be explored in chapter 4.B.3.

43   See Margaret H. Freeman, "Cognitive Mapping in Literary Analysis," *Style* (2002);
     José Sanders and Gisela Redeker, "Perspective and the Representation of Speech and
     Thought in Narrative Discourse," in *Spaces, Worlds, and Grammar*, eds G. Fauconnier
     and E. Sweetser (Chicago: University of Chicago Press, 1996).

important to consider this as a cyclical process in which diachronic historical and cultural study also impact synchronic understandings of the text.

C. Jeremiah 3.6-3.11

Since cognitive packets are "…set up, structured, and linked under pressure from grammar, context, and culture," a thorough grammatical analysis is the first priority for the TD approach.[44] The results of this analysis provide the basis for contextual and cultural inferences and connections. The first step is a comprehensive syntax analysis. Secondly, preliminary decisions regarding the information structure category of *topic* are made for each of the clauses represented in the analysis. Third, preliminary decisions regarding the information structure category of *focus* are made for each clause and for the section in question. Fourth, preliminary decisions regarding the cognitive structuring of the larger section are proposed from a cognitive network perspective. This is based upon the nature of the space-builders involved, and which linguistic construal operations, in addition to information structure, are available for structuring and linking the spaces. Finally, the analysis is refined and finalised, based upon the previous findings, in conjunction with available historical and cultural information.[45]

1.   Clause analysis

The syntax portion of the clause analysis follows the ascendant, recursive model, originally developed for the computer database at VU, Amsterdam and now utilised by the Stuttgart Electronic Study Bible.[46]

---

44   Fauconnier and Sweetser, *Spaces, Worlds, and Grammar*, 11.

45   This process has similarities to that of Sebastiaan Floor, who utilises the information structure categories *topic* and *focus* to examine texts for *theme traces*, or "…clues in the surface form of a discourse that…point to the cognitive macrostructure or theme of the text." Sebastiaan J. Floor, "From Information Structure, Topic, and Focus, to Theme in Biblical Hebrew Narrative." (DLit, University of Stellenbosch, 2004). A major difference between the two approaches involves the notion of *macrostructure*. While a TD approach argues for cognitive structuring and that such structuring is cued by surface level information presented by the text, it abandons the term *macrostructure* in favour of the phrase *on-line meaning construction*, which better reflects the notion of cognitive structuring as a dynamic process which is *prompted by* rather than *contained in* the text.

46   The ascendant process eliminates some of the ambiguity that results from a descendent process, such as that used by Longacre, as it begins by discerning the contours

This ascendant process mimics, to a certain degree, the brain activity involved in the reading process.[47] Initially, the text is segmented into clause-level units.[48] One clause comprises one predication, and a clause may be either verbal or nominal. At minimum, a verbal clause consists of an inflected or participial verbal form plus an implicit or explicit subject. While the TD model begins with clause level segments, it is important to note that the clause-level segments comprise phrase-level segments, or *clause atoms*, and that phrase-level segments comprise lexical-level segments, or *phrase atoms*.[49] This understanding reflects the extremely detailed accounting of surface-level text features that is required for computerised text processing.[50] When parsing a text, the computer delimits the lexical and phrase-level segments by a set of recursive pattern matching processes. It is possible to replicate this manually, however, it is time consuming and possibly less accurate to do so.

Because pattern matching is important for establishing connections at the lexeme and phrase levels, it is hypothesised that clause level patterns may be used to establish connections at the sentence and dis-

---

of the text and then observes for cognitive structural cues and clues, rather than beginning with a structural theory and imposing the theory upon the text. For a critique of Longacre in this respect, see Jean-Marc Heimerdinger, *Topic, Focus and Foreground in Ancient Hebrew Narratives*, JSOT Sup 295 (Sheffield: Sheffield Academic Press, 1999).

47 Cognitive scientists use *event-related brain potential measures* in tracking the two phases of language processing represented by speaking and hearing. In speaking, an area of the brain known as the *Broca* area is responsible for breaking complex ideas into smaller units which are linearised, whereas in hearing the same area is responsible for the analysis and synthesis of incoming information into a meaningful structure. Thus, a bottom-up method of analysis most closely resembles the hearing process of the human brain. W. Raible, "Language Universals and Language Typology," in *Language Typology and Language Universals: An International Handbook*, eds M. Haspelmath et al. (Berlin: Walter de Gruyter, 2001), 13.

48 A clause-level analysis offers benefits for the study of parallelism. The TD clause-level analysis offers a visually stacked display which facilitates observation of constituent order, which is a defining feature of various types of parallelism. Other studies which employ a clause-level analysis include Walter Theophilus Woldemar Cloete, *Versification and Syntax in Jeremiah 2-25: Syntactical Constraints in Hebrew Colometry* (Atlanta, Ga: Scholars Press, 1989); Terence Collins, *Line-Forms in Hebrew Poetry: A Grammatical Approach to the Stylistic Study of the Hebrew Prophets*, Studia Pohl. Series Maior; 7 (Rome: Biblical Institute Press, 1978); Michael Patrick O'Connor, *Hebrew Verse Structure* (Winona Lake, Ind: Eisenbrauns, 1980).

49 The construct phrase is one such pattern that occurs with regularity in BH. See J. H. A. Kroeze, "Semantic Relations in Construct Phrases of Biblical Hebrew: A Functional Approach," *ZAH* 11 (1998), 27-41.

50 This level of detail is also required for language learners. Verheij utilises some of the clause segmentation and pattern matching techniques in his introductory grammar. A. J. C. Verheij, *Basisgrammatica Van Het Bijbels Hebreeuws* (Delft: Eburon, 2002).

course levels as well. For example, clauses might function as *sentence atoms* and sentences as *discourse atoms*.[51] This illustrates that single lexemes do not simply connect as beads on a string, but they demonstrate patterns of combination which are acceptable at each of several processing levels. However, the situation is more complicated when connections at the sentence and discourse level are involved.[52] Lehmann demonstrates that a number of intersecting factors contribute to clause linkage. These include:

- Autonomy versus Integration;
  - o Hierarchical downgrading;
  - o Syntactic level of subordinate clause;
- Expansion vs. Reduction;
  - o Sententiality vs. nominality of subordinate clause;
  - o Independent predicate vs. grammatical operator;
- Isolation vs. Linkage;
  - o Interlacing of two clauses; and
  - o Explicitness of the linking[53]

Each of these parameters involves two sets of scalar contrasts. Lehmann's approach to clause linkage is considered the most analytical of

---

51 Talstra proposes patterns of phrase level connections, i.e. אשר clauses and infinitives connect to the immediately preceding clause. He also proposes sets of clause level connections at the same level, and at unequal levels. Same level connections tend to occur between *wayyiqtol+subject/wayyiqtol+subject* and *wayyiqtol-subject/wayyiqtol-subject* clauses. Unequal level connections appear between *wayyiqtol+subject/wayyiqtol-subject; wayyiqtol-subject/wayyiqtol+subject; wayyiqtol-subject/we-X-qatal*. E. Talstra, "A Hierarchy of Clauses in Biblical Hebrew Narrative," in *Narrative Syntax and the Hebrew Bible*, ed. Ellen van Wolde (Leiden: Brill, 2002), 107.

52 For the VU database, the levels of connection are based upon computer guided proposals and are modified by operator feedback. The programmes process information in several stages. The first stage is an examination of the text for co-occurrences of words in a manner similar to that of a traditional concordance. The second stage involves examining the text for combinations of words and grammatical features. In the third stage, the beginning and ending of individual clauses is noted. At stage four larger constituents are grammatically parsed and tagged as *subject, predicate, adjunct* and so on. At stage five the text is presented as a listing of clauses and clause types, indicating syntax, style and text structure. At stage six, text-types such as narrative, quotation and discursive are noted, along with the embedding each represents. Finally, clause connections are proposed. Talstra, "Text Segmentation and Linguistic Levels," 3-7.

53 Christian Lehmann, "Towards a Typology of Clause Linkage," in *Clause Combining in Grammar and Discourse*, eds John Haiman and Sandra Thompson (Amsterdam: Benjamins, 1988), 217.

the typological approaches and is a useful tool for cross-linguistic analysis.[54] This is noteworthy. Since there are no native speakers of BH, anyone who approaches the ancient text does so by learning the language, which involves a certain amount of translation, particularly at the early stages. The complexity of clause linking highlights both the strengths and limitations of computerised text processing. While research findings from the VU corpus clarify the nature of BH clause connections, the linear analysis requires human intervention in order to account for features such as verbal ellipsis and defective clauses that contribute to irregular patterns. This complexity also contributes to the insufficiency of descendent models for analysing prophetic texts, which may contain similar syntactic information at several hierarchical levels, i.e. a series of *wayyiqtol* clauses with varying semantic content, such as the presence of verbs of speaking and perception.

The choice of clause level segments is significant for information structure in two ways. First, the inherent relation between a predicate and its arguments affects clause structure.[55] This feature, otherwise referred to as verbal valence, affects the number of arguments involved in a particular situation, which in turn affects the construal of topical entities at the sentence and paragraph level.[56] Secondly, constituent order contributes to establishing the type of focus indicated by a clause or sentence. Each verbal predication has a focus element such as a predicate, argument or sentence, which is determined in part by word order and in part by prosody.[57] Moreover, a complement clause might act as an argument, taking the subject or object role in a larger sentence.[58] Such clauses contain a focus element of their own, and in turn

---

54 W. Raible, "Linking Clauses," in *Language Typology and Language Universals: An International Handbook*, eds. M. Haspelmath et al. (Berlin: Walter de Gruyter, 2001), 614.

55 Here the term *argument* is used for nouns/noun phrases and prepositional phrases with the syntactic function of subject, direct object or indirect object. The term *predicate* "…expresses the state of affairs that the referents of the arguments are involved in." Robert D. Van Valin, *An Introduction to Syntax* (Cambridge: Cambridge University Press, 2001), 9.

56 Stative and intransitive verbs take a subject, mono-transitive verbs take a subject and direct object, and di-transitive verbs take a subject, direct object and an indirect object. Some verbs are capable of taking two direct objects, resulting in a double accusative construction.

57 It is widely assumed that prosody is unavailable for BH. Shimasaki proposes that prosody is recoverable. Katsuomi Shimasaki, *Focus Structure in Biblical Hebrew: A Study of Word Order and Information Structure* (Bethesda, Md: CDL Press, 2002), 240. The present author is reluctant to make definitive statements in this regard, as there are no native speakers to provide phonological data for linguistic analysis.

58 Kaoru Horie, "Complement Clauses," in *Language Typology and Language Universals*, ed. M. Haspelmath (Berlin: Walter de Gruyter, 2001); Michel Noonan, "Complemen-

an entire complement clause might act as the focus element within a sentence. The TD analysis presented in this volume is the result of a manual process, which in turn has been checked against the computer-generated analysis and adjusted at some points.[59] A sample analysis of Jeremiah 3.6-10 follows:

Clause Layout	Jer
וַיֹּאמֶר יְהוָה אֵלַי בִּימֵי יֹאשִׁיָּהוּ הַמֶּלֶךְ	3.6a
הֲרָאִיתָ	b
אֲשֶׁר עָשְׂתָה מְשֻׁבָה יִשְׂרָאֵל	c
הֹלְכָה הִיא עַל־כָּל־הַר גָּבֹהַּ וְאֶל־תַּחַת כָּל־עֵץ רַעֲנָן	d
וַתִּזְנִי־שָׁם	e

Jer	Type	Clause Tag	PNG	Focus	MSC
3.6a	N	Wayyiqtol-X	3sgM	PRED	Base
b	NQ	X-Qatal	2sgM	Inter	SB for M¹
c	NQP	X-Qatal	3sgF	ARGU	M¹ Focus
d	NQP	Qotel	sgF	PRED	
e	NQPN	Wayyiqtol-0	3sgF	PRED	

Figure 2.2   Jeremiah 3.6-3.11 Clause Analysis

---

tation," in *Language Typology and Syntactic Description*, ed. Timothy Schopen (Cambridge: Cambridge University Press, 1985), 181.

59 Figure 2.2 uses a text-boxing system to highlight clause constituents. This is a useful method for tracking constituent order, which in turn affects information structure. In this example, verbal forms are boxed by a single line, grammatical subjects are boxed with double lines and the prepositional phrase is boxed with a dashed line. This system provides another way to track anaphoric connections, such as the connection between the subject in 3.6c and the pronoun in 3.6d. The search function in the SESB edition of BHS utilises colour in a similar manner.

The TD linguistic analysis consists of the following categories: Top box: verse identification and analysed text; Bottom box: Column one contains the verse identification, Column two records the discourse type: narrative – N; direct speech – Q; perception – P.[60] Column three presents the clause tag, which contains the verb type (*wayyiqtol, yiqtol, qatal, we-qatal, participle, infinitive*) and basic word order information. Column four contains person, number and gender information. Column five contains information structure notes regarding the verbal stem or the type of *focus*. Column six contains preliminary observations regarding cognitive structuring. Various mental spaces construction tags will appear in this column. In this case, the first clause sets up the base space, tagged *Base*. The second clause opens a mental space for the third clause. In the third clause this space is tagged M[1]. In later examples when perspective is assigned to a narrator, the tag will be N with a superscript number identifying the speaker. When perspective within a space belongs to a character, the tag will be C with a superscript number identifying the character. N and C tags identify the entity whose deictic centre represents primary viewpoint within a space. Cnstituents in this example have been marked for clarity. The verbal forms have a single-lined box, lexicalized subjects have a double-lined box and the direct object as a dashed box.

a.   Differentiating Between Narrative and Discursive Text

Since prophetic text exhibits a high degree of complexity due to multiple shifts in genre and the high degree of reported speech, the TD approach proposes that suitable cross-genre criteria be utilised in the text analysis process. For example, in BH it is possible to make a primary distinction between discursive speech and narrative speech. This is largely a syntax-based distinction, as it depends upon verbal forms and word order. Thus, it is accounted for prior to semantic analysis.[61]

---

60   The first two of these categories are proposed by Wolfgang Schneider and are based upon his observations regarding sets of verbal forms. He notes that, from the perspective of syntax, discursive sections of text tend to contain *yiqtol, qatal* and *we-qatal* forms, while narrative texts tend to contain *wayyiqtol* and *qatal* forms. Schneider, *Grammatik*, 48.48. The perception category is unique to the TD approach. It has been added because verbs of perception act as space-builders, initiating a variety of epistemic spaces.

61   This distinction stands across genres and is not intended to mark text-types such as those observed by Longacre. In this case, the differentiation is significant for establishing viewpoint in the text, which is a matter of *perspective*. The Hebrew verbal system will be addressed in Chapter 4, where Cook's semantically oriented *grammaticalization* approach will be incorporated into the discussion (Cook: 2001).

Wolfgang Schneider discusses the distinction between narrative text and discursive text in his grammar of Biblical Hebrew. His understandings derive from the work of German linguist Harald Weinrich.[62] In his volume *Grammatik des biblischen Hebräisch*, Schneider describes the implications of the syntactic difference between narrative and discursive text.[63] He states, *"Erzählende Rede lässt dem Hörer Freiheit zur Distanzierung. Besprechende Rede engagiert ihn: Sprecher und Hörer haben zu agieren und zu reagieren."* Clearly, there is a significant conceptual distinction between the two types. Viewpoint and perspective account for this distinction: while narrative speech creates distance between the reader and the text, first and second person speech draws the reader into the text. As a result, at the syntactic level, the person and number morphemes attached to the BH verb forms act as primary indicators of viewpoint or perspective in BH text.[64]

Schneider goes on to describe the series of verbal forms that is prevalent in narrative text, *erzählenden Texten*; and the series of forms prevalent in discursive text, *besprechenden Texten*. For Schneider, the main opposition between Hebrew verbal forms is not the paradigmatic distinction between perfect/imperfect, the *qatal /yiqtol* forms. Rather, the distinction is between *wayyiqtol* forms, which are the main forms found in narrative, and *yiqtol* forms, which are the main forms found in discursive sections of text.

At this point cognitive analysis addresses the issue of tense versus aspect with regard to BH verbal forms. The debate is largely about how much perspective-inducing information is included in a given verbal form. On the one hand, if verb forms are viewed as tensed, they become a source of information regarding the perspective-inducing operation of deixis, specifically temporal deixis. On the other hand, if the verb forms are viewed as aspectual, they become a source of information regarding the type of action inherent in the verbal form. In this case, verbal aspect is associated more closely with the viewing arrangement of the activity in question than with the time of the action.[65]

---

62 Harald Weinrich, *Tempus: Besprochene und Erzählte Welt*, 2 ed. (Stuttgart: Kohlhammer, 1971: 49).

63 Importantly, this distinction is not genre based; rather the terms *narrative* and *discursive* are syntactic categories, based upon participant reference information contained in the verbal forms: person/number morphemes. (Talstra 1978: 170).

64 Viewpoint is defined as "... the vantage point (the position from which a scene is viewed) plus the orientation of the viewer." (Langacker 1987: 494).

65 In terms of cognitive grammar, a viewing arrangement may be described as *canonical*, in which case the viewer is distinct from the object of perception, the object of perception is sharply delimited, and the viewer's attention is directed outward. Most importantly, in this viewing arrangement, the viewer construes the perceived object

The distinction between narrative and discursive text is particularly significant for prophetic text. For this reason, the syntactic clause analysis diagrams of Jeremiah 1.1-6.30 document the shifts between narrative and discursive text. These contain the notation N for narrative, D for discursive, in accordance with the WIVU database. In addition, the present author has included a P category of space opened by terms of perception and cognition.

b. Observations

1. Jeremiah 3.6a

Jer	Clause Layout	Type	Clause Tag	PNG
3.6a	וַיֹּאמֶר יְהוָה אֵלַי בִּימֵי יֹאשִׁיָּהוּ הַמֶּלֶךְ	N	Wayyiqtol-S	3sgM

Line 3.6a initiates the section. The clause וַיֹּאמֶר יהוה אלי בימי יאשיהו המלך is tagged *wayyiqtol*+subject. The text-type column contains an N, indicating that this line belongs to a section of narrative. At this point in the discourse, the lexicalised subject יהוה is taken as the topic of the sentence, and the person, number and gender of the verb is 3sgM. Word order is: *verb, subject, indirect object, time margin*. Like other verbs of speaking, וַיֹּאמֶר opens a quotation space.

2. Jeremiah 3.6b

b		הֲרָאִיתָ	NQ	X-Qatal	2sgM

Line 3.6b consists of the single phrase הֲרָאִיתָ, tagged *X-qatal*. In this case, X represents the interrogative prefix, and the verb form is *qatal*. The text-type is NQ, as this is the first quoted line in the narrative. The verb רָאִית derives from √ראה. It is a verb of perception, initiating a new mental space in the following line. The subject of this clause is implicit, the 2sgM *you* of the addressee in the speech event. Although not explicitly mentioned at this point, the larger textual context indicates that this is Jeremiah. For further information, see chapter 5, section F which addresses the problem of identity.

---

with "... maximal objectivity and construes himself with maximal subjectivity." (Langacker 2003:15).

3. Jeremiah 3.6c

c	אֲשֶׁר עָשְׂתָה מְשֻׁבָה יִשְׂרָאֵל	NQP	X-Qatal	3sgF

Line 3.6c, אשר עשתה משבה ישראל, is a relative clause, as indicated by
the initial אשר. The text-type is NQP, as this clause is the complement
of the perception verb, רָאִית. The clause is embedded in a quotation,
which in turn is part of a narrative section. The clause tag *is X-Qatal*. In
this case, the X represents the relative particle אשר, which acts as a syntactic hinge to the preceding clause.[66] The person, number and gender
notation is 3sgF, in agreement with the explicit subject משבה ישראל.
Three different referents are mentioned within three lines: two explicit
subjects, the first person יהוה and the third person משבה ישראל; and the
implicit mention of the second person addressee, Jeremiah. The conceptual significance of these entities will be taken up in the section on conceptual metaphor in chapter 5, section B. Their significance as topical
referents is the subject of chapter 2, section C.2.

4. Jeremiah 3.6d

d	הֹלְכָה הִיא עַל־כָּל־הַר גָּבֹהַּ וְאֶל־תַּחַת כָּל־עֵץ רַעֲנָן	NQP	Qotel	sgF

Line 3.6d is an asyndetic participial clause, which links to the preceding
clause with a high degree of embedding. The phrase הלכה היא continues the perception space introduced in line 3.6b and is in VS order.
Given that SV is the unmarked order for participial clauses, this phrase
is in marked word order, indicating argument focus.

5. Jeremiah 3.6e

e	וַתִּזְנִי־שָׁם	NQPN	Wayyiqtol-0	3sgF

Jeremiah 3.6e is a *wayyiqtol-0* clause. The *0* indicates that there is no
overt subject. The word order is V-Adv. The 3sgF form continues the
participant reference established in 3.6c, where the idea of the doings of
turnable Israel is introduced to the discussion. At this point in the analysis several key terms and concepts have been mentioned. These in-

---

66   This clause connection is used in the WIVU database, where the clause containing
אשר joins immediately to the preceding clause. Talstra, "A Hierarchy of Clauses in
Biblical Hebrew Narrative," 95.

clude: topic, focus word order, maintaining reference and mental spaces. Topic, focus, and word order are information structure categories, which are introduced in chapter 2, section C.2, below and developed in the following section. Maintaining reference and mental spaces are conceptual categories, discussed in chapter 3 and beyond.

2.   Information Structure

a.   Topic

Returning to the computer programme metaphor, information structure involves the semantic and pragmatic layers of the text.[67] Just as clause structure is affected by the inherent relationality between a syntactic predicate and its arguments, information structure involves the inherent relationality between topical referents and propositions about these referents. The information structure term *topic* has been defined as follows: "Topic...has to do with the pragmatic relation of aboutness between discourse referents and propositions in given discourse contexts." [68] This definition reflects the linguistic notion of topic-comment articulation, in which a sentence is *about* something.[69] The identification and function of topical expressions is an important component of information structure theory. Lambrecht states, "The function of topical expressions is either to name a topical referent in the discourse or to express a semantic relationship between a topic referent and a predicate."[70]

Pragmatically speaking, the state of knowledge that a speaker assumes that he or she shares with the hearer or reader determines, in

---

67   Lambrecht discusses information structure under four categories: pragmatic presupposition and pragmatic assertion; identifiability and activation; topic and focus. Lambrecht, *Information Structure*, xiii.

68   Ibid., xiv.

69   Heimerdinger elaborates upon Tomlin's definition of topic by introducing the concepts of *topical frame* and *topical elaboration*. Heimerdinger, *Topic, Focus and Foreground in Ancient Hebrew Narratives*, 106. See also Stephen H. Levinsohn, "Review of *Topic, Focus and Foreground in Ancient Hebrew Narratives*, by Jean-Marc Heimerdinger," *JTTL* 14 (2002); C. H. J. van der Merwe, "Review of *Topic, Focus and Foreground*, by Jean-Marc Heimerdinger," *Biblica* 81 (1999). The difference between the introductory function of the topical frame and the developmental function of the topical elaboration correlates with the difference between the deictic procedure and the anaphoric procedure. Ehlich, "Anaphora and Deixis: Same, Similar, or Different?" 315-338.

70   Lambrecht, *Information Structure*, 335.

part, the informational status of topical referents in a discourse.[71] This is an issue of identifiability and activation. Due to the constraints of short-term memory, topical referents may be in various states of activation at a given point in a discourse. Thus, identifiability and activation involve both *knowing* and *consciousness*. With respect to knowing, a referent is considered to be *identifiable* if the hearer is assumed to have a mental representation of the referent in his or her mind.[72] In similar circumstances, a proposition, or state of affairs, is considered to be *presupposed*. With regard to consciousness, a referent (or proposition) that is presently in the hearer's mind is considered to be *discourse active*. Important for the TD analysis, discourse active referents are cognitively preferred topics and unstressed pronominals are the preferred type of topical expression.[73] If a referent or a proposition is to be part of a discourse, it must be discourse active. Thus, if a referent is identifiable (known to the conceptualiser), but not yet discourse active (not in current consciousness), the speaker may utilise topic promoting constructions, such as fronting, to make the referent discourse active. Topical referents may also be brand new and unanchored in discourse, or brand new but in some way anchored to the discourse. In these cases, a presentational construction such as fronting serves an identificational function.[74]

In the Jeremiah examples mentioned above, Yahweh and Jeremiah have already been introduced, so they are already discourse active at this point in the narrative. At this point the relative clause אשר עשתה משבה ישראל is introduced as a topical referent. In short, the narrator reports, via the voice of Jeremiah, that "Yahweh asked me if I had seen what משבה ישראל had done." Three main referents are involved: two interlocutors: Yahweh and Jeremiah; and the referent in their discussion. At first glance, it appears that the referent in the discussion is משבה ישראל, but this is not the case. Jeremiah is asked if he has seen what משבה ישראל *has done*. Syntactically, the third clause is the object of the sentence *Have you seen what turnable Israel has done?* As such, *what Turnable Israel has done* is an argument which includes both Turnable Israel as an entity and her actions as well. The exact nature of

---

71   Pragmatically speaking, this information structure component will vary depending upon the nature of the speech event as a prototypical face-to-face interchange versus that of the reading process modelled in Figure 2.1.
72   This correlates with the idea of encyclopaedic background knowledge.
73   Lambrecht, *Information Structure*, 335.
74   For information regarding extraposed constructions across a range of Semitic languages, see Geoffrey Khan, *Studies in Semitic Syntax*, London Oriental Series; V. 38 (Oxford: Oxford University Press, 1988).

the behaviour is not known at this point in the narrative, although this section creates a certain amount of tension in the text. This tension builds throughout the following sections.

After identifying and activating topical referents, identifying the *topical theme* of a longer discourse is also possible. As Heimerdinger demonstrates, there is often a topical frame involved. A topical frame is a short summary statement that introduces a discourse topical theme, like the phrase הראית אשר עשתה משבה ישראל at 3.6b-c. It is important to note that this topical frame is embedded in the quotative frame established at 3.6a with the sentence ויאמר יהוה אלי בימי יאשיהו המלך.

The question הראית אשר עשתה משבה ישראל is addressed to Jeremiah and introduces both Turnable Israel and her doings. At this point, Turnable Israel is activated as a discourse referent and her doings as the topical theme. The introductory topical frame is followed by the *topical elaboration* in which the topical theme is developed. This begins with the clause הלכה היא על־כל־הר גבה ואל־תחת כל־עץ רענן at 3.6d, followed by ותזני־שם at 3.6e. The doings of Turnable Israel involve *going upon every high hill and under every green tree and committing adultery there*.

b. Focus

Recent studies in the area of BH syntax have explored the connection between the linear ordering of sentence constituents and the information structure component of focus.[75] Each of these studies makes use of Lambrecht's discussion of focus, in particular the relationship between constituent order and focus type.[76] Regarding *focus*, Lambrecht states, "...the focus of a proposition is that semantic element (or elements)

---

75 Floor, "From Information Structure, Topic, and Focus, to Theme in Biblical Hebrew Narrative;" E. R. Hayes, "Hearing Jeremiah: Perception and Cognition in Jeremiah 1.1-2.2," *HS* 45 (2004); Heimerdinger, *Topic, Focus and Foreground in Ancient Hebrew Narratives*; Martin Pröbstle, "Deixis and the Linear Ordering of Sentence Constituents", *SBL, Denver* (2001); Shimasaki, *Focus Structure in Biblical Hebrew: A Study of Word Order and Information Structure*; C. H. J. van der Merwe, J. A. Naudé and J. H. A. Kroeze, *A Biblical Hebrew Reference Grammar* (Sheffield: Sheffield Academic Press, 1999); C. H. J. van der Merwe and Eep Talstra, "Biblical Hebrew Word Order: The Interface of Information Structure and Formal Features," *ZAH* 15/16 (2001).

76 This volume utilises only Lambrecht's framework in order to avoid confusing terminology and competing theoretical discussions. In this regard, see Holmstedt's review of Shimasaki, in which Holmstedt discusses the differences between Lambrecht's framework and that of Simon Dik. He observes that a synthesis of the two results in a "theoretically unfocused model of BH information structure". Robert Holmstedt, "Review of *Focus Structure in Biblical Hebrew: A Study of Word Order and Information Structure*, by Katsuomi Shimasaki," *HS* 44 (2003); Michael Rosenbaum, *Word-Order Variation in Isaiah 40-55: A Functional Perspective* (Assen: Van Gorcum, 1997).

whose presence makes the proposition into an assertion, i.e. a potential piece of information."[77] Lambrecht proposes three basic focus categories based upon the syntax of the sentence: predicate focus; argument focus and sentence focus. At the risk of provoking the sort of Kugelian response which occurs when studying BH poetry (there is either one type of parallelism or one hundred, not three), this volume will explicate focus under these three major categories.[78]

Predicate focus is the default, or unmarked focus type, and is associated with the topic-comment function. Markedness, according to Bussman, "…is concerned with the distinction between what is neutral, natural, or expected, or *unmarked*, and what departs from the neutral, or *marked*, along some specific parameter."[79] In the case of focus, constituent order is the specific parameter involved in determining focus types, particularly in light of the irrecoverability of BH prosody. This work presupposes that the basic, unmarked constituent order for BH sentences is VSO, and that the constituent order is marked when other constituents are placed before the verbal construction.[80]

---

77   Lambrecht, *Information Structure*, 336.

78   It is worth noting that focus categories, like their Lowthian counterparts in the area of parallelism, are meant to be descriptive rather than prescriptive. They are primary level categories, subject to elaboration and modification when used to describe actual sentences.

79   Bussman, *H. Bussman, Dictionary*, 294.

80   There are three reasons for this. First, several sources present VSO as the unmarked order. Among these are C. H. J. van der Merwe, "Explaining Fronting in Biblical Hebrew," *JNSL* 25 (1996), 173-186; van der Merwe and Talstra, "Interface," 68-108; Bruce Waltke and M. O'Connor, *An Introduction to Biblical Hebrew Syntax* (Winona Lake, Ind: Eisenbrauns, 1990), 694. However, the subject is complicated and not all scholars agree. Dissenting voices include JM §155k; John A. Cook, "The Use of *Wayyiqtol* in Hebrew Poetry," *SBL, Atlanta* (2003); Robert Holmstedt, "Word Order and Information Structure in Proverbs," *SBL, Atlanta* (2003), 1-20. Secondly, pragmatics research demonstrates that "… in language comprehension the privilege of primacy arises from general cognitive processes, those involved in structure building… initialized concepts must serve as the foundation for their sentence level structures." Morton Ann, and David Hargreaves, "The Privilege of Primacy," in *Pragmatics of Word Order Flexibility*, ed. Doris L. Payne (Amsterdam: John Benjamins, 1992), 83-116. Finally, language typology and universals research supports this view. Jongling proposes a typological approach to BH in K. Jongeling, "On the VSO Character of Hebrew," in *Studies in Hebrew and Aramaic Syntax*, ed. K. Jongeling (Leiden: Brill, 1991), 103-111. For language typologists, the main distinction between language types is the difference between VO languages and OV languages. According to Primus, BH exhibits *consistent head-initial order* (VO) as opposed to languages that exhibit *consistent head-final order* (OV). The main distinction between head-initial and head-final languages is based upon *Consistent Head Serialization* or CHS, as indicated by the tendency that "…for all phrasal categories X, the head of X either precedes or follows all dependents." Consistent head-initial order is demonstrated in BH as follows: verb – object as opposed to object – verb; preposition – noun as opposed to

A sentence with predicate focus presents new information about the state or actions of a known topical entity. Typical word order is VSO. It is not surprising that the predicate focus, BH *wayyiqtol* clause, is widely recognised as having sequential, narrative qualities. Jeremiah 3.6a וַיֹּאמֶר יְהוָה אֵלַי בִּימֵי יֹאשִׁיָּהוּ הַמֶּלֶךְ is an example of predicate focus. The sentence gives the answer to the diagnostic question *what did Yahweh do?* The underlying presupposition, Yahweh communicates directly with Jeremiah, is set up by the call account in the first chapter of Jeremiah.

Argument focus is a marked focus type, associated with the identification function.[81] At times in BH sentences, an argument (or non-predicating expression) will occur prior to the verb in a sentence, which results in XVO word order. In these cases, an argument may be fronted for topicalisation (identifying the argument for a particular proposition), or for the sake of focus. Jeremiah 3.6b is an example of argument focus. This is due to a combination of factors. First, the interrogative sentence itself is intended to elicit information from Jeremiah. The question might be rephrased as "Have you seen X?," with X representing the argument אֲשֶׁר עָשְׂתָה מְשֻׁבָה יִשְׂרָאֵל. In this case, the sentence הֲרָאִיתָ אֲשֶׁר עָשְׂתָה מְשֻׁבָה יִשְׂרָאֵל carries the presupposition that Jeremiah is aware of the existence of מְשֻׁבָה יִשְׂרָאֵל, and perhaps aware of the behaviour as well. Second, because phrase includes a verb of perception, the pragmatic focus shifts to the information in the relative clause despite the VO word order. The focus constituent (the assertion) is that מְשֻׁבָה יִשְׂרָאֵל has acted in a certain, as yet unexplicated, way.

---

noun – post-position; noun – possessor as opposed to possessor – noun; adjective – object of comparison versus object of comparison; article – noun versus noun – article; etc. Most relevant to the VSO-SVO debate for BH is the fact that "... the subject is a bad patterner in VO languages since it often precedes V yielding SVO." Beatrice Primus, "Word Order Typology," in *Language Typology and Language Universals: An International Handbook*, ed. M. Haspelmath (Berlin: Walter de Gruyter, 2001), 856. Constituent order in the verbless clause is an area of further research for the TD approach. See Randall Buth, "Word Order in the Verbless Clause: A Functional Approach," in *The Verbless Clause in Biblical Hebrew: Linguistic Approaches*, ed. Cynthia L. Miller (Winona Lake, Ind.: Eisenbrauns, 1999), 79-108; Lenart J. de Regt, "Macrosyntactic Functions of Nominal Clauses Referring to Participants," in *The Verbless Clause in Biblical Hebrew*, ed. Cynthia L. Miller (Winona Lake, Ind.: Eisenbrauns, 1999), 273-296. For studies in post-verbal word order see Lars Lode, "Postverbal Word Order in Biblical Hebrew: Structure and Function," *Semitics* 9 (1984), 113-164; idem, "Postverbal Word Order in Biblical Hebrew: Structure and Function: Part Two," *Semitics* 10 (1985), 24-39.

81 Floor notes that argument focus appears in clauses that present unexpected or contrastive information, and that such information often contains theme macro-words. Floor, "From Information Structure, Topic, and Focus, to Theme in Biblical Hebrew Narrative." 4.

Sentence focus is also a marked focus type and is associated with either presentational or event reporting function.[82] In the case of sentence focus, all of the information presented in the sentence is in focus. Sentence focus entails predicate focus. BH sentences with this type of focus are often preceded by a sentence level marker, such as *hinneh*.[83] There are no sentence focus clauses in Jeremiah 3.6-3.11. While word order is the basic criterion by which information structure is ascertained, Lambrecht also utilises semantic domain information when assessing focus types, as noted in the above quotation, "…the *semantic* element…whose presence makes the proposition into an assertion."[84] Thus, a BH predicate focus clause with a verb of speaking and a quotation as complement, and a predicate focus clause with a transitive verb and a topical entity as a direct object both share similar *syntactic* structure. However, due to differing *semantics*, they do not share the same linguistic construal. Because of this, the three basic focus types might appear to multiply.[85] At this point no further attention to the series of verbal forms is necessary, other than to note that this example demonstrates the insufficiency of verbal forms alone to determine hierarchical levels within the narration.[86] For this analysis, both the information structure of individual sentences and their relationship to one another are pertinent to the conceptual ordering of the text and for establishing text hierarchy.

---

82   To these functions, Floor adds theme-supporting, redirecting and state-reporting. Ibid.

83   van der Merwe and Talstra, "Interface."

84   Lambrecht, *Information Structure*, 336.

85   Such an elaboration has been proposed by Shimasaki, who notes that *predicate focus* might have implications for participant reference or ambiguity resolution and *argument focus* might indicate a closing formula. For Shimasaki, *sentence focus* becomes *clause focus*, thus the pragmatic function of this clause type is confined to the clause-level, rather than to the entire sentence. *Clause focus* functions are proposed for three levels: at the information level, a brand new referent is introduced. At the inter-clausal level, the entire clause might be exclamatory, circumstantial or contrastive. At the text level, the clause might exhibit one of four *onset functions*: initialisation; topicalisation; introductory formula; or contextualisation. Alternatively, the clause might provide background information. None-the-less, the three basic focus types provide the initial departure point for his information structure analysis. Shimasaki, *Focus Structure in Biblical Hebrew: A Study of Word Order and Information Structure*, 241.

86   In this regard, the cognitively oriented TD approach differs from the discourse analysis approach presented by Longacre. While Longacre sees verbal forms and combinations of verbal forms as macrostructural indicators, a TD approach is concerned with conceptual structuring based upon constellations of syntactic features. Thus, a *qatal* form that Longacre assigns to *background* information may actually be used to present information that is quite important to its larger context. Such information might be cued by a meta-linguistic construction, such as *Thus says the Lord*.

3.   Cognitive Structuring in Jeremiah 3.6-3.11

Given the information produced by the syntax analysis, as well as the topic and focus information, it is now possible to make some preliminary observations regarding the cognitive structuring of Jeremiah 3.6-3.11 by examining larger segments of text.

1.   Jeremiah 3.6

Jer	Clause Layout		Focus	MSC
3.6a	וַיֹּ֤אמֶר יְהוָה֙ אֵלַ֔י בִּימֵ֖י יֹאשִׁיָּ֣הוּ הַמֶּ֑לֶךְ	N	Pred	Base
b	הֲרָאִ֕יתָ	NQ		SB
c	אֲשֶׁ֣ר עָשְׂתָ֔ה מְשֻׁבָ֖ה יִשְׂרָאֵ֑ל	NQP	Arg	M¹ *Focus*
d	הֹלְכָ֨ה הִ֜יא עַל־כָּל־הַ֣ר גָּבֹ֗הַּ וְאֶל־תַּ֛חַת כָּל־עֵ֥ץ רַעֲנָ֖ן	NQP	Arg	
e	וַתִּזְנִי־שָֽׁם	NQP	Pred	

The clause hierarchy for 3.6 reflects the narrative-discursive disinction found in the WIVU database, with the addition of the third category – perception. A P in the clause tag indicates this. The addition of the *P* category is significant for prophetic text, which involves a high concentration of interpersonal speech act verbs.[87]

As Raible notes:

> Since one of the most important topics of human communication is communication itself, there exist a lot of verbs expressing, by their semantic content, communicative or related activities: above all *verba decendi, sentiendi et sciendi,* encompassing all the speech act verbs.[88]

This list includes verbs of speaking, perception and knowing, which also act as matrix verbs in space-building constructions (see chapter 4, section B.2). Such verbs do not take an agent as grammatical subject, but rather an *experiencer*.[89] Often, when these verbs occur as matrix verbs, they take relative or complement clauses as the grammatical object, which is the case at 3.6b. The following two examples demonstrate the differences in clause hierarchy when the *P* category is included:

---

87   Jeremiah 3.6-11 contains 22 verb forms, of which six are communication and experiencer verbs.
88   Raible, "Linking Clauses," 599.
89   The issue of verb specific semantic roles will be discussed in the following chapters.

Clause linking hierarchy in Jeremiah 3.6, without perception space

1.	N	*Wayyiqtol-S (3sgM)*
2.	NQ	*X-Qatal (2sgM)*
3.	NQ	*X-Qatal (3sgF)*
4.	NQ	Qotel (fs)—*downgraded by form*
5.	NQN	*Wayyiqtol-0 (3sgF).*

Clause linking hierarchy in Jeremiah 3.6, including perception space

6.	N	*Wayyiqtol-S (3sgM)*
7.	NQ	*X-Qatal (2sgM)*
8.	NQP	*X-Qatal (3sgF)*
9.	NQP	Qotel (fs)—*downgraded by form*
10.	NQPN	*Wayyiqtol-0 (3sgF).*

Because clause 3.6d is downgraded by form (participle versus fully declined verbal form), this hierarchy is identical to the computational linguistics version in the VU database. The difference appears to be slight. However, when combined with focus information, the second hierarchy provides a more accurate template for translation.

Jeremiah 3.6a is a quotation frame which acts as a *space-builder* due to the semantic field of the verb.[90] It sets up a topical frame for the entire section, and is the base space for the following information. Jeremiah 3.6b also acts as a space-builder, due to the semantic field of the verb. It opens a perception space, M^1, which is now the focus space. It is here that new information is accruing in the cognitive structure. In this case, a topical frame is introduced by the question *Have you seen what Turnable Israel did?* Jeremiah 3.6d-e gives a *topical elaboration* upon the topical frame. The asyndetic participle clause הלכה היא joins the previous clause at an unequal level, and the clause is resumptive of the topical referent/argument אשר עשתה משבה ישראל in the previous line. Both of these features contribute to maintaining reference.

---

90   Space-builders include, but are not limited to: temporal references; verbs of speaking and perception and *mental states predicates*, such as *think, believe* and *hope* (see chapter 4.B.2).

2. Jeremiah 3.7

וַיֹּאמֶר	3.7a
אַחֲרֵי עֲשׂוֹתָהּ אֶת־כָּל־אֵלֶּה	b
אֵלַי תָּשׁוּב	c
וְלֹא־שָׁבָה	d
*וַתֵּרֶאה **וַתֵּרֶא בָּגוֹדָה אֲחוֹתָהּ יְהוּדָה	e

3.7a	NQN	Wayyiqtol-0	Pred	SB for M²
b	NQNP	X-Qetol		M²
c	NQNP	X-Yiqtol	Arg	
d	NQN	W-X-Qatal	Pred	Base
e	NQN	Wayyiqtol-X	Pred	

Jeremiah 3.7a contains a conjugated form of the verb אמר, which in this context functions as a *verba sciendi*. יהוה is reported to have *thought*, rather than to have *said*. Phrases containing verbs of speaking, perception and cognition all act as space-builders. However, the spaces opened by these terms differ in one key respect. The new space, M², is an internal cognition space, so it is accessed only through the first person experiencer. This involves perspective as a linguistic construal operation.

Jeremiah 3.7b and 3.7c exhibit irregular word order. The object clause אֶת־כָּל־אֵלֶּה at 3.7b contains the deictic term אֵלֶּה, which points back to the activities of Israel presented in 3.6. Deixis contributes to maintaining reference and will be discussed at length in the following chapters. The adjunct clause at 3.7c connects directly to the *following* clause. The complement clause אֵלַי תָּשׁוּב at 3.7d contains a fronted indirect object. The OV word order is marked, and the term שׁוּב is highlighted as a *theme trace*, according to Floor.[91] The *kethiv-qere* at 3.7e involves two alternate spellings for the 3sF verb form. Although this is of interest for historical linguistics, it is not crucial to the present analysis, which uses the available person, number and gender information included in the verbal form to assess participant reference.

---

91 Jeremiah 3 contains nine verbs from √שׁוּב. There are 111 instances in the entire book of Jeremiah, indicating a localisation of this theme trace. Floor, "From Information Structure, Topic, and Focus, to Theme in Biblical Hebrew Narrative." 2.

3.   Jeremiah 3.8

וָאֵרֶא	3.8a
כִּי עַל־כָּל־אֹדוֹת	b
אֲשֶׁר נִאֲפָה מְשֻׁבָה יִשְׂרָאֵל	c
שִׁלַּחְתִּיהָ	d
וָאֶתֵּן אֶת־סֵפֶר כְּרִיתֻתֶיהָ אֵלֶיהָ	e
וְלֹא יָרְאָה בֹּגֵדָה יְהוּדָה אֲחוֹתָהּ	f
וַתֵּלֶךְ	g
וַתִּזֶן גַּם־הִיא	h

3.8a	NQN	Wayyiqtol-0	Pred	SB for M³
b	NQNP	X-Prep		
c	NQNP	X-Qatal	Sent	M³
d	NQNP	0-Qatal		
e	NQNP	Wayyiqtol-0	Pred	
f	NQN	W-X-Qatal	Pred	
g	NQN	Wayyiqtol-0	Pred	Base
h	NQN	Wayyiqtol-X	Pred	

Jeremiah 3.8a consists of a conjugated form of √ראה, a *verba sentiendi* that opens a perception space, M³. There is some discussion regarding the person, gender and number of this verb, which affects the identity of the perceiver.[92] However, access to a perception space is possible for multiple experiencers, so this type of space is not as restricted as the cognition space addressed in the previous example. The space closes with the shift in addresee from Israel to Judah in clause 3.8f. Israel's sister, Judah, was not afraid, in fact, she went away, and in the end her doings were worse than those of Israel. From this point until 3.10c, the narrative level remains the same.

---

92   LXX, Statenvertalig, ASV use first person; RSV uses 3f/s.

4. Jeremiah 3.9-11

וְהָיָה מִקֹּל זְנוּתָהּ	3.9a
וַתֶּחֱנַף אֶת־הָאָרֶץ	b
וַתִּנְאַף אֶת־הָאֶבֶן וְאֶת־הָעֵץ	c
וְגַם־בְּכָל־זֹאת לֹא־שָׁבָה אֵלַי בָּגוֹדָה אֲחוֹתָהּ יְהוּדָה בְּכָל־לִבָּהּ	3.10a
כִּי אִם־בְּשֶׁקֶר	b
נְאֻם־יְהוָה	c
וַיֹּאמֶר יְהוָה אֵלַי	3.11a
צִדְּקָה נַפְשָׁהּ מְשֻׁבָה יִשְׂרָאֵל מִבֹּגֵדָה יְהוּדָה	b

3.9a	NQN	W-Qatal	Pred	
b	NQN	Wayyiqtol-0	Pred	
c	NQN	Wayyiqtol-0	Pred	Base
3.10a	NQN	W-X-Qatal	Arg	
b	NQN	Ellip		
c	NQN	*focus*		
3.11a	N	Wayyiqtol-S	Pred	SB for M³
b	NQ	Qatal		M³

In Jeremiah 3.10a, the adjunct clause וְגַם־בְּכָל־זֹאת contains the deictic term זֹאת, which refers anaphorically to the description of immorality presented in 3.9. The identity of the offending party in 3.9 is ambiguous. Again, the focus of the sentence highlights a theme trace לֹא־שָׁבָה אֵלַי based upon שׁוּב√ (see 3.7c; 3.7d).

This analysis demonstrates that by observing the interplay of a constellation of features, such as experiencer verbs and shifts in topical entities, it is possible to observe the conceptual format of the text. Accordingly, Jeremiah 3.6-3.11 reflects the following structure:

3.6.a: Base space - report of a speech event by the Lord to *ME* (Jeremiah)
3.6.c: M¹ – content of address
3.7.a: Base – report of cognition event by the Lord
3.7.b: M² – content of cognition
3.7.d: Base – report of non-event
3.8.a: Base – continued report of cognition event
3.8.b: M³ – content of perception/cognition space
3.8.f-3.11b: Base – report of non-event

4. Structuring Conceptual Packets: Speech Frames

One easily recognisable feature of Jeremiah 3.6-3.11 is the communica-
tion/speech act frame at 3.6a ויאמר יהוה אלי בימי יאשיהו המלך, *the Lord
said to me in the days of King Josiah*. For this section of text, the citation
formula is as important for what it does not make explicit as for what it
does. The sentence identifies the first interlocutor in the reported
speech act as the Lord, and the second only as *ME*. The time of the
speech event is expressed as the days of Josiah the King. In the communication situation set up by the text, the narrator, *ME*, is simultaneously onstage, as part of the reported speech event, and offstage, as
the narrator's voice.

While the statement ויאמר יהוה אלי בימי יאשיהו המלך mentions a
speaker, an addressee and the time of the event, this reported speech
event is far from prototypical. Regarding prototypical dialogue, Miller
states:

> A prototypical dialogue involves two participants who alternate speaking
> and listening in paired turns of talk, or adjacency pairs…the dialogue oc-
> curs with the two participants speaking face-to-face, and in the same loca-
> tion, not across a distance.[93]

In this case, there are two participants but no alternation between
speaking and listening. The participants are not speaking face-to-face,
nor (presumably) are they in the same location. From a cognitive
science perspective, the question הראית אשר עשתה משבה ישראל and the
continuing references to perception and cognition serve to compress
the complexities of the situation to human scale. Fauconnier notes,
"…human beings are evolved and culturally supported to deal with
reality at human scale, that is, through direct action and perception
inside familiar frames, typically involving few participants and direct
intentionality."[94]

The issue at hand is enormous: The Lord's displeasure with Israel
and Judah is unmistakable. Here, via conceptual blending, the originator (speaking from Jeremiah's point of view) has created a version of
the situation which is so compressed that the human observer has no
difficulty in understanding the enormity of the problem. The text has
become a material anchor for complex projections. The Lord is not a
prototypical conversation partner, just as Israel and Judah are not prototypical siblings. Even Jeremiah appears to be an irregular human: he

---

93   Miller, *Representation*, 316.
94   Fauconnier and Turner, *The Way We Think*, 322.

is able to speak with the LORD, and is susceptible to actual interchanges, as demonstrated in Jeremiah 1.1-1.10.

D. Cognitive Construction in Jeremiah 3.6-3.11

This short analysis of Jeremiah 3.6-3.11 provides a starting point for the examination of cognitive construction based upon the network model as explained by the TD approach. The analysis demonstrates that Jeremiah 3.6-3.11 consists of several spaces, all connected to the initial base space, or ground. The cognitive configuration begins with the initial base space, Jeremiah 3.6a. For most of the section, the literary point of view remains with Jeremiah. This varies with the spaces opened at 1.3b and 1.4b, where literary point of view is assigned to the character, the Lord, rather than to Jeremiah. The shift to the propositional content space immediately after *I thought that* at 3.7a shifts the cognitive viewpoint directly to the proposition *she would come back to me*, while the literary point of view remains with the character. A glance at the conceptual format of the above texts demonstrates that the conceptual packets cued by the text do not line up as beads on a string. Rather, they cluster as a whole, against the backdrop presented at Jeremiah 3.6a. This short analysis demonstrates that even though reading seems to be a linear process it actually entails a recursive blending process in which meaning accrues as the text is encountered.

Conclusions and Directions

This chapter introduces the theory and method of the TD approach. This approach will be used in the following chapters to analyse and describe the prophetic text of MT Jeremiah 1.1-6.30. It has been demonstrated that the TD approach is cognitive in nature, drawing from the areas of cognitive linguistics, cognitive grammar and cognitive science in order to develop a comprehensive method for understanding prophetic text. The TD method includes a recursive text analysis that begins with a clause level syntax analysis. The syntax analysis provides the basis for information structure analysis, in both the area of topic and that of *focus*. This information is then analysed for the linguistic cues and clues that act as space-builders for cognitive construction. Mental spaces opened in this manner are then observed for linguistic construal operations that structure and link the spaces. Finally, the spaces are integrated through a process of conceptual blending. Information derived from this process is then available for historical and cultural analysis.

The TD approach has several strengths. It is text oriented; it offers a way to map cognitive structure that originates with the author; it provides the reader or analyst with a way to confirm certain intuitions about the manner in which meaning accrues as the text is read and it provides a fresh look at an ancient text and the integrative nature of the method opens the way for gathering and synthesising information from a variety of linguistic and technological studies. Each of these strengths is required for a comprehensive analysis of prophetic text.

3. Traditional and Cognitive Approaches to BH Grammar

He who does not know foreign languages
does not know anything about his own.

~Johann Wolfgang von Goethe

According to the TD approach, grammar is a significant point of contact for the author and reader of an ancient text (see chapter 2). Thus, understanding Biblical Hebrew grammar is a prerequisite for successful analysis of MT Jeremiah. Since TD is a cognitive approach, the aim of this chapter is to explore traditional and cognitive approaches to BH grammar. Traditional approaches undergird the move toward a cognitive grammar of BH, providing shared meta-language and standard grammatical categories. Cognitive Grammar provides a reorganisation of traditional grammatical categories, accompanied by new meta-language that contributes to a fresh understanding of BH grammar.

Since syntactic structure varies across languages, the synchronic analysis of the syntax and semantics of MT Jeremiah 1.1-6.30 necessarily involves dealing with both BH grammar and the grammar of the receptor language, in this case English. Taking human cognitive processes as a starting point for the study of BH grammar is an effective method for addressing translation issues. Premper notes:

> ...the semantic structure of a complex sign (for instance, a sentence) differs in syntactic structure across languages. From a conceptual perspective, however, expressions within a language and across languages can be compared: sentences can express the same proposition, and, in this sense, have the same meaning. Thus, the conceptual level is often considered the locus of *tertia comparationis* and therefore a point of departure for language comparison and universals research.[1]

These comments underscore the role of syntactic structures for text analysis and reinforce the choice of clause-level units as the basic unit of analysis for the TD approach.

---

1   Waldfried Premper, "Universals of the Linguistic Representation of Situations," in *Language Typology and Language Universals: An International Handbook,* ed. M. Haspelmath (Berlin: Walter de Gruyter, 2001), 478.

This chapter integrates information from traditional sources, such as introductory grammars, reference grammars, journal articles and monographs, with information from the field of cognitive grammar.[2] This initial and necessarily elementary foray into the application of cognitive grammar and linguistics to BH text touches upon several interrelated issues. Section A. discusses the relationship between BH syntax and grammatical constructions. This section introduces the grammatical theory that informs the TD approach. Section B., Cognitive Approaches to BH Terms, introduces the idea of prototypical situations and contains a short discussion of perception and cognition terms in Jeremiah. Section C. discusses the central role of the BH verb. There is significant debate regarding whether the verb indicates tense or aspect. For BH, the binyan system indicates situation in given verbal form. Section D. presents cognitive additions to the discussion of BH grammar by introducing the TIME IS MOTION and TIME IS SPACE conceptual metaphors. These metaphors help to describe how the BH verbal forms construe the presentation of situations. Section E. explains the contributions that conceptual blending theory can make to the description of BH situations at the sentence level and presents a brief introduction to cognitive construction at the discourse level. It will be demonstrated that although cognitive approaches cannot solve the tense versus aspect debate, such approaches have much to contribute to the description of the cognitive construal of situations in BH text.

A. Grammatical Theories:
Syntax and Grammatical Constructions

The TD approach utilises selected aspects of three complementary grammatical theories to address BH text: Role and Reference Grammar (RRG); Cognitive Grammar (CG); and Construction Grammar.[3]

---

2   An important introductory essay of particular interest to BH scholars is Langacker, "Context, Cognition, and Semantics: A Unified Dynamic Approach," in *Job 28: Cognition in Context*, ed. E. J. van Wolde (Leiden: Brill, 2003), 179-230.

3   Role and Reference Grammar has its roots in Transformational Grammar, Generative Semantics and Case Grammar. For a synopsis of the historical development of Role and Reference Grammar, see Van Valin, *An Introduction to Syntax*, 218.

1. Role and Reference Grammar

RRG provides a detailed account of the relationship between syntax, semantics and grammatical construction. Its emphasis upon language universals makes it especially useful for typological comparison between languages. Typological comparisons facilitate translation as they clarify the difference between languages that feature VO (verb – object) constituent order and those that feature OV (object – verb) constituent order. Some basic characteristics of Role and Reference Grammar include:

- The representation of the clause as a layered structure;
- the construction-specific nature of grammatical relations;
- the presence of lexical macro-roles; and
- an algorithm for linking syntax, semantics and discourse pragmatics.

Additionally, RRG presents a highly developed approach to language based upon the relationship between oral or manual gestures and their arrangement, morphosyntax and meaning. RRG elaborates upon the role of traditional grammatical categories, such as subject and direct object, by including additional information under the term relational structure.[4] Relational structure accounts for relational characteristics of NPs, such as modifier-modified and possessor-possessed, among others. Concepts drawn from RRG are invaluable for dealing with technological developments such as the WIVU database. For example, relational structure may be used to describe the various phrase atoms created by the computerised database. In general syntactic terms the phrase atom, דברי ירמיהו, *the words of Jeremiah*, (Jeremiah 1.1) may be described as a NP. However, the same phrase atom also exhibits the relational structure of possessor and possessed, which provides additional information for the translator or interpreter.

RRG also accounts for constituent structure by systematically describing "...the nesting of constituents within constituents in a sentence." For example, the sentence *The teacher read a book in the library* consists of the NP, *the library*, which is a constituent of the PP, *in the library*, which is a constituent of the VP, *read a book in the library*.[5] This assessment of constituent nesting demonstrates the interrelationships that hold between computer-generated phrase atoms and clause atoms within a sentence. For example, the NP דברי ירמיהו, is a phrase atom

---

4   Ibid., 4.
5   Ibid., 3.

that is also a constituent of the clause atom דברי ירמיהו בן־חלקיה, which in turn is constituent of the sentence itself.[6] Assessing constituent structure is important for establishing information structure categories such as topic and focus. Relational structure and constituent structure are two interrelated ways of describing syntactic structure, making this approach congruent with and helpful for understanding the information created by the recursive pattern matching process of the computerised database (see chapter 2, section C.1).

2.   Cognitive Grammar

CG explores the relationship between syntax, semantics and pragmatics as a continuum, or as Langacker states, "… manifestations of a single linguistic symbolization process, which has its roots in human cognitive processes."[7] In conceptualising about conceptualising (metaconceptualising), Langacker has developed a comprehensive method for analysing and describing grammatical relations from a cognitive perspective.

a.   Grammar and Perspective

The figure-ground configuration is a basic feature of perspective in human cognition and it plays an important part in Langacker's cognitive grammar.[8] Langacker states "…the prevalence of figure-ground organization in conceptual structure entails its importance for semantic and grammatical structure."[9] This allows Langacker to speak of a *profile* as "The entity designated by a semantic structure … it is a substructure within the base that is obligatorily accessed, functions as the focal point within the objective scene, achieves a special degree of prominence (resulting in one level of figure-ground organization."[10] Thus, a profiled entity will exhibit some of the characteristics that Talmy assigns to the figure in the figure-ground configuration.[11] The figure-ground con-

---

6   The constituent structure of Jeremiah 1.1-1.3 is actually more complicated, and is discussed at length in section 4.A.1.

7   Van Valin, *An Introduction to Syntax*, 223.

8   Viewpoint, deixis and subjectivity are three additional features of perspective that have been taken up in the previous chapters. See chapter 1, section C and chapter 2, sections A and B.

9   Langacker, *Foundations of Cognitive Grammar*, 120.

10   Ibid., 490.

11   The location of the figure is less known than that of the ground; it is smaller than the ground; it is more mobile than the ground; it is structurally simpler than the ground;

figuration is also important to Langacker's definition of relational structure, in which the *trajector* is "...the figure within a relational profile."[12] In addition, the *landmark* is "...a salient substructure other than the trajector of a relational predication or the profile of a nominal predication."[13] A discussion of relational structure follows a short discussion of cognitive grammar categories.

b. Categories in Cognitive Grammar

Rather than subdividing grammatical relations into rigid categories, Langacker argues that there is a continuum between *things* and *relations*.[14] Importantly, the term thing "...makes reference not to physical objects but rather to cognitive events."[15] Thus, the term *thing* indicates conceptualisations that function as subjects or objects in a sentence. The term thing includes not only nouns and noun phrases, but participles and infinitives as well. In certain cases, an entire clause may be termed a thing, such as the object clause that follows a verb of perception. *Relations* may be described as *atemporal,* or "...lacking a positive temporal profile."[16] Atemporal relations are established by prepositional phrases, adverb phrases, appositional noun phrases and stative verbs. Atemporal relations are important to mental spaces construction since these relations are often utilised as space-builders. Alternatively, relations may be described as *processes.* These are indicated by active verbs.

The difference between atemporal relations and processes is a function of the contrasting modes of cognitive processes involved in assessing the conceptualisation. Things and atemporal relations are processed by summary scanning, in which a relation is conceptually scanned to form a single picture. In this case, "...all facets of the complex scene are simultaneously available and through their co-activation...they constitute a coherent gestalt." On the other hand, processes are observed by sequential scanning, in which a relation is conceptually scanned as a moving picture. Sequential scanning "...involves the successive trans-

---

it is more salient than the ground; and it is more recently in awareness than the ground. Croft and Cruse, *Cognitive Linguistics,* 42.

12   Langacker, *Foundations of Cognitive Grammar,* 494.

13   Ibid., 490.

14   This is actually a simplification of Langacker's definition of a *thing* as "a region in some domain of conceptual space." Ibid., 494. Langacker is careful not to limit the definition of a *thing* to substantial physical objects, in order to accommodate abstract entities.

15   Ibid., 183.

16   Ibid., 486.

formations of one configuration into another. The component states are processed in series rather than in parallel."[17]

Langacker uses the terms *trajector* and *landmark* to describe the interconnectedness between profiled participants in a relational structure. The term trajector implies motion and the trajector in a relational structure has special status because it is profiled as the figure against ground. The landmark provides a point of reference for locating the trajector. This results in an asymmetry between the profiled participants in a given expression. Consequently, Langacker is able to describe the cognitive status of grammatical terms. For example, an *adjective* represents an atemporal relation with a *thing* as a trajector, as in the relational predication, *The car is red*. In this predication, the thing *car* is the trajector, the colour term *red* is the landmark. The entire red car is perceived as a figure against ground. Likewise, an *adverb* represents an atemporal relation with a *relation* as a trajector, as in the phrase, *going fast*. In the phrase, *going fast*, the term *going* is the trajector; the adverb *fast* is the landmark. In the relational predication, *The red car is going fast*, the phrase *the red car* is the trajector and the phrase *going fast* is the landmark. In the relational predication, *The red car hit the wall* the phrase *the red car* is the trajector and *the wall* is the *direct object*, or "...nominal whose profile corresponds to the primary landmark of a relation."[18] In this way, Langacker accounts for the cohesion inherent within phrases, within clauses and within sentences. Like RRG discussed above, these facets of CG support the idea (presented in chapter 2) that phrase atoms combine to form clauses, and that clause atoms combine to form sentences, making this approach helpful for understanding the computerised database (see section 2.C.1).

c.   BH Grammatical Categories

The interrelationship between phrase, clause and sentence level trajectors and landmarks contributes towards a re-evaluation of BH grammatical categories. This is actually a simple category shift away from a bifurcation between nouns and verbs towards a scale from noun to verb. The main points on the scale are Langacker's *things, atemporal relations* and *processes*. The *thing* end of the scale begins with nouns, appositional noun phrases, adjective phrases, infinitives and participles (when used as nouns). Following this, the *atemporal relation* point begins with adverb phrases, followed by prepositions and stative verbs. Finally, the *processes* point begins with participles (used as verbs), in-

17   Ibid., 248.
18   Ibid., 217-219.

transitive verbs, singly transitive verbs and doubly transitive verbs. Verbs are categorised by the *binyan* of a given form in the areas of force dynamics, diathesis and verb specific semantic roles.[19]

Langacker has developed a series of diagrams and descriptive symbols as a form of shorthand for these terms and concepts. One of these, the canonical viewing arrangement diagram presented in chapters 1 and 2, has been adapted for use in the description of TD analytical categories.

3. Construction Grammar

Construction Grammar focuses upon the notion of grammatical structures. It is similar to cognitive grammar. Construction grammar is helpful for understanding the BH verbal system, in particular the various options represented by the *binyan* system. Further discussion, based upon Mandelblit's work with the MH *binyan* system, paves the way for the use of construction grammar principles in the TD approach. See section 3.E.2, below.

B. Cognitive Approaches to BH Terms of Perception and Cognition

Because linguistic terms relating to perception and cognition are at the heart of this volume, it is rewarding to investigate these verbs from a cognitive grammar perspective. Justification for grouping verbs of perception and cognition comes from two sources: the study of semantic domains and the RRG assessment of verb-specific semantic roles. According to Louw-Nida's study of semantic domains, verbs of perception are included in domain 24, *Sensory Events and States*. Verbs of cognition are included in domain 28, *Know*. The intervening categories include *Attitudes and Emotions* (25), *Psychological Faculties* (26) *and Learn* (27). Categories that follow verbs of cognition include: *Recall* (28), *Think*

---

19 This is a very basic continuum, which the author plans to develop by additional research in light of the language typology and language universals model. Similar scales are discussed in greater depth in H. J. Sasse, "Scales between Nouniness and Verbiness," in *Language Typology and Language Universals: An International Handbook*, ed. M. Haspelmath (Berlin: Walter de Gruyter, 2001).

(29), *Hold a View* (30), *Believe, Trust* (31), and *Understand (32).* Verbs of speaking follow in domain 33, *Communication.*[20]

1.   Role and Reference Grammar

RRG is useful for understanding the characteristics of groups of terms that occur in various semantic domains. In his study of syntax, Van Valin delimits a continuum with verb-specific semantic roles at one end and grammatical relations at the other. This continuum is marked both by increasing generalisation and by increasing neutralisation of semantic contrasts.[21] For example, terms describing semantic roles such as speaker and hearer are highly specific and indicate a high degree of semantic contrast. On the other hand, terms describing grammatical relations such as subject and object are highly general and indicate a low degree of semantic contrast. Van Valin begins with an analysis of verb-specific semantic roles, such as someone who speaks, someone who thinks, hears or likes, someone who is given to, someone or something that is seen, someone or something that is located and something that is broken. He observes that these roles form a group, which he describes as thematic relations. One who speaks is an *agent*; one who thinks is a *cogniser*; one who hears is a *perceiver*; one who likes is an *emoter*; one who is given to is a *receiver*; something that is seen is a *stimulus*; something that is located is a *theme*; and something that is broken is a *patient*. Additionally, cognisers, perceivers and emoters form a group, the thematic relation of experiencer. Thematic relations, such as agent, experiencer, recipient, stimulus, theme and patient formed groups called semantic macro-roles. Two major semantic macro-roles are *actor* and *undergoer*. Importantly, actor and undergoer are not grammatical relations, but rather are a more general type of semantic role.[22] For this reason both the subject of an active voice transitive verb and the object of the preposition *by* are actors, while the direct object of an active voice transitive verb and the subject of a passive verb are undergoers. Note the following sentences:

---

20   J. P. Louw and E. A. Nida, *Greek-English Lexicon of the New Testament: Based on Semantic Domains*, 2nd ed., 2 vols. (New York: United Bible Societies, 1989). This categorisation specifically covers Greek, but due to the cross-linguistic nature of semantic domains, the categories are relevant for BH as well. Studies are underway for a Hebrew-specific database. See T. Muraoka, *Studies in Ancient Hebrew Semantics*, Abr-Nahrain. Supplement Series, vol. 4 (Louvain: Peeters Press, 1995); idem, *Semantics of Ancient Hebrew*, Abr-Nahrain. Supplement Series, vol. 6 (Louvain: Peeters, 1998).
21   Van Valin, *An Introduction to Syntax*, 30.
22   Ibid., 28.

- John ate the dog biscuit.
- The dog biscuit was eaten by John.

In the first sentence, the grammatical subject *John* is an actor and the grammatical direct object *the dog biscuit* is an undergoer. In the second sentence, the grammatical subject *the dog biscuit* is an undergoer and John, the object of the preposition *by*, is an actor. The presence of semantic macro-roles is a major reason that active and passive constructions induce different construals of the same situation. This in turn plays into the information structure category of *focus*.[23] It is also the reason that purely syntax driven notions of focus are insufficient for identifying the focal element in a sentence or clause, from a syntactic perspective, the two examples are nearly identical SVO sentences, yet the construal of the two is rather different. Finally, semantic macro-roles form a group called grammatical relations: both an *actor* and an *undergoer* may be the subject of a sentence, as the example above demonstrates.

Van Valin notes that some overlap exists between the group of thematic relations that can serve as actor and the group that can serve as undergoer. He introduces both an actor hierarchy and an undergoer hierarchy, as follows:

Actor Hierarchy:

Agent > Instrument > Experiencer > Recipient

Undergoer Hierarchy:

Patient> Theme > Stimulus > Experiencer > Recipient/Source/Goal/Location

According to this assessment, the prototypical actor argument would be an agent (*John* chopped down the tree), and if no agent is present, the actor argument would be an instrument (*The wind* blew down the tree). Likewise, if no instrument is present, the actor argument would be an experiencer (*John saw* the tree blow down) and so on. Note that experiencer and recipient are present in both hierarchies. The role of experiencer is less than prototypical in both hierarchies, indicating that sentences which include experiencer verbs are less prototypical than sentences that contain communication verbs, such as *to say* or *to speak*. This leads to a discussion of the linguistic expression of prototypicality in situations/propositions.

---

23   As this example demonstrates, word order alone in insufficient for determining focus: both of these sentences are SVO, yet there is a perceived difference in construal.

2.   Prototypical Situations

In a prototypical situation, the subject argument appears as the *agent*, or the *doer* of an action, while the object argument appears as the *patient*, or the *receiver* of the action. These prototypical roles are coloured by the verb-specific semantic role of a given lexeme, which is evaluated by the prototypicality scales mentioned above.

As demonstrated above, the hierarchical positions of the verb-specific semantic roles of the subject and object arguments are important for establishing prototypicality. However, establishing prototypicality occurs on other levels as well. Premper notes that situations exhibit both internal relationality between entities and dynamicity as one entity acts upon another. Thus, prototypicality is evaluated both by the animacy hierarchy and by the degree of dynamicity in a given situation. The animacy hierarchy is a scale in which Speech Act Participant 1 (SAP 1) appears at the top and mass nouns, such as *rock* or *salt*, appear at the bottom, as follows:

Animacy Hierarchy

SAP 1 > SAP 2 > SAP 3 > PN > human > animate > inanimate > mass.[24]

As mentioned above, the subject of a sentence is most likely to be selected from the top of the animacy hierarchy.

In his discussion of the linguistic expression of situations, Premper illustrates this situation using several examples from various scholars. He notes that the sentence, *The farmer killed the duckling,* is dynamic and that it contains two animate entities, one of which causes a dramatic change in the other. This is followed by the sentence, *The ducks ate the old bread,* which contains a non-human, animate entity and an inanimate affected entity. The sentence *Man is just* is static, providing information regarding a permanent property of a single entity.[25] The examples highlight the two-fold nature of prototypicality, which is determined both by the position of the respective entities on the animacy scale and by the degree of dynamicity involved in the situation.

In other words, the primary speaker in a dialogue is the most likely candidate for subject, whereas a mass noun such as salt is least likely to appear as subject (and more likely to appear as an object). The reason that the example sentences *John ate the dog biscuit* and *The dog biscuit was eaten by John* are not equally prototypical is now clear. While the entities maintain identical semantic macro-roles and the verbs carry a similar degree of dynamicity, the position of the entities on the animacy hie-

---

25   Premper, "Universals of the Linguistic Representation of Situations," 489.

rarchy contributes to dissimilar prototypicality. In the first example, the animate subject is higher on the animacy scale than the inanimate object, which indicates a higher degree of prototypicality than found in the second example, which contains an inanimate subject and an animate object of the preposition. Thus, although the sentences are identical with regard to word order, the passive construction in the second sentence induces a less-prototypical construal than the active construction in the first. Prototypicality and the animacy hierarchy are important for understanding Jeremiah 1.1-6.30, where grammatical subjects occur at dissimilar points on the animacy hierarchy, resulting in less than prototypical situations throughout the section.

It is now possible to make some general observations regarding prototypicality with regard to situations of perception, cognition and communication. First, perception and cognition terms are grouped within the thematic relationship of experiencer and are less than prototypical in two ways: the subject argument is an experiencer rather that an agent and these verbs tend to take complement clauses as object arguments, so a second situation might be embedded within the first. Second, communication terms occur with the thematic relationship of agent, which is highly prototypical. However, communication verbs also tend to take complement clauses or even whole paragraphs as object and the degree of dynamicity is less than that of an active voice, transitive verb such as "throw". Miller has demonstrated that communication verbs also differ in degree of prototypicality based upon the markedness of the grammatical constructions in which they occur.[26] Doubtless, this is also the case for perception and cognition verbs as well. Further research, using Miller's stringent analytical process, is surely in order.

3. Perception and Cognition Terms in Jeremiah 1.1-6.30

Terms of communication, perception and cognition abound in MT Jeremiah 1.1-6.30, thus grammatical subjects from the high end of the animacy hierarchy are prevalent in this section. The generality that the subject of a sentence is most likely to come from the top of the animacy hierarchy is born out in Jeremiah's report of the interaction between Yahweh and himself in Jeremiah chapter 1. Throughout this report, Yahweh is SAP 1 and Jeremiah is SAP 2, these being the two highest-ranking positions on the hierarchy. The proper nouns Israel and Judah

---

26 Miller, *Representation*.

also occur, again in a high-ranking slot on the hierarchy. Terms of communication, perception and cognition show a strong tendency to take complement clauses as objects, thus creating sentences that express more than one situation/proposition. The embedding of one situation within another is a prime reason that this group of verbs act as space-builders. These characteristics contribute to establishing the prototypicality of a given situation, which manifests itself in a grammatical construction.

C. The BH Verb in Context

The syntax portion of the TD clause level analysis follows an ascendant, recursive model, originally developed by the WIVU (see chapter 2.C.1). The verb is central to this analysis. Initially, the text is divided into clause-level units, as one clause comprises one predication. A clause may be either verbal or nominal. At minimum, a verbal clause consists of a verbal form (inflected or participial) plus a subject (either implicit or explicit). A nominal clause consists of a subject plus predicate.

The selection of a clause level analysis is significant on three counts. First, a given clause is the linguistic representation of a particular *situation*. Based upon the centre-periphery image schema, the wholeness presented by such linguistic representations subsumes both central elements and peripheral elements. The verb itself is the central element because the verbal form controls the occurrence of other elements. Premper describes this as the *inherent relationality* of the verb.[27] In other words, the inherent relationality, or transitivity, of the verb establishes the number of arguments that may be included in a given predication.[28] Second, Binnick notes that tense and aspect are sentence-level semantics categories.[29] Person/gender/number information associated with a given verb helps to establish participant reference for various arguments that are relationally associated with the verb. Finally, dynamicity, voice and transitivity represent the internal structure of the verb.

---

27 Premper, "Universals of the Linguistic Representation of Situations," 480.
28 Ibid., 490.
29 Robert I. Binnick, *Time and the Verb: A Guide to Tense and Aspect* (New York and Oxford: OUP, 1991), 456. Tense and aspect are also discourse level phenomenon. See Paul Hopper, "Aspect and Foregrounding in Discourse," in *Syntax and Semantics 12: Discourse and Syntax*, ed. T. Givon (New York: Academic Press, 1979), 213-241 (216); Stephen Wallace, "Figure and Ground: The Interrelationship of Linguistic Categories," in *Tense-Aspect: Between Semantics and Pragmatics*, ed. Paul J. Hopper (Amsterdam: John Benjamins, 1982).

1. Overview

Providing a comprehensive analysis and solution to the problems of the BH verbal system is not the goal of this volume, as it would be presumptuous, indeed, to propose a radical new solution to the problems of the "enigmatic" BH verbal system.[30] Nonetheless, it is inevitable that any approach that takes seriously the interrelationships between the syntax, semantics and pragmatics of the text at hand must account for the morphological and semantic information included in the BH verbal forms, as well as the interrelationship between the verbal forms and the information indicated by other lexical elements in a given predication. Therefore, whether the state of the discussion of the BH verb is a quagmire, an enigma or simply a baffling puzzle, it is vital to arrive at a working hypothesis that will move the TD analysis and description of prophetic text forward.

The following section contains definitions for the relevant linguistic terms. A short analysis of the tense/aspect debate follows. Finally, some cognitive linguistic additions are presented. These include the use of cognitive metaphor to describe verbal aspect and an introduction of conceptual blending to describe the *binyan* system.

2. Terminology

Because the discussion of tense, aspect and mood is important for understanding the Hebrew verbal system, it is necessary to review the use of these terms both in contemporary linguistic discussions and in BH studies.[31]

---

30 For a review of major historical trends, see Leslie McFall, *The Enigma of the Hebrew Verbal System: Solutions from Ewald to the Present Day*, Historic Texts and Interpreters in Biblical Scholarship; 2 (Sheffield South Yorkshire: Almond Press, 1982); Tryggve N. D. Mettinger, "The Hebrew Verb System: A Survey of Recent Research," *ASTI* 9 (1974), 64-84. Specific studies include C. Brockelmann, 'Die "Tempora" des Semitischen', *ZP* 3 (1951), 10-154; Diethelm Michel, *Tempora und Satzstellung in Den Psalmen*, Abhandlungen zur Evangelischen Theologie (Bonn: H. Bouvier, 1960).

31 Binnick has created a significant resource for the study of the verb. See Robert I. Binnick, *Project on Annotated Bibliography of Contemporary Research in Tense, Grammatical Aspect, Aktionsart, and Related Areas*. (2002, accessed); available from http://www.utsc.utoronto.ca/~binnick/TENSE.

a.   Tense

Tense is defined as "… a deictic device by which a situation is evaluated as before, overlapping with, or after a temporal position."[32]
Comrie notes that three tense categories occur cross-linguistically. First,
absolute tense, which is "… a tense that refers to time in relation to the
moment of utterance." Secondly, *relative tense,* which is "… a tense that
refers to a time in relation to a contextually determined reference point,
regardless of the latter's temporal relation to the moment of utterance."
Finally, *absolute-relative* tense, which is "… a tense that refers to time in
relation to a temporal reference point, that in turn is referred to in a
relation at the moment of utterance."[33] Somewhat more helpful is the
following definition by Bhat, who argues for a contrast between deictic
tense and non-deictic tense. He states:

> We may use the terms 'deictic' and 'nondeictic' in order to differentiate be-
> tween (i) tenses which have the utterance time as the reference point and
> (ii) the ones that have some other event as the reference point, respectively.
> Traditionally these are called 'absolute' and 'relative' tenses…but the dif-
> ference between the two does not depend upon one of them being relative
> and the other non-relative (or absolute); both are relative to a reference
> point; the difference between the two is only that the former uses a *deictic
> event* (an event that is connected with the speech act) as the reference point
> whereas the latter use some other event for that purpose.[34]

Thus, the crucial difference is not relative tense as opposed to absolute
tense, but rather the specific reference point involved: is the reference
point associated with the speech act itself, or is it associated with some
other event? While many scholars agree that BH does not have tense in
a strict sense, a relative tense model that uses context induced reference
points for determining the temporal ordering of states and events is a
possible option for describing tense in BH. However, a relative tense
theory does not account for all of the details present in the *binyan* system.

---

32   Cook, "Grammaticalization," 123.
33   Bernard Comrie, *Tense,* Cambridge Textbooks in Linguistics (Cambridge: CUP,
     1985), 36.
34   D. N. Bhat, *The Prominence of Tense, Aspect, and Mood* (Amsterdam: John Benjamins,
     1999), 14.

b.   Aspect

The linguistic assessment of aspect takes place under two headings: *viewpoint aspect* and *situation aspect,* or *aktionsart.*[35] Viewpoint aspect is concerned with the various *viewpoints* of the structure of a situation, and situation aspect describes the universal distinctions between situation types, such as *states, activities, accomplishments* and *achievements.*[36] In the case of viewpoint aspect, there is an opposition between *imperfective aspect* and *perfective aspect.* Regarding this distinction, Bhat states:

> ...The most important aspectual distinction that occurs in the grammars of natural languages is the one between perfective and imperfective. It primarily indicates two different ways of viewing or describing a given event. Perfective provides the view of an event as a whole from the outside whereas imperfective provides the view from the inside. The former is unconcerned with internal temporal structure of the event whereas the latter is crucially concerned with such a structure. The former views the situation as bounded, and forming a unified entity whereas the latter views it as ongoing or habitual.[37]

BH scholars of the aspectual school, including Cook, who views BH as an aspect prominent language, are in agreement with Bhat's conclusion that the primary opposition between perfective and imperfective is the most important aspectual distinction in BH. However, it is not the only distinction. As Waltke and O'Connor observe, the central role of predication in BH is shared between the verbal forms (perfect – imperfect) and the verbal stems, or *binyanim,* (i.e. *qal, piel* and *hiphil*). The verbal forms contribute viewpoint aspect information regarding the contour of the situation in time indicated by the form, while the *binyan* system contributes *aktionsart* information, regarding the kind of situation indicated by the verb. Because the *binyan* system is a rich source of morphologically marked aspectual information, it is somewhat surprising that discussions of the BH verb often downplay the importance of the *binyanim.* The aspectual subclasses indicated by the BH *binyan* system are discussed in chapter 5, section A, below.

---

35   See Carl Bache, "Aspect and Aktionsart: Towards a Semantic Distinction," *JL* 18 (1982), 57-72.

36   Cook, "Grammaticalization," 124.

37   Bhat, *The Prominence of Tense, Aspect, and Mood,* 46.

3.   Categories and the Biblical Hebrew Verb: Tense versus Aspect

Tense or Aspect? The debate is ongoing, with scholars arguing that the BH verbal system is a tense system, countered by other scholars who argue that it is an aspect system. Hendel notes that both tense alone and aspect alone theoretical models work passably well and have existed side by side for over a century.[38] The aspectual theory has flourished since the German scholar Heinrich Ewald produced his *Syntax of the Hebrew Language of the Old Testament* in 1835/1870. The work of British scholar S.R. Driver followed. Driver wrote his *Treatise on the Use of the Tenses* in 1874/1892.[39] Modern scholars continue to discuss the BH verb utilising the paradigmatic perfect-imperfect aspectual distinction, which Ewald described as *completed* and *incompleted*, and Driver termed as *complete* and *nascent*.[40] Although linguists use the terms *perfective* and *imperfective* to describe these primary aspectual categories, the distinction is effectively the same. The perfect/perfective BH verb form describes a completed action or state while the imperfect/imperfective form describes an ongoing action or state.

Scholars interested in analysing BH text from a discourse perspective, such as Longacre and Niccacci, tend to utilise verbal forms as structural markers, or signals that indicate a particular type of discourse.[41] This creates two difficulties. First, as Cook notes, the argument for categorising text-types based upon verbal forms is inherently circular: one must decide which discourse type is present in a text before deciding which verbal forms are characteristic of the type.[42] However, it is worth mentioning that Longacre's text-types are descriptive rather

---

38   Ronald S. Hendel, "In the Margins of the Hebrew Verbal System: Situation, Tense, Aspect, Mood," *ZAH* 9 (1996), 152.

39   J. A. Emerton, "Samuel Rolles Driver, 1846-1914," in *A Century of British Orientalists 1902-2001*, ed. C. E. Bosworth (Oxford: OUP, 2001), 130.

40   S. R. Driver and W. Randall Garr, *A Treatise on the Use of the Tenses in Hebrew and Some Other Syntactical Questions* (Grand Rapids, Mich.: William B. Eerdmans, 1998), xxxix; Emerton, 'Samuel Rolles Driver, 1846-1914', 131; Heinrich Ewald, *Syntax of the Hebrew Language of the Old Testament*, trans. James Kennedy (Edinburgh: T and T Clark, 1881; reprint, Georgias Press, 2005), 2.

41   Alviero Niccacci, "Essential Hebrew Syntax," in *Narrative and Comment*, ed. Eep Talstra (Amsterdam: Societas Hebraica Amstelodamensis, 1995), 111-125; Alviero Niccacci and W. G. E. Watson, *The Syntax of the Verb in Classical Hebrew Prose*, JSOT Sup 86 (Sheffield: JSOT Press, 1990).

42   Cook is referring to the term *text-type* as used by Longacre, who distinguishes between the sets of verbal forms used in hortatory text, narrative text, and so on. This volume uses the term *text-type* differently, as the term is used to categorise stretches of text based on Schneider's differentiation between narrative and discursive text. Cook, "Grammaticalization," 117.

than prescriptive. This is also the case with Schneider's distinction between narrative and discursive text. Hebrew scholars in general approach the verb forms from a discourse perspective when discussing
the *waw*-conversive theory, as this theory moves the discussion to the
relationship between multiple predications.[43]

Secondly, the perfective-imperfective inflection of verbal forms is
not sufficient for establishing the structure of a text, nor does this distinction exhaust the quantities of morphologically marked information
available in the verbal forms. This volume argues that conceptually
blended syntactic and semantic information, such as the space building
terms described in MST, proves to be more useful in determining
boundaries and connections in a text. Information Structure findings
are also significant. Primarily a sentence level phenomenon, information structure is the product of the interrelationship between topic and
focus information in a given predication. At the discourse level, this
sentence level information combines with other text level features, such
as text-deictic particles and anaphoric terms to indicate cognitive structuring of the text. The verbal forms are crucial, yet not the only deter-
minative factor for textual structuring.

4.   The TD Approach: Mapping the Syntax-Semantics Interface

As previously explained, the TD approach begins with a syntactic analysis of the text. The syntactic analysis provides a blueprint of the text,
which is then realised via conceptual blending of information derived
from semantic and pragmatic text analyses. Nowhere is this multi-
staged analytical approach more important than when dealing with the
Biblical Hebrew verbal forms and their role in BH text.

The TD approach shares Talstra's interest in exhausting the syntactic information presented in the BH text before proceeding with further
analysis. However, even in the syntax driven WIVU database and its
realisation in the SESB format, semantic information is included at the
distributional level. Two semantic fields are marked: verbs of speaking
and forms of the verb היה. Following Schneider, Talstra utilises verbs
from the semantic field of speaking to differentiate between narrative,
discursive and quoted levels in the text.

---

43   In her review of Goldfajn, Zewi states "… verbal forms and discourse functions go
     together in Biblical Hebrew to create the complete pattern of the verbal sentence in-
     volving certain verbal forms and a certain word order incapable of being separated.
     Thus, discourse factors do play an important role in the Biblical Hebrew verbal sys-
     tem." Tamar Zewi, "Review of *Word Order and Time,* by Tal Goldfajn," *JSS* 46.

Semantic information is also important for Information Structure analyses, as indicated by Lambrecht's foundational statement: "The focus of a proposition is that semantic element (or elements) whose presence makes the proposition into an assertion, i.e. into a potential piece of information."[44] The role of semantics in determining space building terms and constructions in MST is illustrated by the examples in chapter 4, section B.2, where space-builders are indicated by semantic domain information.

Several recent studies utilise both morphological and semantic categories for the description of the BH verb.[45] Cook's grammaticalisation approach, which omits discussion of the *binyan* system, does include a strong semantic component.[46] Hendel's study of the "margins" of the verbal system includes discussion about the *binyan* system and introduces the categories of situation and mood as well. The following section presents findings from Cook's approach and Hendel's lexicalization and grammaticalisation study. These studies help to clarify the categories utilised by the TD approach to the BH verb.

a.   Cook: The Grammaticalisation Approach

In *The Hebrew Verb: A Grammaticalization Approach,* Cook addresses two issues that also motivate the TD approach: the asymmetrical relationship between form and meaning and the problem of language change over time. The asymmetry between form and meaning, where a particular form may represent more than one function and where a particular function might be fulfilled by more than one form, is addressed in the discussion of space building terms (see chapter 4.II.B). The second issue is quite important for synchronic aspects of the TD approach, because the realities of language change over time impinge upon a synchronic reading at the lexical and syntactic levels. Since Cook's approach is effective in addressing both of these questions, the TD approach adopts and elaborates upon his discoveries. A brief summary of the grammaticalisation approach is in order.

Cook notes that linguists employ the term grammaticalisation in two different ways: it describes both grammaticalisation *phenomena* and grammaticalisation *theory*. According to Cook, *grammaticalisation phe-*

---

44   Lambrecht, *Information Structure,* 336.

45   Bill T. Arnold and John H. Choi, *A Guide to Biblical Hebrew Syntax* (Cambridge: CUP, 2003); Galia Hatav, *The Semantics of Aspect and Modality: Evidence from English and Biblical Hebrew,* SLCS, vol. 34 (Amsterdam: John Benjamins, 1997); Waltke and O'Connor, *An Introduction to Biblical Hebrew Syntax.*

46   Cook, "Grammaticalization," 121.

nomena are "…changes that result in increased grammaticality of items – either lexical > grammatical or grammatical > more grammatical', while *grammaticalisation theory* "…refers to claims made about gram- maticalisation phenomenon, such as unidirectionality."[47] Since certain linguists view grammaticalisation theory as derivative, Cook utilises the term *grammaticalisation approach* for his approach to the description of changes in the BH verbal system over time.

In his discussion of form-meaning asymmetry, Cook employs two grammaticalisation principles: First, he notes, "…the grammaticalisa- tion process is cyclical."[48] Language change occurs as a multi-layered process in which new layers emerge and may interact with older layers still in existence.[49] He notes that the layering effect combines with a second principle, the *persistence of meaning*, which describes the tenden- cy for traces of the original meaning to remain as long as the form is grammatically viable.

Finally, regarding the problem of language change over time, Cook notes, "…*universal paths* exist within broad semantic domains along which relevant forms develop."[50] These universal paths are reflected cross-linguistically and are unidirectional; if a form exhibits change, it does not revert to a former stage, but rather will stay the same or progress to the next stage of change.[51] These characteristics of language change constrain possibilities, thus the grammaticalisation process is not haphazard.[52]

Cook posits grammaticalisation paths for the *wayyiqtol, qatal, yiqtol,* participle, imperative and jussive forms. The (purported) origin of the *wayyiqtol* form was the pronoun + **q(u)tul* (infinitive). In Pre-BH, the form moved from resultative > perfect aspect > perfective aspect. In BH the form represents past tense. The origin of the *qatal* form was **qatil* + pronoun. This form moved from resultative > perfect aspect. In BH, the form represents perfective aspect. The origin of the *yiqtol* form was the pronoun + **q(u)tul* (infinitive) + locative *u*. In Pre-BH the form represented progressive aspect, while in BH the form represents imper- fective aspect. The origin of the participle was the **q(u)tul* form and the

---

47   Ibid., 119.

48   Ibid., 120.

49   Regarding the process of language change in BH, see J. A. Naudé, "The Transitions of Biblical Hebrew," in *Biblical Hebrew: Studies in Chronology and Typology*, ed. Ian Young, JSOT Sup (Sheffield: T & T Clark, 2003).

50   Cook, 'Grammaticalization', 121.

51   For a complete theoretical discussion, see Joan L. Bybee, Revere Perkins and William Pagliuca, *The Evolution of Grammar: Tense, Aspect, and Modality in the Languages of the World* (Chicago: UCP, 1994), 1-26.

52   Cook, "Grammaticalization," 121.

form indicates progressive aspect in both Pre-BH and BH. The origin of the imperative was *q(u)tul* and that of the jussive was pronoun + *q(u)tul* (imperative), both of which indicated deontic modality in Pre-BH and BH. According to this analysis, there is a basic meaning discernible for each form and there is a certain amount of semantic overlap between forms as well. Some secondary meanings might persist from earlier stages in the grammaticalisation process. Meanings that do not share any of the semantic parameters of the basic meaning are the result of "context induced reinterpretations."[53] Cook notes that there is an obvious discourse pragmatic distinction between *qatal* and *wayyiqtol* forms, in that *wayyiqtol* forms express foregrounded narrative events.[54]

It is significant for the TD approach that Cook concludes that Hebrew is an aspect prominent language. At the time of BH, the *wayyiqtol* form functioned as the narrative tense verb, indicating sequential, past time action. *Qatal* forms developed along the same grammaticalisation path. They indicate *perfective aspect*. On the other hand, the *yiqtol* and participle forms developed along a grammaticalisation path from progressive to imperfect, resulting in forms that expressed *imperfective action*. In addition, *imperfective action* exhibits a *past: non-past* opposition.[55]

This analysis is compelling in that it accounts for both diachronic change and the synchronic nature of the forms as they appear in the BH text. In analysing and describing the information structure of the Jeremiah text, the TD approach will draw upon Cook's conclusions regarding BH verbal forms as follows. The main use of each of the forms is in bold type and selected subsidiary uses are in normal type.[56]

wayyiqtol	past tense, narrative verb: simple past; counterfactual
qatal	**perfective aspect**: perfect; immediate future; performative
yiqtol	imperfective aspect: general future; future in past; directive
Participle	**progressive aspect**: expected future; present/past progressive
Imperative	deontic modality: directive; volitive
Jussive	deontic modality: directive; volitive

Cook's approach does not address the *binyan* system, which is the main means of establishing transitivity and as a result is quite important for determining the relations that hold between topical entities in a given predication. However, Hendel does make some very helpful prelimi-

---

53   Ibid., 122.
54   This analysis is in accord with that of Schneider and adopted by Talstra.
55   Cook, "Grammaticalization," 137.
56   For the complete range of uses, see Ibid., 136.

nary observations that include both the semantics of the BH verb and the influence of the *binyan* system as well.

b. Hendel: Lexicalization and the Binyanim

Hendel examines the margins of the Hebrew verbal system, as "… it is often in the domain of marginal phenomena that the right – or more analytically precise – distinctions can be made."[57] In doing so, Hendel demonstrates that accurate analysis of the Hebrew verbal forms is a matter of both morphological form and semantic function.[58] Hendel sidesteps the tense/aspect debate by advocating for a relative tense model that interacts with the categories of situation, aspect and mood.[59] He states:

> The system of relative tense, as with any tense system, involves the relationships among three temporal points: that of the speaker, or speech-act (S), the event (E), and the reference point (R)…In an absolute tense system, the reference point is always the time of the speaker or speech-act (R=S). In a relative tense system, R may or may not coincide with S. R may be past to the speaker (R<S), it may be simultaneous (R=S), or it may be future (R>S). As a result of this non-identity of R and S in a relative tense system, the event (E) may be in a different temporal relationship to R and S.

In this definition, the term *relative tense* correlates with Bhat's description of *non-deictic* tense. Importantly, this definition of relative tense holds at the level of the single predication; no explicit claims are made for discourse level sequencing of multiple predications.[60] Establishing discourse-level temporal reference in prophetic literature would present difficulties for an absolute tense model, because the time frame of the text, the meta-linguistic "speech-act," is in competition with embedded time frames. It may be possible that a relative tense theory taken to the discourse level would offer additional options for the analysis of such a text, which opens a door for further research.

Hendel then addresses three significant features of the BH verb, all of which are associated with the binyan system: *situation; transitivity; and voice.*

---

57 Ronald S. Hendel, "In the Margins of the Hebrew Verbal System: Situation, Tense, Aspect, Mood," *ZAH* 9 (1996), 152.

58 This is also the case for Talstra, for whom establishing the limits of syntax is a main goal. He still finds it necessary to include notation of verbs from the semantic domain of direct speech in the syntax oriented WIVU database.

59 Hendel's relative tense model follows that of Reichenbach with modifications by Bernard Comrie (Comrie 1985; Binnick 1991: 109-116).

60 Goldfajn has developed the relative tense model for the discourse level analysis of narrative text with good results. Goldfajn, *Word Order and Time in Biblical Hebrew Narrative.*

Situation

The introduction of the linguistic category *situation* into the discussion of the BH verb is quite helpful.[61] Premper, speaking of *situation* as a linguistic category states, "In typical situations something is happening and one or more entities are involved. Thus a situation is something which is internally relational, implying at least two entities (in a wider sense)."[62] Situations may be more or less typical, based upon the degree of dynamicity involved and upon the types of entities involved.[63] For Hendel, the term *situation* refers to "...the inherent meaning of the circumstance signified by the verb."[64] He notes that *dynamicity* is morphologically marked in the Hebrew *Qal*, where the dynamic versus static opposition is most clearly observed. Some scholars perceive dynamicity as a gradual concept, rather than an opposition. Consequently, it is possible to develop a scale from more static to more dynamic actions.[65] These additional gradations are found at the lexical level for the BH verb. Exploring situation as a linguistic category has implications for the information structure component of the TD analysis, because the semantic difference between a dynamic, or *fientive* verb, and a stative verb may be significant.[66]

Transitivity

The relationship between the situation in *Qal* and situation in the derived conjugations, i.e. the stative *Qal* and the factitive *Piel*; as well as the dynamic *Qal* and the causative *Hiphil*, is related to the issue of transitivity. The contrasts found between transitive and intransitive con-

---

61   See F. W. Dobbs-Allsop, "Biblical Hebrew Statives and Situation Aspect," *JSS* XLV (2000), 21-52.

62   Premper, "Universals of the Linguistic Representation of Situations," 478.

63   Comrie describes *dynamicity,* or the difference between *states* and *processes*, as follows: "States are static, i.e. continue as before unless changed, whereas events and processes are dynamic, i.e. require a continual input of energy if they are not to come to an end." Bernard Comrie, *Aspect: An Introduction to the Study of Verbal Aspect and Related Problems*, Cambridge Textbooks in Linguistics (Cambridge: Cambridge University Press, 1976), 13. See also Binnick, *Time and the Verb: A Guide to Tense and Aspect*, 170-197.

64   Hendel, "In the Margins of the Hebrew Verbal System: Situation, Tense, Aspect, Mood," 154.

65   Premper, "Universals of the Linguistic Representation of Situations," 495.

66   In addition to the term *dynamic*, the term *fientive* is used for verbs that describe action, motion or change of state, since the term *active* is used to denote voice (Arnold 2003: 38).

structions in *Qal* and those in the derived conjugations are also significant.[67] Hendel summarises as follows:

Qal	Piel	Hiphil
• Stative>	factitive>	intransitive
• Dynamic/intransitive>	frequentative>	causative/singly transitive
• Dynamic/transitive>	resultative>	causative/doubly transitive

The choice of a verbal form will affect the number of arguments in a
given predication. Evaluation of the verbal forms from the perspective
of quantitative valence provides the following information: a stative
verb requires one argument: *The boy* is young. A dynamic, intransitive
verb also requires one argument: *The boy* fell. A dynamic, singly transitive verb requires two arguments: *The boy* kicked *the ball.* A doubly
transitive verb requires three arguments: *The boy* gave *Mary the ball.*[68]
For this reason, the number and identity of topical entities in a BH predication will interact with the number and type of arguments required
by a particular verbal form. For example, a *Qal* stative form requires
one argument, as does a *Qal* intransitive form. A *Qal* transitive form
requires two arguments. A dynamic, singly transitive *Hiphil* form requires two arguments, and a dynamic, doubly transitive *Hiphil* form
requires three.

This summary has implications for sentence-level Information
Structure analysis, because a particular conjugation will constrain the
relationship that holds between a verb and its arguments. For Information Structure analysis, argument(s) may function as topical entities, so
the use of a particular verbal form will affect tracking of such entities.

Voice

The second issue is the relationship between situation in the *Qal* and
the semantics of voice, or *diathesis*. For example, the *niphal* "...effects a
change of voice and situation for dynamic/transitive verbs."[69] This may
be summarised as follows:

---

67 The most recent elaboration of this material is Arnold and Choi, *A Guide to Biblical
    Hebrew Syntax*, 193. See also the *Expanded Stem Chart*, Arnold and Choi, *A Guide to
    Biblical Hebrew Syntax*, 194.

68 Quantitative valence is a widely accepted means of evaluating transitivity. A second
    means of evaluating transitivity is the *semantic decomposition of verbs*, which may be
    done by analysing the internal time structure, or *inherent aspectual properties* of the
    verbal form, i.e. *dynamicity* – which results in the dynamic-stative opposition. Prem-
    per, "Universals of the Linguistic Representation of Situations," 495.

69 Hendel, "In the Margins of the Hebrew Verbal System: Situation, Tense, Aspect,
    Mood," 157.

Qal

    Dynamic/transitive

Niphal

    Reflexive/transitive

    Or middle/intransitive

    Or passive/intransitive

    Resultative/stative

The *niphal* signals an intransitive construction and the form is underspecified with regard to the causal force, source of energy or agent.[70] The *niphal* form gives rise to one mapping configuration, but at least two types of pragmatic, context-induced elaboration. In the first elaboration, the causal force is associated with an external agent. This is a passive, agent-oriented understanding.[71] Often the agent is encoded as a prepositional phrase, as in the sentence *The ball was thrown by Harry*. Harry caused the motion of the ball. In the second elaboration, the causal force has something to do with the internal characteristics of the theme. This contributes to a *middle*, or non agent-oriented, understanding.[72] The sentence: *The ball rolled from the table and bounced on the floor* illustrates this. The ball is no longer on the table, but whether the ball was pushed off by Harry, or was set in motion by a breeze from the window, or by vibrations from the street-repairers below, is not specified.

This marginal issue might have significant consequences for exegesis, as Keith Grüneberg demonstrates in his discussion of the Genesis 12.3. Grüneberg differentiates between three possible translations of the *niphal* בְּרֵךְ in Genesis 12.3, offering options such as the passive *be blessed*; the middle *find blessing*; and the reflexive *bless themselves*. The passive option, *be blessed*, accords with the presence of the explicit agent in the prepositional phrase *by you*, and seems to be the best choice.[73]

---

70   Mandelblit, "Grammatical Marking," 229.
71   Waltke and O'Connor, *An Introduction to Biblical Hebrew Syntax*, 383.
72   Mandelblit, "Grammatical Marking," 229.
73   Grüneberg proposes that middle *niphals* come from roots derived from several semantic domains, such as action for one's own benefit, reciprocal activities, grooming, self-movement, separation, performative speech and so on. He includes the root לָחַם, *to fight* in the category of reciprocal activity, thus having a "middle" nuance. So the English clause *they fought* might appear in Hebrew as an intransitive construction with a *niphal* verb form. Keith Grüneberg, *Abraham, Blessing and the Nations: A Philological and Exegetical Study of Genesis 12:3 in Its Narrative Context* (Berlin: Walter de Gruyter, 2003).

Again, these category shifts will affect the topical entities (arguments) involved in a text, potentially altering the relationships established via functional roles in a given discourse. For example, the argument in the position of grammatical subject often holds the functional role of *agent*, or "...the instigator of the action" in a given predication. Likewise, the argument in the position of grammatical direct object will often hold the functional role of *patient*, who is "...the entity undergoing the effect of the action" in a given predication. [74] The role of *agent* is often encoded as the grammatical subject, whereas the role of *patient* is often encoded as the grammatical indirect object, making the entity in the role of *agent* more salient than the entity in the role of *patient*. [75] During the reading process, the role of *agent* and that of *patient* might shift between entities as discourse progresses. Alternatively, one entity might retain the role of subject, the other of object over several predications.

The latter situation occurs in Jeremiah 1.4-1.10, in which both Jeremiah and Yahweh are active discourse topical entities. Jeremiah reports the interchange, but Yahweh occurs as the subject, or *agent*, in many of the following clauses, while Jeremiah is represented as the direct object, or *patient*, in the same clauses (see Jeremiah 1.4a; 1.5a, b, d, e; 1.7a, d, f; 1.9a, b, c, d; 1.10b). Clearly, while this section includes both discourse topical entities in nearly equal proportions, Yahweh appears to be the more active of the two. He is the initiator of most of the action and Jeremiah appears to be the less active interlocutor as he is the recipient of much of the action.

D. Space and Time in Biblical Hebrew Text: Cognitive Additions

As previously noted, one difficulty with the Hebrew verbal system is determining the role of various verbal forms in the mapping of temporal information. [76] This difficulty arises for two reasons. First, the

---

74 Finch describes these as *theta* roles. Geoffrey Finch, *Linguistic Terms and Concepts* (Basingstoke: Palgrave Macmillan, 2000), 120.

75 The reverse is also the case. Premper states, "There is a universal tendency such that the less 'salient' or animated, or individuated a participant is, the less likely it is to be coded as subject." Premper, "Universals of the Linguistic Representation of Situations," 489.

76 Among others, Waltke and O'Connor note, "Biblical Hebrew has no tenses in the strict sense: it uses a variety of other means to express time relations." Waltke and O'Connor, *An Introduction to Biblical Hebrew Syntax*, 347.

Hebrew verb is not the primary source of temporal information in BH text, where temporal adverbs, such as בטרם, *before*, and אחרי, *after*, and constructions such as בימי יאשיהו המלך, *in the days of King Josiah* (Jeremiah 3.6), contribute to time reference.[77] Second, the verb contains far more information than simple time reference. The verb indicates the type of activity represented by a particular lexical choice. It also provides information regarding its adjuncts (subject and object) and their functional roles in the sentence.[78]

1.   Cognitive Metaphor and Time: TIME IS MOTION

Some fresh insight into the expression of time in Biblical Hebrew is gained when the issue is examined from the perspective of the TIME IS MOTION conceptual metaphor because this metaphor underlies much discussion of this widely debated subject. As discussed in chapter 5, section B.4, a conceptual metaphor is not in itself a literary metaphor, although conceptual metaphor has a role in establishing the basis for literary metaphor. Rather, a conceptual metaphor is an experientially derived cognitive construction. The concept of motion is experiential: humans experience a wide variety of motion, such as walking, running, carrying and being carried. Similarly, humans regularly observe other kinds of motion, such as flowing rivers, flying birds and the shifting of heavenly bodies. This common experience makes the source domain, MOTION, available for understanding the target domain, TIME, in the conceptual metaphor TIME IS MOTION. The conceptual metaphor TIME IS MOTION is a structural metaphor.[79] The source domain, MOTION, is a rich

---

77   Other features that map temporal relations are expressions headed by nouns, adverbs, adjectives and prepositions. See C. H. J. van der Merwe, "Reconsidering Biblical Hebrew Temporal Expressions," *ZAH* 10 (1997), 42-59.

78   Categories relevant to the description of the BH verb include: person, number and gender; tense; modality; voice; aspect, i.e. *perfective-imperfective*; and aspect (aktionsart), i.e. *voice, fientivity-transitivity and causation*. Waltke and O'Connor, *An Introduction to Biblical Hebrew Syntax*, 344.

79   Conceptual metaphors perform three basic functions. Structural metaphors include "… a source that is a rich source of knowledge for the target." A structural metaphor "… enables speakers to understand target A by means of the structure of source B,"(i.e. time is motion). Ontological metaphors "… provide less conceptual structure than a structural metaphor," while "… giving ontological status to general categories of abstract concepts" (i.e. society is a person). Orientational metaphors provide even less conceptual structure while "… making a set of target concepts coherent in our conceptual system, based upon coordinates established by basic human spatial orientation" (i.e. more is up). Kövecses, *Metaphor: A Practical Introduction*, 33-35.

source of knowledge for understanding the target domain, TIME. Linguistic expressions such as *time flows by, time flies, times change; he is running out of time, the days ahead will be challenging* are a few examples of this structural metaphor. The source domain, MOTION, also gives rise to a certain amount of confusion, because the motion inherent in this conceptual metaphor may be construed in two quite different ways. The first way of construing the TIME IS MOTION metaphor is *time passing is the motion of an object.* In this construal the observer is fixed, while time is an object moving with respect to the observer. Linguistic expressions such as *time flows by, time flies* and *times change* are overt examples of this construal. The second way of construing the TIME IS MOTION metaphor is *time passing is an observer's motion over a landscape.* In this case, time is fixed and the observer is moving with respect to time. Linguistic expressions such as *he is running out of time* and *the days ahead will be challenging* are examples of the second. Lakoff and Johnson see the two options as reversals of the figure-ground configuration, as two related ideas. Talmy lists the following features that characterise the figure and ground opposition:

Figure	Ground
location less known	location more known
smaller	larger
more mobile	more stationary
structurally simpler	structurally more complex
more salient	more backgrounded
more recently in awareness	earlier on scene; in memory[80]

This information informs the construal of the TIME IS MOTION metaphor in the following ways: In the first construal, *time passing is the motion of an object,* time is moving toward a fixed observer. In this case, the fixed observer is the ground: his location is more known, he is more stationary and is backgrounded. Time is the figure. The location of time is less known, it is more mobile, it is structurally simpler and it is more salient. In this construal, time is in focus. In the second construal, *time passing is an observer's motion over a landscape,* time is the ground: its location is known, it is more stationary and it is backgrounded. The observer is the figure. His location is less known, he is smaller, more mobile, structurally simpler and more salient. The observer is in focus. For both of these understandings, time is moving in a linear, one-dimensional manner. The metaphors make full use of the human cogni-

---

80   Croft and Cruse, *Cognitive Linguistics,* 42.

tive ability to manipulate abstract structure in mental space.[81] Because the relationship between time and the observer is relational, rather than absolute, these metaphorical understandings are compatible with the relative tense view of the BH verb. They are also compatible with mapping temporal ordering along a time line based upon alternative temporal indicators, such as adverbs and temporal constructions. For this reason, it is important to determine the identity of the observer in order to map the temporal contours of a text. In terms of MST, this will determine which space is the *viewpoint space*. In terms of cognitive grammar, the identity of the observer will interact with the viewing arrangement: in first and second person speech, the reader is brought into the situation, perhaps identifying with the observer, whereas in third person narration, the reader will most likely view the situation from afar. It is then important to observe the manner in which verbal forms, in combination with other linguistic cues, are used to construe the issue of time: Is time moving with respect to the observer (viewpoint space), or is the observer (viewpoint space) moving with respect to time? What linguistic cues allow the reader to track time from the observer's perspective (viewpoint space) in either construal? Are these cues the same or different in each case?

2.   Extending Aspectual Boundaries: TIME IS SPACE

As discussed in chapter 4, section A.3, the cognitive metaphor TIME IS A CONTAINER structures Jeremiah 1.1-1.3. The TIME IS A CONTAINER metaphor is a subset of the conceptual metaphor TIME IS SPACE because of the metaphorical association of time with matter, in this case a container. For Jeremiah 1.1-1.3, the series of temporal references at 1.2b, בימי יאשיהו; 1.2d, בשלש־עשרה שנה למלכו and at 1.3a, בימי יהויקים, indicate the extent of the container's metaphoric boundaries.

---

81   Johnson notes that Lakoff's image schema transformations are "…more general and abstract that particular mental images." Four image schema transformations are relevant to this analysis of the BH verb. Path-focus to end-point focus is the transformation by which it is possible for one to follow, in the imagination, the path of a moving object, then to focus upon the point where it comes to rest. Multiplex to mass is the transformation by which one is able to imagine a group of several object, then move away (in the mind) until the cluster turns into a single homogenous mass, then to move back until the mass turns into a cluster. Following a trajectory is the transformation by which one is able mentally to trace the path traversed by a continuously moving object, and superimposition is the transformation by which one is able to manipulate abstract structure in mental space. Johnson, *The Body in the Mind: The Bodily Basis of Meaning, Imagination, and Reason*, 24-25.

The time is a container metaphor is an *orientational* metaphor. Orientational metaphors are cognitive metaphors that provide less conceptual structure than do structural metaphors, such as the time is motion metaphor mentioned above. In the case of Jeremiah 1.1-1.3, the metaphorical container sets the major parameters for locating the events in time and space, but the container itself is relatively unstructured.

However, the metaphor TIME IS SPACE is a structural metaphor in which the structure of the source, SPACE, enables speakers to understand the target, TIME. While space might seem even less structured than the aforementioned container, this is not necessarily the case. In her study on Slavic aspect, Janda notes:

> Space is occupied by matter. If space consisted merely of empty dimension, it would provide little (if any) structure for metaphorical imagination. Indeed, spatial metaphors almost invariably refer to the parameters of material objects of various sorts. Aspect refers very specifically to the physical forms of matter and maps this parameter to the domain of space.[82]

In order to account for the complexities of Slavic aspect, Janda proposes "... a version of the universal TIME IS SPACE metaphor, according to which SITUATIONS ARE MATERIAL ENTITIES and, more specifically, PERFECTIVE IS A DISCRETE SOLID OBJECT versus IMPERFECTIVE IS A FLUID SUBSTANCE."[83] In this assessment, perfective situations are objects that occupy time as discrete solid objects occupy space, while imperfective situations are objects that occupy time as fluid substances occupy space. Janda divides the properties of matter into three groups: inherent properties, interactional properties and human interactional properties. In this scheme, inherent properties, such as edges, shape and integrity, correspond to inherent situation aspect. Interactional properties, such as dynamism and salience, correspond to discourse phenomena of aspect. Human properties, such as grasping and impact, correspond to pragmatic phenomena of aspect. Inherent properties are default motivators, while the interactional properties "...can be used to motivate subjective construal."[84]

Janda's assessment of Slavic aspect is experientialist. She notes, "... the human body is the instrument through which (the above) properties are explored and it also plays a role on the location of situations in time." Regarding her Russian examples, Janda states, "... the solid

82   Laura A. Janda, "A Metaphor in Search of a Source Domain," *CL* 15 (2004), 485.
83   Ibid., 471.
84   Ibid.

body of the human observer helps to disambiguate the tense."[85] As in the TIME IS MOTION examples discussed in the previous section, the presence of the human observer in the timeline has an effect upon temporal construal, in that the observer becomes the deictic centre for the construal of the situation.[86] Additionally, Marmaridou notes that the TIME AS A MOVING OBJECT metaphor gives time "... a front-back orientation facing the direction of motion. In these terms the future is facing toward us while it is moving toward us...when time is constructed as a moving object, it is also moving toward or away from the speaker. Future, present, past are calculated from the perspective of the speaker/observer."[87] Additionally, "... the tense distinction results form the fact that two solid objects (the human body of the observer and the discrete solid of the perfective situation) cannot occupy the same spot on the timeline. A solid object (the human body of the observer) can, however, be enveloped in a fluid substance (the imperfective situation), permitting the two to co-exist at the same moment."[88]

3.   Biblical Hebrew: TIME IS SPACE

Examining the Hebrew verbal system via the cognitive metaphor TIME IS SPACE provides insight into the cognitive construal inherent in each of the verbal forms and into discourse-conditioned cognitive construal as well. A synthesis of Janda's metphorical description of PERFECTIVE IS A DISCRETE SOLID OBJECT versus IMPERFECTIVE IS A FLUID SUBSTANCE with Cook's findings regarding the aspect prominent nature of BH makes it is possible to explore the implications of the cognitive metaphor TIME IS SPACE.

    Cook has observed that both the *wayyiqtol* (past tense form) and the *qatal* (perfective aspect form) developed along the *resultative > perfect >*

---

85   At any given point in a discourse, the observer has a place in the canonical viewing arrangement for a given predication, even though the observer is not physically present in the event. Ibid., 490.

86   From an experientialist perspective, Marmaridou proposes that deixis is an Idealized Cognitive Model, an ICM, and that this ICM "...gives rise to the emergence of the CENTRE vs. PERIPHERY image schema." Additionally, she states, "...the proposed construal of the ICM of deixis structures all categories of deixis. In this analysis, person and place deixis mutually co-evolve, whereas social deixis is based on the metaphorical understanding of social space as physical space, time deixis is based on the metaphorical understanding of time as space, and discourse deixis is based on the metaphorical understanding of discourse as time, and time as space." Marmaridou, *Pragmatic Meaning and Cognition*, 97.

87   Ibid., 102.

88   Ibid., 491.

perfective > simple past grammaticalisation path, while the *yiqtol* (imperfective aspect form) and the participle (progressive aspect form) developed along the *progressive > imperfective* grammaticalisation path. When approached according to Janda's categories, the first set of forms indicates situations that occupy time as discrete solid objects occupy space, and the second set of forms indicates situations that occupy time as fluid substances occupy space.

4.   Inherent Properties of Matter and BH Aspect: Sentence Level

This section presents three characteristics regarding inherent aspect in BH verbal forms. These characteristics deal with individual forms, so they concern sentence level predications. (For discourse level characteristics, see section D.5, below.)[89]

1. *Edges*: Discrete solid objects have edges, thus perfective situations (*wayyiqtol, qatal*) exhibit boundedness. On the other hand, fluid substances have no inherent edges, so imperfective situations (*yiqtol*, participle) tend to exhibit unboundedness and a lack of reference to beginning and end.[90]

2. *Homogeneity vs. Heterogeneity*: A discrete solid object has integrity as a whole, so perfective situations (*wayyiqtol, qatal*) may be characterised as single, one-time accomplishments and achievements, exhibiting wholeness, definiteness and totality. On the other hand, fluid substances tend to be uniform, continuous and divisible, so imperfective situations (*yiqtol*, participle) may be characterised as ongoing activities and states that have temporal stability and sometimes exhibit indefiniteness.

3. *Penetrability*: A discrete solid object is impenetrable and only experienced from the exterior, so perfective situations (*wayyiqtol, qatal*) are perceived from the outside. On the other hand, the observer can reach, see or be inside a fluid substance, so imperfective situations (*yiqtol*, participle) may be viewed from the inside.

The above characteristics correlate with Bhat's definition, highlighting the conceptual nature of aspect as a linguistic category. To reiterate, Bhat states:

---

89   The relevant characteristics are renumbered from Janda's alphabetical list, where they occur as A, C and F. Janda, "A Metaphor in Search of a Source Domain."

90   The participle is included with the *yiqtol* in the *imperfective* category because, according to Binnick, "Perfective and imperfective are universally accepted as aspects; the progressive is widely considered to be a variety of the imperfect" (Binnick: 2001, 563).

...perfective provides the view of an event as a whole from the outside whereas imperfective provides the view from the inside *(see point 2, above)*. The former is unconcerned with internal temporal structure of the event whereas the latter is crucially concerned with such a structure *(see point 3, above)*. The former views the situation as bounded and forming a unified entity whereas the latter views it as on-going or habitual *(see point 1, above)*.[91]

The three characteristics also have points in common with Cook's scope and distance metaphor. He uses the idea of a camera to explain that a *perfective* form (*qatal*) indicates the entire interval of a situation, as viewed from a distance. A *perfect* form (*wayyiqtol*) provides a resultant view of situation, while presuming a prior event nucleus. An *imperfective* form (*yiqtol*) provides a close-up view without endpoints and a *progressive* form (participle) indicates an agent in the midst of a situation at reference time. On the other hand, these characteristics do not require the distance factor employed by Cook. A situation described using a *yiqtol* form may be perceived as either close up or far away from the perceiver; being fluid, it simply does not have endpoints. Similarly, a situation described using a *qatal* form may also be perceived as either close up or far away from the perceiver; being solid, it simply is a bounded whole.

Four additional properties relate to sentence level verbal forms. These are *shape, countability, streamability* and *convertibility*.[92]

1. Shape: A discrete solid object can have various shapes and can be perceived as thin stable slices, so perfective situations (*wayyiqtol, qatal*) can have various durations. They may also be punctiliar. Fluid substances do not exhibit shape, although they do have thickness, so imperfective situations (*yiqtol*, participle) must have some duration and can extend indefinitely.

2. Countability: Discrete solid objects are countable, while fluid substances are uncountable masses that can fill a space, so imperfectives (*yiqtol*, participle) occur with indefinite time reference, or with references that form boundaries.

3. Streamability: Discrete solid objects do not stream, fluid substances stream.

4. Convertibility: Discrete solid objects can convert to substances when many are viewed from a distance, while fluid substances can be converted into solids.

The first two of these four categories show some promise for BH verbal aspect, while the second two are not available for BH as they are for Slavic aspect.

---

91   Bhat, *The Prominence of Tense, Aspect, and Mood*, 46.
92   Janda, "A Metaphor in Search of a Source Domain."

5.   Interaction of Matter and Discourse Structure in BH

The aforementioned inherent characteristics of matter are associated with individual forms, while the following four categories give insight into the interaction of matter with discourse structure. These categories function when two or more predications combine at the discourse level. At this point, the status of the *waw* becomes a matter of discussion. Talstra has observed that clauses tend to form hierarchies based upon various sets of clause connections. Discourse approaches, such as those of Longacre and Niccacci, also utilise some of the following characterisations.

Four characteristics interact metaphorically with discourse structure. These are *compatibility, dynamicity, salience* and *contiguity*.

1.   Compatibility: Discrete solid objects cannot share space with other solids. This results in sequencing of perfectives (*wayyiqtol, qatal*) with each other and with the human observer (a solid) in the present moment. On the other hand, fluid substances can share space with both substances and solids, so imperfective situations (*yiqtol*, participle) often demonstrate simultaneity with each other, with the human observer in the present moment (particularly participles).

This feature contributes to Schneider's bifurcation between the solid *wayyiqtol* forms, which predominate in narrative speech, and liquid *yiqtol* forms, which predominate in discursive speech. The imperfective situation envelops the solid body of the observer. Thus first and second person speech situations that feature the presence of the speaker and hearer utilise many *yiqtol* forms, while third person narration distances the observer and utilises many *wayyiqtol* forms.

2.   Dynamicity: Discrete solid objects can provide a firm path of stepping stones, so perfectives (*wayyiqtol, qatal*) are dynamic and move the narrative along, while imperfectives (*yiqtol*, participle) are essentially static and encourage dwelling on characteristics and setting.

This feature accords with Goldfajn's relative time theory. She states, "Both *we-qatal* and *wayyiqtol* verb forms seem to have the temporal function of continuity, that is, the function of advancing the R times in the BH text... There is a close correspondence between the specific location function and the evident bounded, telic nature of the situations described by these two verb forms."[93]

3.   Salience: Discrete solid objects are perceptually salient, so perfectives (*wayyiqtol, qatal*) can act as figure or foreground in narration. Fluid substances are perceptually diffuse masses, so imperfectives (*yiqtol*, participle) might act as ground, or background, in narration.

---

93 Goldfajn, *Word Order and Time in Biblical Hebrew Narrative*, 140.

This discussion of salience is insufficient on two counts. First, as was observed in the metaphors for time, the foreground-background distinction may experience a reversal. It is possible that Schneider's opposition between *wayyiqtol* and *yiqtol*, in narrative and discursive speech respectively, reflects such a reversal. Thus, if perfective forms were fore-grounded in narrative, they would be backgrounded in discursive speech. It would follow, then, that if the imperfectives were back-grounded in narrative speech, they would be fore-grounded in discursive speech. This is (slightly) plausible, but simplistic. Second, salience as an information structure category is affected not by the verbal form alone, but by the amalgamation of the specific verbal form and the word order in a given clause. The complexities that develop due to the interaction between verbal forms and the *binyanim* will follow.

> 4. Contiguity: Discrete solid objects can serve as barriers, while fluid substances can be bounded by solids or mixed with other substances (not applicable for BH).

While the analysis of *aspect* from the perspective of the TIME IS SPACE conceptual metaphor does not solve the problems of the BH verbal system, it does provide some new vocabulary for discussing the verbal forms at both the sentence and discourse levels.

Three characteristics of matter (edges; homogeneity versus heterogeneity; and penetrability) are already included in the definition of aspect and are applicable to BH predications. Two additional qualities (shape and countability) show some promise and suggest an area of further research. Discourse level discussion of aspect from the TIME IS SPACE conceptual metaphor demonstrates a mixed result. BH scholars discuss the categories of compatibility, dynamicity and salience in a limited way. Compatibility and dynamicity have proven to be useful categories for discussing the role of the verb at the level of discourse. This metaphor does not sufficiently describe saliency, based upon the foreground-background distinction.

The primary distinction between *perfective* and *imperfective* aspectual categories is syntax based and the TIME IS SPACE conceptual metaphor provides a rich set of concepts for understanding the temporal contours of the verbal forms in BH sentences and discourse. This distinction provides a certain amount of structural information, but does not take into account the entire range of information indicated by the verbal forms in a particular communication event, where each verbal form is marked for viewpoint aspect (perfective, imperfective, progressive), for participant reference (person/gender/number) and for features that delineate situation aspect (dynamicity, voice, transitivity and causality). Situation aspect is a function of the *binyan* system, thus it is time to return to the margins.

E. Returning to the Margins: The Binyan System

TD is a cognitively based approach to text, in which the author/speaker and the reader are engaged in a cooperative, constructive process. In his discussion of centrality and predication, Premper proposes that the decision as to what is central in a given predication depends upon the perspective of the speaker. The speaker decides upon what he or she may leave out when expressing a situation (valence); what perspective or orientation he or she gives to the expression of the situation (point of view); the option of inducing valence change by shifting voice; and the choice of selecting a predicate.[94] As a result, a given predication is a partial representation of a given situation, and the speaker's choices provide the hearer/reader with information for reconstructing the re-presentation.

BH verbs are highly marked and the choice of a particular BH verbal form contributes three important types of information: viewpoint aspect (*perfective, imperfective, progressive*), participant reference (*person/gender/number*) and situation aspect (*dynamicity, voice, transitivity and causality*). Traditional categories are reviewed below and the following section will introduce *conceptual integration* as a productive means for elaborating upon the linguistic categories of *situation, transitivity* and *voice* (see section 5.2, below).

1. Traditional Categories

Arnold and Choi, citing Waltke and O'Connor and assisted by Lawson Stone, have produced an expanded stem chart, which is a useful starting place for discussing the *binyan* system.[95] The contents of the chart appear on two axes: the axis of *voice*, presented vertically; and the axis

---

94 Premper, "Universals of the Linguistic Representation of Situations," 480.

95 Arnold and Choi, *A Guide to Biblical Hebrew Syntax*, 194. Recent technical studies in the area of the BH *binyan* system include Ernst Jenni, *Das Hebräische Pi'el: Syntaktisch-Semasiologische Untersuchung Einer Verbalform Im Alten Testament* (Zürich: EVZ-Verlag, 1968); P. A. Siebsma, *The Function of the Niph'al in Biblical Hebrew* (Assen, NL: Van Gorcum, 1991); Arian J. C. Verheij, *Bits, Bytes, and Binyanim: A Quantitative Study of Verbal Lexeme Formations in the Hebrew Bible*, Orientalia Lovaniensia Analecta; 93 (Leuven: Peeters; Departement Oosterse Studies, 2000).

of *causation*, presented horizontally. The *axis of voice* comprises three main sections: *active*, *passive* and *middle*. The active voice comprises the stative and fientive (dynamic). Fientive comprises intransitive and transitive. The *axis of causation* also comprises three sections: *no causation* (*qal, niphal*); *brings about a state* (*piel, pual, hithpael*); and *causes an action* (*hiphil, hophal* and *hishtaphal*).

Within the axis of causation, the first section, *no causation*, has three divisions. *Qal* is the active voice and niphal is both the passive voice and the middle voice. The middle voice divides into middle and reflexive-reciprocal. The second section, *brings about a state*, has divisions in the active voice between factitive (1 makes 2 be X) and resultative (1 makes 2 be X-ed), in conjunction with transitive constructions. *Pual* is the passive voice. *Hithpael*, the middle voice, is reflexive-reciprocal. The third section, *causes an action*, is most complex. Stative *hiphil* forms may be two-place ingressive (1 makes 2 become X), or one-place internal (1 makes self do/become X). Fientive, intransitive constructions are two-place causative (1 makes 2 do X). Fientive transitive constructions are three-place causative (1 makes 2 do X to 3). *Hophal* is the passive voice. Each of these categories represents a basic clause structure construction, so each form is associated with a certain type of event structure. This contributes to the conceptual blending process as described in the following section.

2.   Cognitive Additions: Conceptual Blending

The preceding sections of this chapter have established three presuppositions regarding clause level predications:

- One predication designates one situation.
- A predication includes both the verb and associated entities.
- The verb is central, as it controls the number of entities involved.

These presuppositions form the basis for the following discussion, which examines Nili Mandelblit's work on the Modern Hebrew (MH) verbal system and its implications for BH. In her article *"The Grammatical Marking of Conceptual Integration"*, Nili Mandelblit offers a principled methodology for describing the conceptual integration process. This process occurs as a speaker selects the elements of a conceptualisation that he or she wishes to articulate and maps these onto an appropriate linguistic construction. Mandelblit's insights are particularly useful for tracking BH verbal forms from a cognitive perspective. Her argument is as follows:

- Languages possess basic clause structure constructions.

- Each construction is associated with a generic conceptual event schema.

- These constructions serve as integrating frames for expressing situations.

- Speakers project partial information from an initial (conceptual) representation of the situation onto an integration construction, thereby highlighting some aspects of the event over others.

- The *binyanim* provide a grammatical formalism to mark conceptual integration operations. Different grammatical meanings associated with different *binyanim*, such as causative, passive, middle or reflexive are produced directly by the projection schemes.[96]

The TD clause analysis allows access to clause level information from MT Jeremiah 1.1-6.30, which may be approached from the same conceptual integration perspective. According to Mandelblit's argument, each clause represents a novel conceived event mapped onto a basic syntactic structure and its *generic event schema*. The author/speaker has projected partial information from novel conceptual events on to an appropriate construction, such as causative, passive, middle or reflexive, in order to assist the reader in reconstructing the original novel conceived event. Significantly, the syntax and morphology of a given clause construction "...formally marks the speaker's subjective construal of the communicated event."[97]

---

96 Mandelblit, "Grammatical Marking," 197.
97 Ibid., 233.

Mapping Conceptual Integration of BH Binyanim

Although Mandelblit utilizes bi-scope blending diagrams to map the variables of the MH clause constructions, this method is useful for sorting and mapping the variables of the BH *binyanim* as well.[98] A blending configuration consists of two input spaces and a space representing the blend. For the speaker, all three spaces are active when a given clause is articulated. A clause in written text represents the blended space, which acts as a set of instructions that allow the reader to recreate the conceived event.[99] The conceptual integration operation for representations of the BH clause is similar. Input 1 contains elements of the conceived situation. Input 2 contains the integrating syntactic construction. Elements undergo cross-space mapping, with common elements occurring in the blended space.

The following schematic diagram represents a BH intransitive construction. Input 1 contains elements of the conceptualisation; the single star represents the NP, or subject, while the double stars represent the verb. Empty boxes represent aspects of the situation that are not linguistically coded but are part of the conceptualisation. Input 2 contains the elements of an intransitive construction, in the typical word order: Verb and Noun Phrase. Cross-space mapping connects the single star with the NP and the double stars with V, the verb. The blended space maps the elements of the conceived event onto the intransitive syntactic structure: V – NP, resulting in the linguistic representation of the situation.

Mandelblit observes, "…since the conceptual structure of the conceived event to be blended is typically richer (has more predicates and arguments than the target construction), there are *a priori* a large number of possible blends, depending on which cross-space mapping is selected."[100] The schematic diagram presented below maps an autonomous predicate and a single argument, such as *Jack ate quickly.*

98   For a concise explanation of the diagramming method proposed in this section see G. Fauconnier and Mark Turner, "Blending as a Central Process of Grammar," in *Conceptual Structure, Discourse and Language*, ed. Adele E. Goldberg (Stanford: CSLI, 1996), 113-129.

99   Mandelblit's diagramming method is illuminating for language learners, as it isolates features that the verbal forms may obscure, such as the missing agent in a *niphal* clause.

100 Mandelblit, "Grammatical Marking," 206.

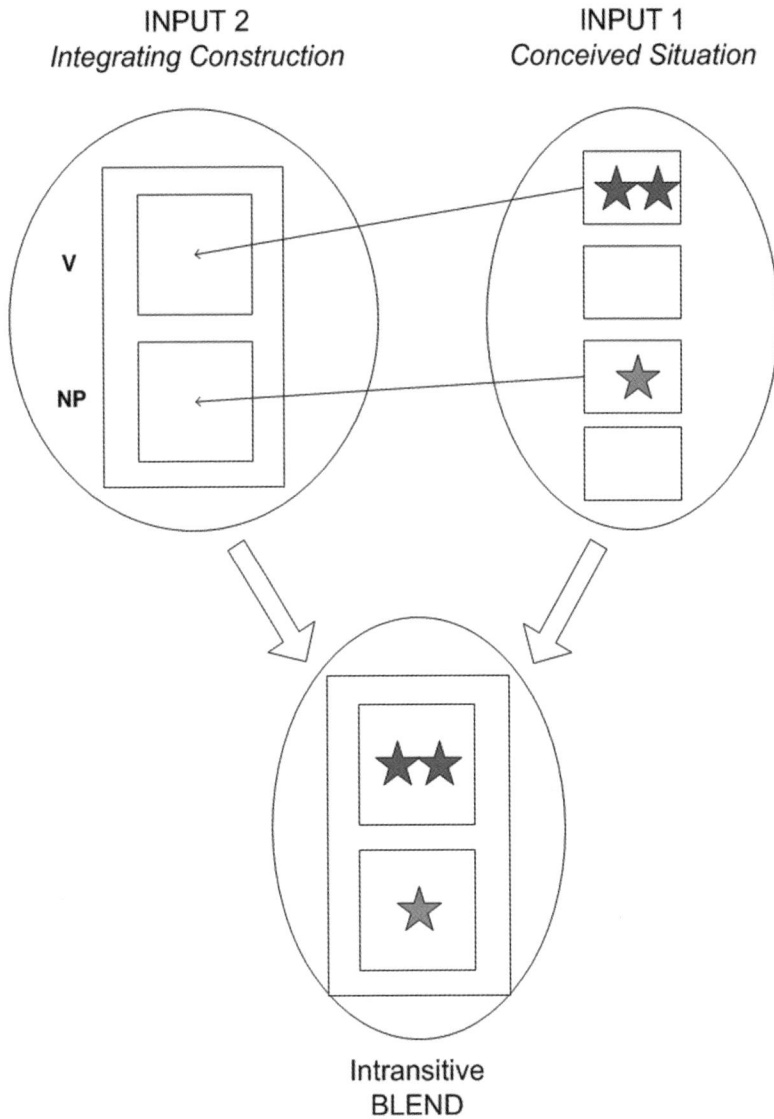

INPUT 2
Integrating Construction

INPUT 1
Conceived Situation

V

NP

Intransitive
BLEND

Figure 3.1 Intransitive Construction Blend

The diagram below presents BH constituent order for a caused motion, *hiphil* construction.

Jeremiah 1.10, הפקדתיך היום הזה על־הגוים ועל־הממלכות, demonstrates that a NP' might appear as an object suffix in such a clause.[101]

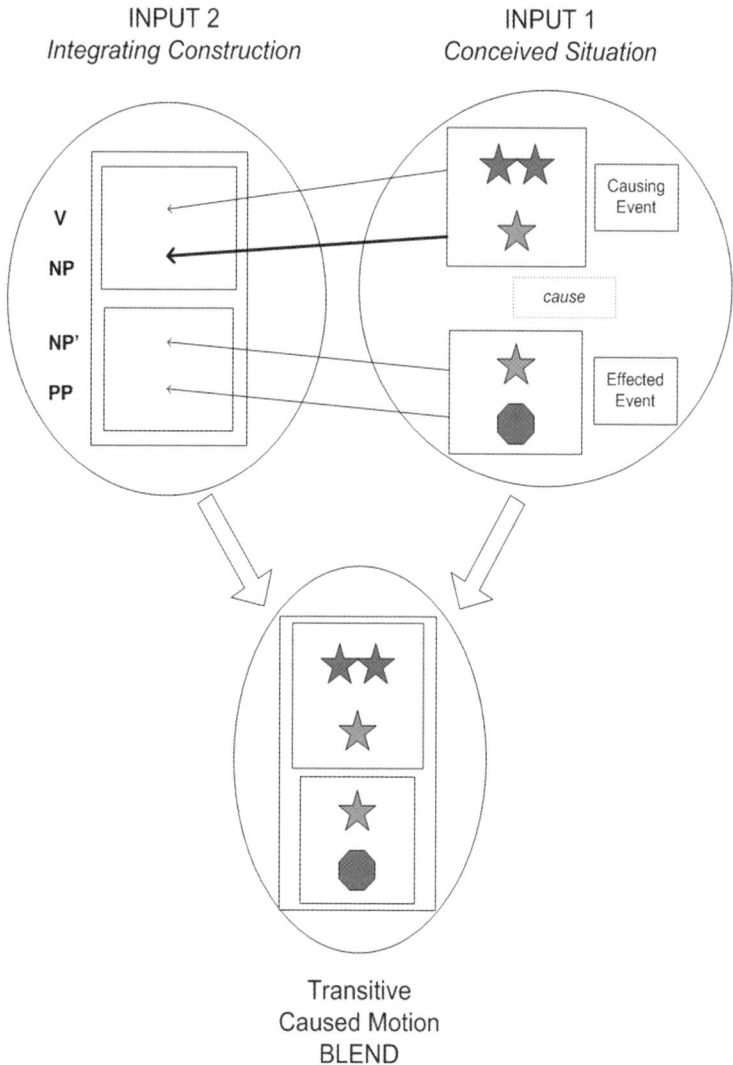

Figure 3.2 Transitive Caused Motion Blend

---

101 This example is not strictly a caused motion construction, since the construction involves a performative speech act that changes Jeremiah's status.

The causal event sequence is illustrated by the English sentence *Rachel sneezed the napkin off the table*. This sentence contains three principle semantic predicates. Rachel's sneeze is the *causing* predicate, the napkin's motion off the table is the *effected motion predicate* and the *causal link* is the implied predicate.[102] Since the integrating construction (NP[1], V, NP[2] PP) contains only one verbal slot to express the semantic predication, the speaker must choose one of the predicates from the causal event sequence to map onto the verbal slot of the integrating construction. In this case, it is the *causing* predicate. In a sentence such as *She trotted the horse into the stable*, the *effected motion* predicate is mapped onto the integrating construction. Finally, there are certain verbs such as *threw*, in a sentence such as *She threw hay to the horse*, that integrate the three predicates, due to the lexical semantics of the verb. Thus, while the syntactic constructions are the same for all three of the example sentences, the underlying cross-space mapping is different for each. Mandelblit has isolated three types of predicate mapping:

- The *causing* predicate within a causal event;
- the *effected* predicate within an effected event; and
- the *autonomous* predicate.

Additionally, there are three types of participant mapping:

- The *causal agent* within a causal event (active voice);
- the *affected entity* within a causal event (passive voice); and
- the *autonomous entity* (middle voice).

While it is not practical to map each individual clause in MT Jeremiah 1.1-6.30, creating conceptual integration diagrams for selected examples would illustrate some of the "hidden" features of the BH predications, such as which of the three predicates is mapped by a transitive form, and the impact of the "absent" agent in the passive voice forms. This would be an effective teaching tool and is an area for further research and documentation.

Conclusion

This initial foray into the application of cognitive grammar and linguistics to BH contributes toward understanding BH prophetic text. First, grammatically, RRG provides additional metalanguage for bridging the gap between traditional grammatical description and the fresh termi-

---

[102] Mandelblit, "Grammatical Marking," 202.

nology employed in cognitive grammar. Because human perception is the basis for cognitive grammar, CG brings greater understanding to the issue of perspective in BH grammar. Second, the presentation of situations as more or less prototypical assists in the discussion of the speech frames that include both human and divine characters. Third, the BH verb has a central role in a given situation. There is significant debate regarding whether the verb indicates tense or aspect, however. The TD approach follows Cook's assessment that the verb is aspect prominent. Fourth, cognitive additions to the discussion of BH grammar, such as the TIME IS MOTION and TIME IS SPACE conceptual metaphors provide additional metalanguage for discussing this complex issue. Fifth, conceptual blending theory is a valuable tool for the description of BH situations at the sentence level. Cognitive approaches have much to offer for the BH text analyst and interpreter.

4. Cognitive Structuring in Jeremiah 1.1-6.30

Dreams, books, are each a world;
books we know, are a substantial world, both pure and good.

~ William Wordsworth

As described in Chapter 1, the TD approach utilises a network model to describe the interaction between the author/originator of a text, the written text and the reader/hearer of the text. The dynamic mappings proposed by the TD approach are mappings of cognitive activity on the part of the originator and the reader alike. The mapping process takes place at the cognitive level, *level C.* [1] In this volume, such mappings are represented by a series of figures, each utilising nested Chinese box diagrams to model the emergent cognitive network. Cognitive construction involves opening, structuring and linking mental spaces. *Space-builders* are grammatical terms and constructions that set up new spaces, and the cognitive network is extended as the new spaces are structured and linked. Information structure, frames and cognitive models structure mental spaces. [2] As discussed in Chapter 2, information structure is an integral part of the TD clause analysis. Perspective, the space-building and structuring device that encompasses viewpoint, deixis and subjectivity-objectivity is foundational for understanding prophetic text.

Jeremiah 1.1-6.30 exhibits three major breaks, based upon text-level shifts in text-type: [3]

---

1   According to Fauconnier, constructions at *level C* are distinct from the language structure (they may be imagistic), although they relate language structure to the real world. Additionally, such constructions are partial, in that they are not representations of models of the world, or representations of possible worlds. Rather, such structures are highly schematic and are subject to further elaboration. Fauconnier, *Mappings*, 36.

2   For an extended list of linguistic construal operations that includes the work of both Langacker and Leonard Talmy, see Croft and Cruse, *Cognitive Linguistics*, 46.

3   Discerned by VU database information, which reflects Schneider's categories mediated by Talstra.

A. Jeremiah 1.1- 3.25;

    1. Jeremiah 1.1-2.1: N with embedded Q and P;

    2. Jeremiah 2.1-3.25: Q at 3.1-3.5; N with embedded Q and P 3.6-3.25;

B. Jeremiah 4.1- 4.31;

    1. Jeremiah 4.1-4.9: D with embedded Q;

    2. Jeremiah 4.10: N with embedded Q;

    3. Jeremiah 4.11-4.31: N with embedded D; and

C. Jeremiah 5.1-6.30: Q.

Section A is largely narrative, with embedded quotation and perception spaces. Section B is mainly discursive, with embedded quotation and narrative spaces. Section C comprises quotation with embedded quotation spaces. Chapter 4 in this volume covers examples from section A.1, Chapter 5 covers examples from section A.2, and Chapter 6 covers examples from sections B and C.

This chapter contains an analysis and description of a perceptible cognitive network in section A.1, Jeremiah 1.1-2.1. This analysis and description will follow the pattern set in Chapter 2, where the network model is explained using Jeremiah 3.6-3.11 as a sample text. As in that analysis, observations will be made regarding the syntax, semantics and pragmatics of each section of text (see sections A.1 and B.1, below). An analysis of cognitive structuring in the text follows, with special reference to the linguistic construal operation of perspective (see sections A.2 and A.3, below). The examination of perspective-inducing space building terms from the semantic fields of deixis, communication, perception and cognition is an important aspect of this process (see section B.2, below). Finally, the interface between conceptual metaphor and literary metaphor will be examined (see section 4B.3, below).

A. Jeremiah 1.1-1.3: Establishing Text-Level Perspective

1. Perspective in Jeremiah 1.1-1.3

Jeremiah 1.1-3 has been described as a *prologue*, a *superscription* and a *rubric*.[4] Each of these terms reflects the introductory nature of the material. The terms used to describe this section are also indicative of the perspective-inducing nature of the text as presented in Figure 1, below. At this point in the analysis, the relationship between originator, text and reader is as follows:

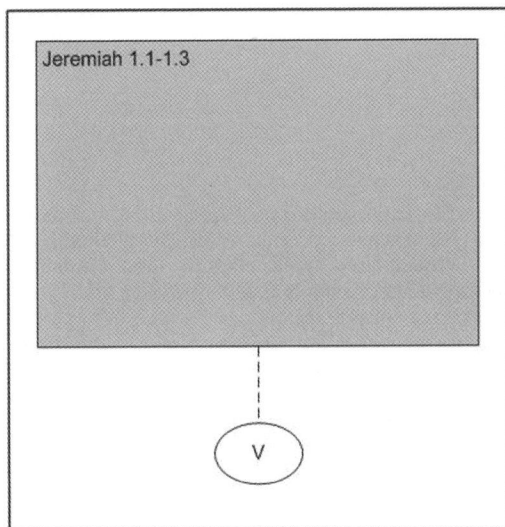

Figure 4.1 Perspective in Jeremiah 1.1-1.3

Figure 4.1 presents the scope of conceptualisation for Jeremiah 1.1-1.3. The text is in the on-stage, objective position. The identity of the viewer, V, is determined by the fact that Jeremiah 1.1-1.3 consists of third

---

4   Carroll is among those who describe this section as a prologue, while McKane uses the term superscription, and Meier utilises the term rubric. Robert P. Carroll, *Jeremiah: A Commentary*, Old Testament Library (Philadelphia: Westminster, 1986), 89; William McKane, *A Critical and Exegetical Commentary on Jeremiah*, 2 vols., International Critical Commentary on the Holy Scriptures of the Old and New Testaments (Edinburgh: T. & T. Clark, 1986), 1; Samuel A. Meier, *Speaking of Speaking: Marking Direct Discourse in the Hebrew Bible*, VT Sup 46 (Leiden: Brill, 1992), 21.

person narration or indirect speech in the form of narrative sentences.[5] The speaker/narrator and hearer/reader correspond to V in the canonical viewing arrangement. This simplified representation conflates the shared gaze of the speaker and hearer, which appears as a single dashed line. As viewers, the speaker and hearer are wholly distinct from the object of perception, which is the text. The object of perception is sharply delineated and "perceived with full acuity."[6] Thus, in the case of Jeremiah 1.1-1.3, the narrator and the reader share the V position, and the text is clearly perceived.[7] This configuration of communication participants and text has been tagged N[1].

---

5   Van Wolde observes that a narrator may speak directly or indirectly to his or her audience. Two types of sentences result: direct speech takes the form of a commentary sentence, whereas indirect speech takes the form of a narrative sentence. E. J. van Wolde, *Ruth and Naomi* (London: SCM Press, 1997), 146.

6   Langacker, "Deixis and Subjectivity," 15.

7   At first glance, the TD diagrams resemble Kamp's cognitively oriented, world-building diagram. Kamp presents a diagram of the nested worlds in the book of Job. The *Outer World* represents the reality of the reader. Within this, the *discourse world* represents the context of communication, in which the *narrative world* represents the Book of Job, and the *embedded discourse world* represents Job 28, the subject of Kamp's article. Kamp notes that three types of sub-worlds might be found within the *embedded discourse world*. These are based upon belief, probability and temporal alteration, which are all features that the TD approach recognises as space-builders. However, Kamp's worlds are somewhat less fluid than the cognitive spaces proposed by the TD approach, and Kamp's account of the linguistic specifics that open and structure spaces is somewhat limited. Kamp bases his analysis upon the work of Paul Werth. Werth, in turn, bases his world-building analysis upon Fauconnier's space-building terms. However, Werth populates his conceptual worlds by means of *Possible Worlds* philosophy as understood by Saul Kripke and David Lewis. The TD approach avoids a close association with this philosophy for two reasons. First, Fauconnier himself dissociates his MST proper from *Possible Worlds* philosophy. Secondly, because of the nature of MST. This theory proposes that human conceptualisation is similar for a range of communication processes. Thus, *Possible Worlds* philosophy may be said to represent a specific instantiation of mental spaces construction that is exceptionally detailed and operates without explicit reference to frames and cognitive models. On the other hand, because mental spaces and conceptual blending are features of human communication that operate on many levels, the TD analysis is also a specific instantiation of these conceptual theories but includes explicit reference to space structuring features, specifically with regard to frames and cognitive models. See Albert Kamp, "World Building in Job 28," in *Job 28: Cognition in Context*, ed. Ellen Van Wolde (Leiden: Brill, 2003), 309; Werth, "How to Build a World (in a Lot Less Than Six Days, Using Only What's in Your Head)," 53.

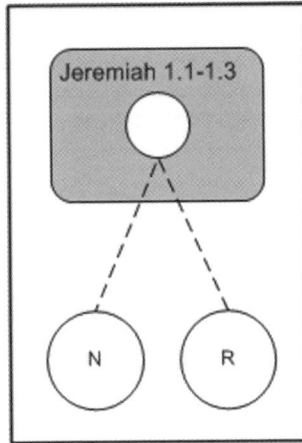

Figure 4.2   Viewing Arrangement N1 for Jeremiah 1.1-1.3

From a cognitive grammar perspective, Jeremiah 1.1-1.3 presents the *ground* of the text-level communication event.[8] In terms of MST, this section represents the *base-space*, the space from which further cognitive construction occurs. The immediate circumstances of the communication event are indicated by a series of terms and constructions indicating atemporal relations. Schweizer uses the term *Relationswörter* to describe the trajector terms for this set of atemporal relations (see cognitive grammar definitions in chapter 3, section A.2). He includes prepositions and the relative particle within this group of BH terms.[9] The atemporal relationships indicated by these terms and constructions delineate social, locative and temporal coordinates for establishing the *base-space* in a cognitive network that extends throughout the text of MT Jeremiah. In the following clause analysis diagram, boxes surround the relational terms.

8   For a discussion of how deictic expressions invoke alternate grounds in speech situations see Jo Rubba, "Alternate Grounds in the Interpretation of Deictic Expressions," in *Spaces, Worlds, and Grammar*, eds G. Fauconnier and E. Sweetser (Chicago: UCP, 1996), 227-261.

9   Schweizer, *Metaphorische Grammatik: Wege zur Integration von Grammatik und Textinterpretation in der Exegese*, 236-237.

Clause Layout	JER
דִּבְרֵי יִרְמְיָהוּ בֶּן־חִלְקִיָּהוּ מִן־הַכֹּהֲנִים	1.1a
אֲשֶׁר בַּעֲנָתוֹת בְּאֶרֶץ בִּנְיָמִן	b
אֲשֶׁר הָיָה דְבַר־יְהוָה אֵלָיו	1.2a
בִּימֵי יֹאשִׁיָּהוּ	b
בֶן־אָמוֹן מֶלֶךְ יְהוּדָה	c
בִּשְׁלֹשׁ־עֶשְׂרֵה שָׁנָה לְמָלְכוֹ	d
וַיְהִי בִּימֵי יְהוֹיָקִים	1.3a
בֶּן־יֹאשִׁיָּהוּ מֶלֶךְ יְהוּדָה	b
עַד־תֹּם עַשְׁתֵּי עֶשְׂרֵה שָׁנָה לְצִדְקִיָּהוּ	c
בֶן־יֹאשִׁיָּהוּ מֶלֶךְ יְהוּדָה	d
עַד־גְּלוֹת יְרוּשָׁלַ͏ִם בַּחֹדֶשׁ הַחֲמִישִׁי	e

JER	Type	Clause Tag	PNG	*Focus*	MSC
1.1a	?	NmCl			BASE
b	?	X-NmCl			VP= N[1]
1.2a	?	*X-Qatal*	3sgM	Pred	
b	?	PreP			
c	?	NmCl NmCl			
d	?	X-Qetol			
1.3a	N	*Wayyiqtol-X*	3sgM	Pred	
b	N	NmCl NmCl			
c	N	X-Qetol			
d	N	NmCl NmCl			
e	N	+Qetol			

Figure 4.3   Clause Analysis for Jeremiah 1.1-1.3

a.   Syntax

The syntax of Jeremiah 1.1-1.3 contributes to the introductory character of these verses. The three verses are written in the third person, cuing the narrator's viewpoint and viewpoint perspective (MSC column, above). Jeremiah 1.1 is devoid of verbal forms, containing instead a series of construct and prepositional phrases, or *clause atoms*. The first conjugated verbal form, היה, appears in the relative clause אשר היה דבר־יהוה אליו at 1.2a. The second conjugated form, ויהי, appears in the *wayyiqtol* clause ויהי בימי יהויקים at 1.3a. Another series of construct and prepositional phrases follows this verbal clause.

A few short comments regarding the functions of the *X-qatal* and *wayyiqtol* forms are appropriate here. First, according to Schneider, the function of *X-qatal* clauses in either narrative or discursive text is to provide background information.[10] This is indeed the case in 1.2a, where Jeremiah is identified as the one to whom דבר־יהוה came. From Cook's grammaticalisation perspective, *qatal* forms represent perfective action, which is not inappropriate in 1.2a. Secondly, according to Schneider the function of the *wayyiqtol* forms is to provide foreground information in narrative text. For both Cook and Goldfajn, *wayyiqtol* forms indicate sequential, past tense events.[11] Although the *wayyiqtol* clause at 1.3a does give sequential past tense information, it does not appear that the verb form contributes to foregrounding in this case.

b.   Information Structure

The Information Structure categories of *topic* and *focus* provide insight into this section of text. Topic, according to Lambrecht, is "...the thing which the proposition expressed by the sentence is about."[12] Often the topical entity is the grammatical subject of the sentence, but this is not always the case. On a scale of pragmatic acceptability, topical entities range from *accessible*, to *unused* but available, to *brand new* and anchored within the discourse, to *brand new* and unanchored. The preferred topic expression is an unaccented pronominal.[13] In order to engage fully with the category of topic, one must also engage with another of Lambrecht's categories, that of *identifiability and activation*. Because most hearers have limited short-term memory, the topical entities may be in

---

10   Schneider, *Grammatik*, 186.
11   Cook, "Grammaticalization;" Goldfajn, *Word Order and Time in Biblical Hebrew Narrative*, 146.
12   Lambrecht, *Information Structure*, 119.
13   Ibid., 165.

various states of activation at any given point in a discourse. For this reason, when initiating a discourse, the topical entities must first be *activated*, or made identifiable. Like other languages, BH does use topic-promoting devices, such as fronting and presentational constructions, to introduce new topical entities.[14] Topical entities may also be part of the interlocutors' shared information at a given point in the discourse, needing only to be activated.

Because Jeremiah 1.1-1.3 stands at the beginning of the book of Jeremiah, appropriate topical entities must be identified. This process begins at 1.1a, with the presentation of several significant terms within the series of construct phrases. The clause דברי ירמיהו בן־חלקיהו at 1.1a introduces both the *words of Jeremiah* and, by extension, *Jeremiah*. The relative clause אשר היה דבר־יהוה אליו at 1.2a introduces both *the word of Yahweh* and, by extension, Yahweh. This is represented schematically in the following figure.[15]

		דברי ירמיהו	ירמיהו	דבר־יהוה	יהוה
1.1a	1	1.00			
1:2a	2	0.50	0.50	0.50	
1:2b	3	0.33	0.66	0.33	
1:3a	4	0.25	0.50	0.50	

Figure 4.4 Cumulative Referential Density in Jeremiah 1.1-1.3

In this diagram, each time a topical entity appears, it is recorded by line. Then, the total number is divided by the most recent line number and a percentage is calculated. The percentage indicates the cumulative density for each entity, allowing for an evaluation of both frequency and density as the discourse unfolds (for full analyses of Jeremiah 1.1-2.2, see the chart at the end of the current chapter). When Jeremiah 1.1-1.3 is evaluated in this way, the following hierarchy of topical entities emerges: דברי ירמיהו, *the words/deeds of Jeremiah*, with mentions in 25 percent of the lines analysed; ירמיהו, *Jeremiah*, with mentions in 50 percent of the lines analysed; דבר־יהוה, *the word of Yahweh*, with mentions in 50 percent of the lines analysed; and Yahweh, but only by extension here.

---

14 For a discussion of extraposed constructions in BH and other Semitic languages, see Khan, *Studies*.

15 Heimerdinger has adapted this methodology from the work of Russell Tomlin. See Heimerdinger, *Topic, Focus and Foreground in Ancient Hebrew Narratives*, 105.

After identifying and activating the topical entities involved in a stretch of text, identifying the topical theme of a longer discourse is also possible. As Heimerdinger demonstrates, there is frequently a topical frame involved.[16] A topical frame is a short summary statement that introduces a discourse topical theme such as ... *and God tested Abraham* in Genesis 22:1. In this case, *God* and *Abraham* are re-introduced as topical entities and *tested* is introduced as the topical theme. In the MT, this short statement exhibits marked word order, as both a temporal clause and a proper noun phrase precede the verb. This word order shift indicates sentence focus. The entire sentence is important to what follows, setting up topical interests to be discussed as the discourse unfolds. The introductory topical frame is followed by the *topical elaboration* in which the identified topical concerns are developed.

The manner in which the topical entities are introduced and activated in Jeremiah 1.1-1.3 provides the first indication that this section is acting as a topical frame for the following discourse. Examining the section from the information structure category of *focus* contributes to this assessment. Focus, according to Lambrecht, is "the semantic component of a pragmatically structured proposition whereby the assertion differs from the presupposition." In BH sentences focus is a function of both verbal forms and word order.[17] As noted above, Jeremiah 1.1 is devoid of verbal forms. Instead, the concatenation of construct and prepositional phrases in 1.1 is "used to establish (promote) identifiable but non-active entities to a state of discourse activeness (topic frame) as far as a subsequent utterance is concerned."[18] In this case, the activated referent is דברי ירמיהו, the words of Jeremiah. Constituent order indicates that 1.2a (X-VSO) and 1.3a (VO) are examples of predicate focus.[19] Like the topic-comment articulation, this sentence type predicates a property of the subject. In this case, the subject for each form is דבר־יהוה, which is explicit at 1.2a and implicit at 1.3a.

c.   Cognitive Construction

Cognitive structuring in Jeremiah 1.1-1.3 begins with the series of construct and prepositional phrases at 1.1a. This series of space-building terms initiates a cascade of atemporal relationships based upon social,

---

16   Ibid., 106.

17   van der Merwe and Talstra, "Interface," 78.

18   Ibid., 86.

19   Regarding BH constituent order, this volume follows the view that BH is a VSO language. This decision is based upon several factors. See chapter 2, n.82 for a full discussion.

locative and temporal cues. The atemporal relationships are cued by a variety of *Relationswörter*, or trajectors, including the relative particle אֲשֶׁר (1.1b; 1.2a) and the prepositions מִן (1.1a), בְּ (1.1b; 1.1b; 1.2b; 1.2d; 1.3a), אֶל (1.2a) and עַד (1.3c; 1.3e). The resulting phrase atoms contribute to the formation of relative clauses and prepositional phrases, or clause atoms. The relations established between entities provide the social, spatial and temporal coordinates that cue the topical frame, and form the parameters of the *base-space* for the Jeremiah text.

At first glance, the term אֲשֶׁר (at 1.b and 2.a) appears to need little explanation beyond that presented in the standard grammars.[20] Syntactically, the relative particle אֲשֶׁר functions as a clause-level relational word, which connects the given clause to the immediately preceding clause.[21] However, for the first three clauses of Jeremiah 1.1-1.2, this relationship is more than a matter of addition. While the אֲשֶׁר clause in 1.2b does refer to the term הַכֹּהֲנִים in the immediately preceding clause at 1.1a, the clause אֲשֶׁר הָיָה דְבַר־יְהוָה אֵלָיו at 1.2a does not refer to the phrase בְּאֶרֶץ בִּנְיָמִן at 1.1b, but to the term יִרְמְיָהוּ in 1.1a, as indicated by the m/s pronominal suffix on אֵלָיו.

Cognitive studies have much to contribute to the understanding of the prepositions בְּ; מִן; אֶל; and עַד. GKC contains an explanation for this grammatical category that moves the discussion in a cognitive direction, stating, "In the case of most prepositions, some idea of a relation of *space* underlies the construction, which then, in a wider sense, is extended to the ideas of time, motive, or other relations conceived in the mind."[22] However, even more can be said regarding the manner in which these terms act as prompts for establishing relationships by evoking particular *image schemata*. For example, the terms אֶל and עַד act as prompts for relationships based upon the *path schema*. This schema "…involves physical or metaphorical movement from place to place and includes a starting point, a goal and intermediate points."[23] In this way, a metaphorical trajectory, or path, underlies the statement אֲשֶׁר הָיָה דְבַר־יְהוָה אֵלָיו at 1.2a. The path includes Yahweh as the starting point and Jeremiah as the goal, with דְבַר־יְהוָה moving across the

---

20 This term, which introduces a relative clause, was originally a demonstrative pronoun. According to GKC, a relative clause is immediately dependent upon the substantival idea to be defined, which is in the same case, thus it belongs syntactically to the main clause (GKC: 138). According to JM the term is a relative conjunction meaning "that" (JM: 536). The term is a relative pronoun. It also introduces object clauses, especially after verbs of observation and mental process (BHRG: 296).

21 Talstra, "A Hierarchy of Clauses in Biblical Hebrew Narrative," 95-96.

22 GKC: § 377.

23 Johnson, *The Body in the Mind: The Bodily Basis of Meaning, Imagination, and Reason*, 115.

points of the trajectory conceptualised between the two. In this example, one may easily recognise traces of the *conduit* metaphor for communication. The immediate problem is, of course, that Yahweh himself is non-localised. Thus, the reader is left without the spatial coordinates for the starting point of the trajectory. To make a claim for the presence of Yahweh in the Temple highlights the turmoil present in the historical setting, as Jeremiah speaks out against the Temple elite in Jeremiah 7. Thus, while Jeremiah claims to have heard from Yahweh, there is significant ambiguity as to the manner in which the communication was received. This persists throughout Jeremiah 1.1-6.30. The main emphasis is upon the fact of Jeremiah's perception, rather than the mode of perception.

2.   The Containment Schema

Grammatical constructions that include the terms בְּ and מִן evoke the *containment* schema.[24] This schema is basic, rooted in the every-day human experience of containers, such as pails, bowls, buckets, open mouths and holes in the ground. The containment schema is characterised by a physical or metaphorical boundary, an enclosed area or volume, or an excluded area or volume. The *transitivity of enclosure principle* is an optional property of the containment schema. In brief, if object A is enclosed in container B and container B is enclosed in container C, object A is also enclosed in container C.[25] This is essentially a spatial version of a *modus ponens* argument, demonstrating that such arguments might have an embodied correlate.

---

24   Jenni argues that prepositions operate at three levels of generality: the prefixed prepositions בְּ, לְ and כְּ are the most general. Because this is the case, it is important to consider the atemporal relationship as a whole – both the trajector and the landmark function together. See Ernst Jenni, *Die Hebräischen Präpositionen*, vol. 1 (Stuttgart: Kohlhammer, 1992), 18.

25   Johnson, *The Body in the Mind: The Bodily Basis of Meaning, Imagination, and Reason*, 21-22.

A rich image example of the transitivity principle allows the hearer to throw out the bath water (grammatically) and still leave the baby soaking in the tub (conceptually). One might imagine that Happy Baby (object A) is sitting in bath water (container B), which is enclosed in a baby bathtub (container C). In this case, one might correctly observe, "The baby is in the bathtub." The fluidity of the bath water (container B), in combination with the transitivity principle, allows the bathwater to be thrown out of the statement (grammatically), while remaining in the rich image prompted by the statement: baby, water, rubber duck, tub and all.

In Jeremiah 1.1-1.3, the containment schema is evoked by the atemporal relationship established by the trajectory, the prefixed preposition ב, in conjunction with its landmark. This occurs at 1.1b בענתות; 1.1b בארץ בנימן; 1.2b בימי יאשיהו; 1.2d בשלש־עשרה שנה למלכו; and at 1.3a בימי יהויקים. The partial nature of the evocation is due to the idea that relations are conceptually dependent. According to Langacker, "...one cannot conceptualize interconnections without also conceptualizing the entities they interconnect."[26] Thus, in order to make sense of the atemporal relations invoked by terms such as ב, מן, אל and עד, all of the entities involved in the relation must be included: the trajector and landmark of the atemporal relationship, and the elements in the larger clause of which the PP/phrase atom is a part. This will be demonstrated by the examples below, in which the previously identified topical entities play a large part.

Each instance of ב in Jeremiah 1.1-1.3 indicates an atemporal relation based upon the *containment* schema. In 1.1b, בענתות, the city of Anathoth is construed as a container with a physical boundary and the priests are construed as physical objects found inside the container. Jeremiah's father, Hilkiah, is selected from this group (also construed as a container of sorts) by the preposition מן in the phrase מן־הכהנים. In 1.1b the land of Benjamin is construed as a container, and Anathoth is construed as an object contained in the land of Benjamin. Due to the transitivity of containment principle, the priests are also contained in the land of Benjamin. Because the priesthood was an inherited position, Jeremiah, related to his father the priest, is also localised.

---

26 Langacker, *Foundations of Cognitive Grammar*, 215.

3.   Conceptual Metaphor: TIME IS A CONTAINER

In the following three instances, the preposition בְּ also indicates the containment schema.[27] However, the entities in the phrases בִּימֵי יֹאשִׁיָּהוּ, *in the days of Josiah,* בִּשְׁלֹשׁ־עֶשְׂרֵה שָׁנָה לְמָלְכוֹ, *in the thirteenth year of his reign,* and בִּימֵי יְהוֹיָקִים, *in the days of Jehoiakim,* all contain information from the semantic domain of time. This indicates that the TIME IS A CONTAINER conceptual metaphor is the structuring device for these phrases. In this case, the containment schema is metaphoric, due to the abstract nature of the boundaries. Two temporal boundaries are initiated by the introduction of segments of time indicated by the reigns of Josiah and Jehoiakim, and are extended to include the reign of Zedekiah and the date of the exile to Babylon, as indicated by the phrases עַד־תֹּם עַשְׁתֵּי עֶשְׂרֵה שָׁנָה לְצִדְקִיָּהוּ at 1.3c. and עַד־גְּלוֹת יְרוּשָׁלַ͏ִם בַּחֹדֶשׁ הַחֲמִישִׁי at 1.3e. Jeremiah's reception of the word of the Lord becomes an object contained within this boundary. This conceptual metaphor is somewhat more elaborate that the image schematic construal presented in the first three examples.

While the interface between cognitive construction and literary metaphor will be discussed later in this chapter, a brief introduction to conceptual metaphor is relevant at this point.[28] Kövecses states:

> When one conceptual domain is understood in terms of another conceptual domain, we have a conceptual metaphor. This understanding is achieved by seeing a set of systematic correspondences, or mappings, between two domains.[29]

Two conceptual domains are involved in a conceptual metaphor. The domains are labelled as either the *source domain,* which is the domain that is used to understand another domain, or as the *target domain,* which is the domain that requires understanding. Typically, the source domain is less abstract or less complex than the target domain. Conversely, the target domain is more abstract and subjective than the source domain.[30] In the case of the conceptual metaphor TIME IS A CONTAINER the *source domain* is the containment schema, aspects of which are used to understand the *target domain,* TIME. Mappings between the source and target domains occur as the characteristics of TIME in the

---

27   In conceptual metaphor studies, established cognitive metaphors are indicated by small capital letters.

28   The choice of the term *metaphor* in conceptual metaphor studies is unfortunate, as the term is most commonly understood as a literary device, rather than a descriptive term for a model of cognitive processing.

29   Kövecses, *Metaphor: A Practical Introduction,* 248.

30   Ibid., 252.

target domain are associated with features of the containment schema, such as boundary, inside, outside and objects within the boundary, in the source domain.[31]

This example demonstrates that utilising the conceptual metaphor TIME IS A CONTAINER allows for the location of an object, such as the reception of דבר־יהוה, to be mapped by establishing a series of temporal coordinates, much as the location of an object in space may be mapped by a series of spatial coordinates. In this case, the coordinates are indicated by the prepositions ב and עד, and the temporal units of *day* and *year* are used to establish the boundary that *contains* instances of Jeremiah's reception of דבר־יהוה. In this way, temporal coordinates are added to the social and locative information that contributes to cognitive construction in MT Jeremiah. The series of relationships involved in these examples provides a cluster of social and locative coordinates and parameters given by the author to assist the reader in conceptualising the setting of the text. This section of text also provides an example of conceptual metaphor that is completely dissociated from literary metaphor. The conceptual construction demonstrates in part that while literary metaphor is an instantiation of conceptual metaphor, conceptual metaphor may be observed in a variety of non-literary contexts and is in fact much more widely used in everyday speech and thought than is often recognised.

In the TD analysis for Jeremiah 1.1-1.3, this section represents the starting point, the *base-space*, in the mental space configuration. Thus, topical entities and other elements of the setting that have been established are available for cognitive construction for the following text. These include Jeremiah and Yahweh, as well as the spatio-temporal situation that has been established. Significantly, the elements in this section are presented at normal scale. Whether Jeremiah 1.1-1.3 is described as an introduction, a superscription or a rubric, the section is indeed the beginning of something.

---

31   This description of cognitive metaphor has affinities with Fauconnier's conceptual blending theory, specifically the use of spaces and cross-space mapping. However, conceptual blending is a more sophisticated theory, in that it includes both a generic input space and a newly formed blended space. Not only does the newly formed blend draw from the input spaces, but it also has its own logic as well.

B. Jeremiah 1.4-2.3: Space Building Terms

1. Perspective in Jeremiah 1.4-2.3

There is a shift in perspective at 1.4, where the first person pronominal suffix on the term אֵלַי in the phrase וַיְהִי דְבַר־יְהוָה אֵלַי shifts participant reference from the unidentified narrator to Jeremiah as speaker/narrator. Jeremiah's voice replaces that of the anonymous third person narrator in the subjective Originator, or O space. Consequently, Jeremiah is simutaneously present both in the subjective viewing position, which is now shared by Jeremiah and the reader, and in the onstage, objective position in the viewing arrangement. This configuration of communication participants has been tagged as N^2.

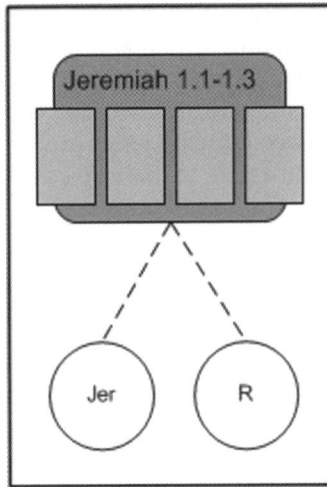

Figure 4.5 Viewing Arrangement N^2 for Jeremiah 1.4-2.2

Some of the consequences of this shift will be explored in this section. Cognitive construction in Jeremiah occurs via terms and constructions that function at various levels, or in terms of the computer programme metaphor, various *layers*. As previously discussed, computer programmes use a series of layers to build up a unified image. Two important features emerge: first, each additional layer adds detail to the final product. This is a sequential process in which layers are added from the bottom up. Thus, while the final product appears to be a complete whole, the layers themselves have a sequential character – reflecting the

creative processes evident in visual art and in writing, where the originator must plan for the final effect and work in an orderly fashion. Secondly, like the focus space in a mental spaces network, only one layer
may be active at a given time. New information may be added to spaces that are already part of the image, but only one space may be selected for this task at a time. This reflects the reading process, which
may be either linear or recursive. (In actuality, it is most likely both, as
a reader may refer back in order to re-focus on a previously read section of text in order to understand the text at hand.) Thus, cognitive
constructions evoked by a text may be modelled as a series or sequence
of mental spaces which coalesce to form a whole.[32] Cognitive spaces, or
conceptual packets, may comprise the information of a single sentence
or of larger clusters of sentences.[33] Spaces are opened by space-builders,
and meaning accrues as the spaces are structured by various linguistic
construal operations. Space-builders from the semantic domains of
perception, cognition, communication and epistemic modality are particularly important in the process of cognitive construction because
these terms are experiencer-oriented and open spaces that are embedded to a particular character. Such spaces are constrained by the character's deictic centre, and access to these spaces is thus restricted to the
character's perspective.

2.   Space-builders in Biblical Hebrew

Perspective-inducing space-builders include text-deictic terms and
constructions (see the *Deictic Terms* chart on page 41) and terms from
the semantic domains of communication, perception and cognition.
These will be examined in turn in the following sections.

a.   Text Deictic Terms

According to Ehlich, certain BH terms and constructions are used text-
deictically. The difference between deixis *per se* and text-deixis has to
do with the different deictic spaces to which the deictic procedure is

---

32 In this instance, the term coalesce is shorthand for conceptual blending. According to
conceptual blending theory, this process is ubiquitous in human cognition.

33 Fauconnier utilises both terms. He uses *spaces* in his earlier work and *cognitive packets*
in his later work. This volume utilises the term *spaces*, as it is foundational to MST.
However, the term *cognitive packet* is slightly more sophisticated. Importantly, in
keeping with the network metaphor, such packets are created in the mind of the
conceptualizer as discourse is processed. In other words, they are not convenient en-
velopes for sending and receiving information, as in the conduit metaphor.

related. In other words, for text deixis, the deictic space is the text it-self.[34] Under certain circumstances, BH terms such as וֹהָיָה and וֹיְהִי are used text deictically.[35] This appears to be the case in Jeremiah 1.4, 1.11, 1.13 and 2.1, where the term appears in the repeated phrase וַיְהִי דְבַר־יהוה אֵלַי לֵאמֹר.[36] However, the term וַיְהִי alone is not responsi-ble for creating the structuring effect. Rather, this is a function of the entire construction. Miller, in her study of reported speech, notes that this type of phrase is a "metapragmatic phrasal expression."[37] The syn-tax of the sentence is *wayyiqtol*+subject, indirect object, complementiser. The VSO word order in the first part of the sentence indicates that without the complementiser לֵאמֹר the sentence would be an example of unmarked, predicate focus. However, the presence of the complemen-tiser indicates that the sentence is a marked construction, functioning at the metapragmatic level.

The difference between a marked term or construction and an un-marked term or construction is significant. Markedness itself may be understood in two quite different ways.[38] First, there is the idea of a polar opposition: if one term is marked, the unmarked form implies its polar opposite. Alternatively, there is an asymmetrical *privative* opposi-tion. In this case, a marked term demonstrates the presence of a feature, while an unmarked term does not imply its logical opposite – it simply is not stated. The phrase וַיְהִי דְבַר־יהוה אֵלַי לֵאמֹר is marked in the priv-ative sense. Thus, while the phrase marks the following speech act as non-prototypical, it does not follow that the unmarked conjugated forms of אמר in the remainder of the speech situation *are* prototypical. In these cases, it is simply not indicated.

What may be said is that the phrase וַיְהִי דְבַר־יהוה אֵלַי לֵאמֹר is a marked metapragmatic phrasal expression; thus each repetition of this clause opens a new mental space at the meta-linguistic level. These spaces might be labelled as *speech domains*. The first domain extends from 1.4-1.10. The second is 1.11-1.12, and the third is 1.13-1.19. The fourth begins at 2.1 and extends into chapter 2. The same phrase links

---

34 Ehlich, "Anaphora and Deixis: Same, Similar, or Different?" 331.

35 This correlates with findings of van der Merwe. See C. H. J. van der Merwe, "The Elusive Biblical Term *WHYH*: A Perspective in Terms of Its Syntax, Semantics, and Pragmatics in I Samuel," *HS* 15 (1999), 99.

36 Parunak includes the phrase in his cline of disjunctive structural markers in the Jeremiah text. See H. Van Dyke Parunak, "Some Discourse Functions of Prophetic Quotation Formulas in Jeremiah," in *Biblical Hebrew and Discourse Linguistics*, ed. Ro-bert D. Bergen (Dallas: SIL, 1994).

37 Miller, *Representation*, 240.

38 A full discussion of markedness is found in Edwin L. Batistella, *The Logic of Marked-ness* (New York: OUP, 1996).

the spaces to one another, due to repetition. Connections are also established between each of these sections and the introductory material in Jeremiah1.1-1.3, due to the repetition of the term דברי ירמיה at 1.1a, and the phrase אשר היה דבר־יהוה אליו at 1.1c.

Jeremiah 1.4-2.3 provides an illustration of scalar adjustment.[39] At this point in the construction, Jeremiah 1.1-1.3 recedes to the background and the speech domains form layers in the foreground. Additionally, as new information comes into view, it is perceived as being more detailed, or more finely-grained, while certain details diminish as previous information recedes. This may be described as something of a visual doppler effect. Only selected details from previous spaces will remain activated within the current focus space. However, previous information will remain available for reactivation as discourse progresses.[40]

---

39   Along with *focus* and *scope, scalar adjustment* is a sub-category of *attention*. The term focus is used to describe the locus of attention, the term scope is used to describe the limits of attention and the term scalar adjustment is used to describe an adjustment in the *scale* of attention. These three terms describe static construals of a scene. Croft and Cruse, *Cognitive Linguistics*, 52.

40   Langacker proposes that a process of consolidation also occurs as discourse is processed. He states, "While the essential content may be retained, memory of how it was presented linguistically will soon be lost. We can usefully speak of a process of *consolidation*, whereby the essential content is abstracted from the specifics of its linguistic presentation… it is simply an apprehension of the overall situation described in its own terms, as an integrated conceptual structure… the consolidated structure continues to grow or be otherwise modified, even as the discourse structure effecting its earlier evolution fades from memory. It is the consolidated structure that we retain from earlier stages in the discourse and store in long-term memory." Ronald W. Langacker, "Discourse in Cognitive Grammar," *CL* 12 (2001), 180.

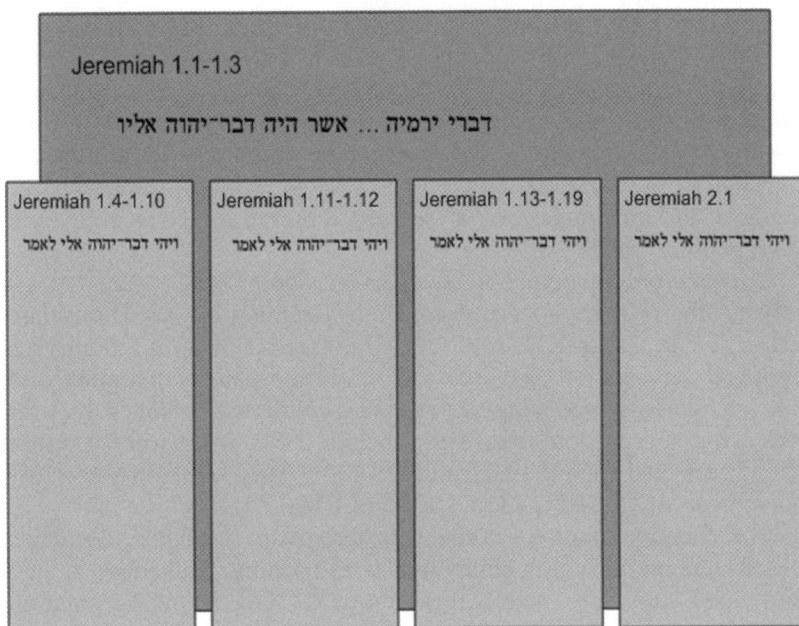

Jeremiah 1.1-1.3

דברי ירמיה ... אשר היה דבר־יהוה אליו

Jeremiah 1.4-1.10	Jeremiah 1.11-1.12	Jeremiah 1.13-1.19	Jeremiah 2.1
ויהי דבר־יהוה אלי לאמר	ויהי דבר־יהוה אלי לאמר	ויהי דבר־יהוה אלי לאמר	ויהי דבר־יהוה אלי לאמר

Figure 4.6   Speech Domains in Jeremiah 1.1-2.3

As demonstrated in Figure 4.6, the speech domains stand out against the ground created by Jeremiah 1.1-1.3. This basic representation of the figure-ground configuration details how the degree of granularity changes as new information comes into view.

b.   Communication

The second semantic domain that cues space-building includes verbs of speaking. The Louw-Nida Dictionary of Semantic Domains includes these terms in domain 33, *Communication*. The communication domain is familiar territory. English convention delineates cognitive spaces that are cued by verbs of speaking by the use of inverted commas, in the case of UK English, or by quotation marks, in the case of US English.

Verbs of speaking, such as conjugated forms of the BH term אמר, may be used to indicate instances of direct speech on the part of characters within the text, thus acting as space-builders for linguistic level embedded quotation spaces within a primary speech domain.[41] A quo-

---

41   Similarly, other citation formulae might act as conceptual space-builders as well. Thus, phrases such as "As it is written" might indicate new cognitive construction

tation space might introduce an alternate ground that includes previously unknown characters, their speech events and new spatio-
temporal circumstances as well. Because this is the case, instances of
direct speech introduce a degree of complexity into the text.[42] The series of verbal forms within the quotation space may be quite different
from that of the series of verbal forms that set up the primary speech
domains, and thus must be analysed at a different level – as a different
layer, in other words.[43]

The metapragmatic phrasal expression, ויהי דבר־יהוה אלי לאמר, establishes the primary speech domains in Jeremiah 1.4-2.2. The phrase
occurs at 1.4a, 1.11a, 1.13a and 2.1a. This *wayyiqtol* clause initiates the
reported conversation between the adjacency pair of Jeremiah and
Yahweh. Verbs of speaking act as space-builders, opening subspaces
within the speech domains. These include ואמר, a *wayyiqtol-0* clause
that appears at 1.6a and 1.11d; and ויאמר יהוה אלי, a *wayyiqtol-X* clause
that appears at 1.7a, 1.9c, 1.11a, 1.12a and 1.14a.

The primary cognitive domain for Jeremiah 1.4-2.2 is a discursive
speech domain, in which Jeremiah acts as narrator. Embedded quotations open subspaces within these domains. The following diagram
zooms in on the information in Jeremiah 1.4-2.2, bringing it into sharper
focus, and adding additional details to the cognitive construction in
this section. The N^2 viewing arrangement remains in place at this point
in the construction.[44]

---

when read in context. See Kevin Spawn. *"As It Is Written" and Other Citation Formulae
in the Old Testament*, ed. Otto Kaiser, BZAW (Berlin: Walter de Gruyter, 2002).

42   Some have proposed that BH also exhibits free direct discourse. For example, see
Galia Hatav, "(Free) Direct Discourse in Biblical Hebrew," *HS* 41 (2000), 7-30. While
this question is beyond the scope of this volume, the conceptual role of free direct
discourse is discussed in Sanders and Redeker, "Perspective and the Representation
of Speech and Thought in Narrative Discourse," 290-317.

43   De Regt proposes a similar idea in Lenart J. de Regt, "Domains and Subdomains in
Biblical Hebrew," in *Narrative and Comment: Contributions to Discourse Grammar and
Biblical Hebrew*, ed. Eep Talstra (Amsterdam: Societas Hebraica Amstelodamensis,
1995), 147-161.

44   Langacker proposes an elaborate account of cognitive construction at the discourse
level in his 2001 article *Discourse in Cognitive Grammar*. In this account, Langacker la-
bels the space that is currently in focus as the Current Discourse Space, or CDS. He
discusses the manner in which new information updates the CDS as discourse is
processed. Significantly, he utilises attention frames that comprise the scope of conceptualisation, and the speaker and hearer. Langacker orders the series of frames in
a linear fashion, including a zero frame and the CDS in any given diagram. The TD
model of cognitive construction is presented as a series of vertical frames, and is presented at a lower degree of granularity than that of Langacker, who begins with sentence-level segments. Langacker, "Discourse in Cognitive Grammar."

Figure 4.7   Secondary Speech Domains in Jeremiah 1.4-2.2

Figure 4.7 demonstrates that the production of new mental spaces via verbs of speaking can be a recursive process, representing many layers of embedding. It is important to recognise that any new space might introduce a shift in ground, with new characters, new conversations and new spatiotemporal parameters. Verbs of speaking, then, provide perspective within a text by registering the identity of various characters as speakers. This in turn affects the construal of the situation of speaking, which is deictically indexed relative to the character as speaker.

This cognitive analysis of Jeremiah 1.1-2.2 demonstrates the high degree of salience produced by the use of space building terms derived from the semantic domain of speaking. This has implications for historical-critical study of prophetic text. In his article, *The "Word Of Yahweh": A Theological Concept in the Book of Jeremiah*, Christoph Levin examines this section from an historical-critical perspective and develops a sophisticated argument for a "word of Yahweh" revision of the book of Jeremiah. He notes that the use of this term is a relatively late development, based upon the fact that the term "word of Yahweh" is used most heavily in the books of Jeremiah and Ezekiel. Additionally, he claims that "… the concept 'word of Yahweh' is derived, not from the divine address itself, but from subsequent reflection on that address". He argues that this thought process is reflected in the literary growth of the book and that one of the earliest redactions of the book depended upon the concept of "Yahweh's word".[45]

Levin's argument is of interest for two reasons. First, he bases his partitioning of the text upon the use of the metapragmatic phrasal expression ויהי דבר־יהוה אלי לאמר.[46] Thus, Levin's argument confirms the salient nature of space building terms from the semantic domain of speaking. Secondly, he sees the concept of "Yahweh's word" as the earliest stage in the literary development of the book of Jeremiah and builds a compelling argument for a redaction of the book that is based upon theological reflection upon this motif.[47]

c.   The Intersection of Verbs of Communication and Cumulative Referential Density in Jeremiah 1.1-2.2

According to the above analysis, the metapragmatic phrasal expression ויהי דבר־יהוה אלי לאמר establishes the primary speech domains in Jeremiah 1.4-2.2 at 1.4a, 1.11a, 1.13a and 2.1a. Each instance of this phrase introduces reported conversation between Jeremiah and Yahweh, who are the main interlocutors throughout this section. An examination of the cumulative referential density of topical entities in Jeremiah 1.1-2.2 provides additional confirmation regarding their status as primary topical entities. Jeremiah is mentioned in 86 percent of the clauses, and Yahweh in 34 percent of the clauses.

---

45   Christoph Levin, "The 'Word of Yahweh': A Theological Concept in the Book of Jeremiah," in *Prophets, Prophecy, and Prophetic Texts in Second Temple Judaism*, ed. Michael H. Floyd and Robert D. Haak, Library of Hebrew Bible/Old Testament Studies (New York: T&T Clark, 2006), 43. For Levin's earlier treatment of this section see: Christoph Levin, *Die Verheissung Des Neuen Bundes: In Ihrem Theologiegeschichtlichen Zusammenhang Ausgelegt* (Göttingen: Vandenhoeck & Ruprecht, 1985), 150-153.

46   Levin includes explanations of Jeremiah 1.4-10, (Jeremiah's call); Jeremiah 1.11-14, (the visions of the almond branch and boiling pot); 2.1 (transition from the call to the book) and the symbolic actions in Jeremiah 13.1-11; 16.1-9; 18.1-6 and 32.1-5.

47   Levin, "The 'Word of Yahweh'." For further discussion regarding the redaction of the book of Jeremiah, see Konrad Schmid, *Buchgestalten Des Jeremiabuches: Untersuchungen Zur Redaktions- Und Rezeptionsgeschichte Von Jer 30-33 Im Kontext Des Buches*, Wissenschaftliche Monographien Zum Alten Und Neuen Testament (Neukirchen-Vluyn: Neukirchener Verlag, 1996).

JER		דברי ירמיהו	ירמיהו	דבר־יהוה	יהוה		
1.1a	1	1.00					
1:2a	2	0.50	0.50	0.50			
1:2b	3	0.33	0.66	0.33			
1:3a	4	0.25	0.50	0.50			
1:4a	5	0.20	0.60	0.60			
1:5a	6	0.16	0.66	0.50			
1:5b	7	0.14	0.71	0.43			
1:5c	8	0.12	0.77	0.37			
1:5d	9	0.11	0.80	0.33			
1:6a	10	0.10	0.82	0.30	0.10		
1:7a	11	0.09	0.83	0.27	0.18	everyone	
1:7b	12	0.08	0.84	0.25	0.17		
1:7c	13	0.08	0.84	0.23	0.15		
1:7d	14	0.07	0.86	0.21	0.14		
1:8a	15	0.06	0.87		0.20		
1:8b	16	0.06	0.87		0.19		
1:9a	17	0.05	0.88		0.24	my words	your mouth
1:9b	18	0.05	0.83		0.28		
1:10a	19	0.05	0.84			nations	kingdoms
1:11a	20	0.05	0.85	0.20		almond branch	
1:12a	22	0.04	0.86		0.27	my word	
1:13a	24	0.04	0.83	0.20	0.33	boiling pot	
1:13b	25	0.04	0.84				
1:13c	26	0.03	0.85				
1:14a	27	0.03	0.85		0.33	disaster	
1:15a	28	0.03	0.85			peoples / north	kings/Jeru.
1:16a	29	0.03	0.85			my judgments	other gods
1:17a	30	0.03	0.86				
1:18a	31	0.03	0.86		0.34	kings/officials	priests/people
1:19a	32	0.03	0.87		0.37		
1:19d	35	0.03	0.88				
2:1a	36	0.02	0.84		0.35		
2:2a		**0.02**	**0.86**	**0.14**	**0.34**	Jerusalem	

Figure 4.8 Cumulative Referential Density in Jeremiah 1.1-2.2

While more will be said regarding this array of topical entities at a later point in this chapter, it is worth noting that Jeremiah and Yahweh are well entrenched as speech act participants by 1.19d. It is only after this extended section that a third speech act participant, Jerusalem, is mentioned in 2.2a. Secondary topical entities occur within the speech frames established by the main interlocutors. Both the viewpoint and cognitive construal of the secondary entities is restricted to the character's perspective – that of the human, Jeremiah, on the one hand, and that of the divine, Yahweh, on the other. Reconciling the difference in animacy between the human and the divine as interlocutors in a communication situation is discussed in section B.3, below. The relative animacy of the almond branch and the boiling pot will also be addressed in that section.

d. Perception and Cognition

The third group of terms that cue space building in a cognitive network are verbs of perception and cognition. As noted in Chapter 2, verbs of perception and cognition share several characteristics. First, the grammatical subject of these verbs is an experiencer, rather than a prototypical agent.[48] Secondly, the verbs demonstrate non-prototypical transitivity, as evidenced by the tendency of these verbs to take complement clauses as grammatical objects. Finally, these verbs demonstrate a low degree of dynamicity.

Verbs of perception are included in LN semantic domain 24, *sensory events and states*. This domain includes the subdomains *see, hear, smell, taste, touch/feel, pain/suffering* and *general sensory perception*. The primary function of verbs of perception is to indicate "the sense modality and the experiencer which is the source of information."[49] From a typological perspective, the term *see* is the most unmarked of the perception terms. This is followed by *hear*, then *touch, taste* and *smell* as a group.[50] This has implications for understanding Jeremiah 1.1-6.30, because there is a certain amount of ambiguity regarding the sense modality by which Jeremiah perceives the word of the Lord. Terms from this semantic domain also tend to extend their meaning into the area of cogni-

---

48   Viberg notes that verbs of perception may be either experiencer-based or phenomenon-based. Experiencer-based verbs may signal activity, as in the phrase *Peter was looking at the birds*; or experience, as in the phrase *Peter saw the birds*; whereas phenomenon-based verbs indicate the phenomenon itself, as in the phrase *Peter looked happy*. Åke Viberg, "Verbs of Perception," in *Language Typology and Universals: An International Handbook,* ed. M. Haspelmath (Berlin: Walter de Gruyter, 2001), 1295.

49   Ibid.
50   Ibid., 1297.

tion.[51] For example, in English the phrase *I see* may refer both to physical perception and to understanding as well.

Verbs of cognition are also known as *mental states predicates*. This term refers to the LN semantic domains of *knowledge*, 28; *memory and recall*, 29; *thinking*, 30; and *belief and trust*, 31. According to Croft and Cruse, these terms relate directly to the issue of perspective based upon knowledge, belief and attitudes.[52] This understanding of perspective relates to the issue of modality, which is a semantic rather than a syntactic or formal category. Modality refers to 'the attitude of the speaker towards that expressed in the sentence', or to 'the speaker's subjective judgment concerning the factuality of the events.'[53] Thus, once again, these space building terms are directly associated with a speaker: either the author/originator of the text, or a character within the text. The terms index information from the character's *internal* perspective, thus the term *epistemic modality* is appropriate here.

According to Jan Nuyts, *think* is the prototypical term within the semantic field of epistemic modality. He then lists *believe, doubt, know, suppose* and *guess* as further examples.[54] Because the terms index information from the character's internal perspective, the new spaces opened by the terms are somewhat restricted within the mental spaces network. They will connect directly to their space of origin, but might not connect directly back to the base space, that connection might well be inherited from the space of origin. Thus, a mental space opened by a *mental states predicate* will be highly dependent upon the identity of the speaker for its interpretation, and by definition is a subspace in a larger network. This is demonstrated in the following diagram, which zooms in on the discourse spaces in Jeremiah 1.4-1.19 in order to present a finely-grained view of this section of text. In this diagram the spaces opened by the term ראה are indicated by a dashed line, and are encapsulated within their speech frames, demonstrating restricted access due to the embedding within a character's perspective. In this case, the term ראה seems to be used as a verb of perception. However, once again the nature of Jeremiah's perception is debated. Was it a full-fledged vision? Was it an observation of ordinary objects made in passing? Simply stated, the perception itself is the important aspect of the experience.

---

51   Ibid., 1304.
52   Croft and Cruse, *Cognitive Linguistics*, 58.
53   Bussman, H. Bussman, *Dictionary*, 307; van der Merwe, Naudé and Kroeze, C. *Van der Merwe, J. Naudé and J. Kroeze, BH Reference*, 361.
54   Nuyts, *Epistemic Modality, Language, and Conceptualization*, 110.

Jeremiah 1.1-1.3

Jeremiah 1.4 a

ויהי דבר־יהוה אלי לאמר

1.5

ואמר

1.6

ויאמר יהוה אלי

1.7

ויאמר יהוה אלי

1.9

Jeremiah 1.11

ויהי דבר־יהוה אלי לאמר

1.11c   ?

ואמר

1.11e   almond branch

ויאמר יהוה אלי

1.12b

Jeremiah 1.13a

ויהי דבר־יהוה אלי לאמר

1.13c   ?

ואמר

1.13d   boiling pot

ויאמר יהוה אלי

1.14

1.15b   נאם־יהוה

1.19   נאם־יהוה

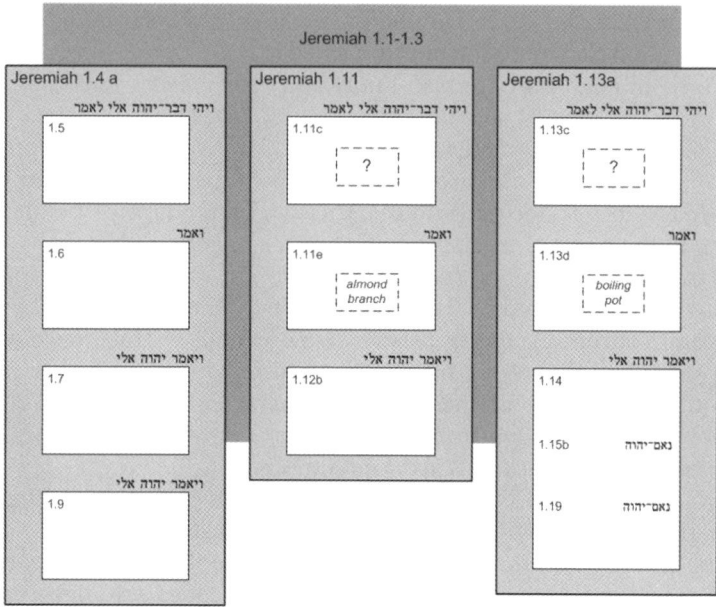

Figure 4.9   Cognitive Construction in Jeremiah 1.1-1.19

Figure 4.9 demonstrates that cognitive construction in Jeremiah 1.1-1.19 is a multi-layered process. Space-builders, including text-deictic terms and terms from the semantic domains of communication, perception and cognition contribute to the formation of numerous interconnected cognitive packets. The cognitive packets are structured by the containment schema in the N^1 section at Jeremiah 1.1-1.3 and by the set of speech frames in the N^2 section at 1.4-1.19. Furthermore, the speech frames in 1.11 and 1.13 contain perception spaces initiated by the unmarked perception term ראה. Within the perception spaces, Jeremiah is asked to report what he perceives visually and does so. Two observations are relevant. First, despite the communication frame, ambiguity still exists regarding the mode of perception by which Jeremiah apprehends the communication event. Secondly, although this section does not contain a high number of literary metaphors, it does exhibit a literary quality that extends beyond a simple narrative. More specifically, the speech frames introduce a type of leveling between the human and the divine as Jeremiah reports his communication with Yahweh. This may be accounted for by the Great Chain of Being conceptual metaphor, which will be discussed in the following section.

3.   Conceptual Metaphor and Literary Metaphor

Because conceptual metaphor provides information from the perspective of human experience and makes this embodied perspective available for understanding abstract experiences and concepts, this study utilises a weak experientialist approach for analysing and describing conceptual metaphor. The approach is necessarily weak because a strong experientialist approach would rule out non-embodied experiences, creating untold difficulties for discussing the non-embodied characteristics of humankind and, more importantly, for discussing the Divine.

Kövecses describes the relationship between conceptual metaphor and human experience as follows:

> Conceptual metaphors are grounded in, or motivated by human experience...Specifically, we experience the interconnectedness of two domains of experience and this justifies us conceptually linking the two domains...the experiences on which the conceptual metaphors are based may be not only bodily but also perceptual, cognitive, biological, or cultural.[55]

Conceptual metaphor research is a relatively new field, yet the issues involved in cognitive studies are reflected in biblical interpretation as far back as the 1190 AD work of Maimonides.[56] For example, in his exposition of the term *temunah*, Maimonides states:

> ...in the Bible, this term is used in three different senses: to signify the outlines of things that are perceived by our bodily senses; to signify the impressions retained in imagination when the objects have ceased to affect our senses; and to signify the true form of an object which is perceived only by the intellect – and it is in this third signification that the term is applied to God.[57]

The experientialist approach proposes that the "outlines of things we perceive with our eyes" contribute to the formation of images and image schemata, which are akin to the "impressions retained in imagination." Additionally, some would propose that the impressions retained in the imagination are derived not only by visual perception, but by other sensory experiences as well. Jackendoff, a cognitive scientist, pro-

---

55   Kövecses, *Metaphor: A Practical Introduction*, 249.
56   Lakoff and Johnson are two important figures in conceptual metaphor research. See George Lakoff, *Women, Fire, and Dangerous Things: What Categories Reveal About the Human Mind* (Chicago: UCP, 1987); Lakoff and Johnson, *Metaphors We Live By*; George Lakoff and Mark Johnson, *Philosophy in the Flesh: The Embodied Mind and Its Challenge to Western Thought* (New York: Basic Books, 1999). See also Gerard J. Steen, "Identifying Metaphor in Language," *Style* (2002), 1-19.
57   Moses Maimonides, *The Guide for the Perplexed*, trans. M. Friedlander (New York: Barnes and Noble, 2004), 25.

poses a model in which visual representations are joined by haptic representations and auditory localisations in this process.[58] Additionally,
image schemata represent one way of organising the impressions retained in the imagination. Image schemata, such as *containment, end of
path, scale, centre-periphery, cycle, force, link, part-whole, path* and *verticality*
are based upon human experiences and structure many of our abstract
concepts metaphorically.[59]

a.   The Extended Great Chain Metaphor

Before moving on to the description and analysis of the interface between cognitive metaphor and literary metaphor in Jeremiah 1.13, it is
necessary to examine the issue of metaphor systems. Kövecses proposes that conceptual metaphors are not isolated occurrences, but function
in larger clusters, which he describes as metaphor systems. Two major
metaphor systems have been proposed: the Extended Great Chain of
Being metaphor, and the Event Structure metaphor. The Extended
Great Chain of Being metaphor correlates with *objects*, while the Event
Structure metaphor correlates with *actions*, or *states of being*.

Grammarians will likely note the connection between nouns and
the Extended Great Chain metaphor, and the connection between verbs
and the Event Structure metaphor. Cognitive linguists might associate
entities with the first, and relations with the second. Linguists at large
will note the connections between the Great Chain of Being metaphor
and the animacy hierarchy, which is used to analyse agency in various
types of sentences.

Animacy Hierarchy
Speech act participant 1
Speech act participant 2
Speech act participant 3
Proper Noun
Animate
Inanimate
Mass

---

58   The term *haptic* refers to the sense of touch. Jackendoff, *Languages of the Mind*, 100.
59   Kövecses, *Metaphor: A Practical Introduction*, 37.

Extended Great Chain of Being
Divine
Creation/Cosmos
Society
Humans: *higher order attributes, behaviour*
Animals: *instinctual attributes, behaviour*
Plants: *biological attributes, behaviour*
Complex objects: *structural attributes, functional behaviour*
Natural physical things: *natural physical attributes, behaviour*

Significantly, the Extended Great Chain is not a metaphorical system in and of itself. Rather, it becomes a metaphorical system when "... a particular level of the chain is used to understand another level."[60] This is precisely what occurs in the first chapter of Jeremiah. As previously noted, Jeremiah and the LORD are presented as the main interlocutors in an extended section of reported speech, and Jerusalem is included as an addressee at 2.2. Cognitively speaking, the speech domain is non-prototypical due to the characterization of the LORD as a speech participant.[61] This portrayal shifts the LORD down by three slots in the Great Chain hierarchy. In this section of text, the LORD is understood in human terms, specifically in the areas of perception, cognition, communication and emotion. Additionally, in Jeremiah 2.3 the term Israel refers to society as a whole. Thus society is also presented at human scale, which is a single slot shift on the hierarchy.

When the LORD and Israel are presented at human scale, the Extended Great Chain of Being hierarchy is being used as a metaphor system. The "reality space" in the text is construed metaphorically – it is plausible, yet does not represent a one to one correspondence with the world outside of the text, where both the LORD and Israel/Judah are entities extending far beyond human scale. The conceptual metaphorical construal of all three entities at human scale makes the experientialist approach an effective approach to this section of the text.

Kövecses proposes that both the Great Chain and the Event Structure conceptual metaphors are available as source domains for the tar-

---

60 Ibid., 126.
61 The speech situation is also non-prototypical according to Miller's linguistic analysis, due to the presence of the marked metapragmatic phrasal expression ‏ויהי דבר־יהוה אלי לאמר‎.

get domain *Abstract Complex System*, i.e. society, government, career and relationships.[62] The abstract complex system *target domain* may then be understood by correlations, technically known as mappings, between such *source domains* as the human body, buildings, machines, and plants. These mappings result in complex conceptual metaphors such as SOCIETY IS A BUILDING, SOCIETY IS A PLANT and so forth. The appeal of this approach for understanding the conceptual metaphor systems present in MT Jeremiah is immediately apparent upon perusal of the specifics of Jeremiah's instructions to uproot and tear down...*to build* and *to plant*. The *what* of these statements surely moves beyond physical buildings and natural plants, to the complex abstract systems present in the society of Jeremiah's day, including temple, covenant, king, and the dichotomy between insider and outsider.[63]

b.   Scoping In: Cognitive Construction in
Jeremiah 1.11-1.12 and 1.13-1.19

This section presents a sentence-level analysis of Jeremiah 1.11-1.12 and 1.13-1.19 in order to examine the most deeply embedded mental spaces in the cognitive network –the perception spaces at 1.11 and 1.13.

---

62   Kövecses, *Metaphor: A Practical Introduction*, 48.
63   Stulman follows this line of reasoning in his discussion of the "dismantling of Judah's sacred world." Louis Stulman, *Order Amid Chaos: Jeremiah as Symbolic Tapestry*, Biblical Seminar; 57 (Sheffield: Sheffield Academic Press, 1998), 31.

Clause Layout	JER
וַיְהִי דְבַר־יְהוָה אֵלַי	1.11a
לֵאמֹר	b
מָה־אַתָּה רֹאֶה יִרְמְיָהוּ	c
וָאֹמַר	d
מַקֵּל שָׁקֵד אֲנִי רֹאֶה	e
וַיֹּאמֶר יְהוָה אֵלַי	1.12a
הֵיטַבְתָּ לִרְאוֹת	b
כִּי־שֹׁקֵד אֲנִי עַל־דְּבָרִי לַעֲשֹׂתוֹ	c

Figure 4.10　Clause Analysis for Jeremiah 1.11-1.12

JER	Type	Clause Tag	PNG	Stem Focus	MSC
1.11a	N	Wayyiqtol-S	3sgM	Pred	VP=N²
b	N	Qetol			SB
c	NQP	X-Qotel		Pred inter	M=N²
d	N	Wayyiqtol-0	1sg	Pred	SB
e	NQP	X-Qotel	sgM	Arg	M=N²
1.12a	N	Wayyiqtol-S	3sgM	Pred	SB
b	NQ	Qatal—Qetol	2sgM	Pred	M=N²
c	NQ	+Qotel PreP; Qetol	sgM	P	

Figure 4.11　Explanation of Clause Analysis for Jeremiah 1.11-1.12

Clause Layout	JER
וַיְהִי דְבַר־יְהוָה אֵלַי שֵׁנִית	1.13a
לֵאמֹר	b
מָה אַתָּה רֹאֶה	c
וָאֹמַר	d
סִיר נָפוּחַ אֲנִי רֹאֶה	e
וּפָנָיו מִפְּנֵי צָפוֹנָה	f
וַיֹּאמֶר יְהוָה אֵלָי	1.14a
מִצָּפוֹן תִּפָּתַח הָרָעָה עַל כָּל־יֹשְׁבֵי הָאָרֶץ	b
כִּי הִנְנִי קֹרֵא לְכָל־מִשְׁפְּחוֹת מַמְלְכוֹת צָפוֹנָה	1.15a
נְאֻם־יְהוָה	b
וּבָאוּ	c
וְנָתְנוּ אִישׁ כִּסְאוֹ פֶּתַח שַׁעֲרֵי יְרוּשָׁלַ͏ִם	d
וְעַל כָּל־חוֹמֹתֶיהָ סָבִיב	e
וְעַל כָּל־עָרֵי יְהוּדָה	f

Figure 4.12   Clause Analysis for Jeremiah 1.13-1.15

JER	Type	Clause Tag	PNG	Focus	MSC
1.13a	N	Wayyiqtol-S	3sgM	PF	VP=N²
b	N	Qetol			SB
c	NQP	X-Qotel	sgM	PF inter	M=N²
d	N	Wayyiqtol-0	1sg	PF	SB
e	NQP	X-Qotel	sgM	AF	M=N²
f	NQ	NmCl			N²
1.14a	N	Wayyiqtol-S	3sgM	PF	SB
b	NQ	X-Yiqtol	3sF	Niphal PF	M=N²
1.15a	NQ	+Qotel	sgM	SF	
b	NQ	focus			
c	NQ	W-Qatal	3pl	PF	N²
d	NQ	W-Qatal	3pl	PF	
e	NQ	PreP			
f	NQ	PreP			

Figure 4.13 Explanation of Clause Analysis for Jeremiah 1.13-1.15

c. Syntax

Jeremiah 1.11-1.12 and 1.13-1.15 exhibit a high degree of syntactic similarity. This is evident in Figure 4.9, where the mental spaces diagrams
show identical patterning, with the exception of the insertion of the
focus phrase נאם־יהוה at 1.15. Jeremiah 1.11a and Jeremiah 1.13a both
contain the identical metapragmatic clause, ויהי דבר־יהוה אלי, but 1.13
includes the term שנית, which implies a second communication event.
Thus, while on one level the information in each section is segmented,
it is also intricately enmeshed in the cognitive structure on another
level. Commentators differ as to the degree of connection (new segment
versus two connected segments), but in a sense it is an issue that includes both types of connection.

The word order in 1.11c and 1.13c is interrogative particle – pronoun –Verb (Int) SV, which appears to be irregular. The word order in 1.11e and 1.13e is NP – personal pronoun – participle (OSV). In this case, the object is fronted and the word order indicates that these sentences are examples of *sentence focus*. Thus, 1.11e and 1.13e might introduce a discourse topical frame. This appears to be the case at 1.13e, because the phrase וּפָנָיו מִפְּנֵי צָפוֹנָה is echoed in the phrase מִצָּפוֹן תִּפָּתַח הָרָעָה עַל כָּל־יֹשְׁבֵי הָאָר at 1.14b. Implications for interpretation will be discussed below.

d. Information Structure

The sentences in the *P* spaces (Jeremiah 1.11c and e; 1.13c and e) are of particular interest, as the four sentences exhibit marked word order. All four are X-*Qotel* clauses.[64] The fronted element in the first set of clauses מַה־אַתָּה רֹאֶה יִרְמְיָהוּ and מָה אַתָּה רֹאֶה is the interrogative pronoun מַה. This indicates only that the clauses are questions, not that the interrogative pronoun is in focus. Indeed, the sentence initial position is normal for BH interrogative particles.[65] Thus, the first two clauses are instances of predicate focus, underscoring the presupposition that Jeremiah is seeing some, yet to be identified, entity.

In Jeremiah 1.11c the interrogative particle is joined to the personal pronoun אַתָּה by *maqqep* and the clause includes Jeremiah in the vocative. Neither is the case for Jeremiah 1.13c. The two clauses provide an example of the difference between the deictic procedure and the anaphoric procedure. In the first instance the vocative reference to Jeremiah functions deictically Jeremiah is reactivated as a topical entity. In the second instance, Jeremiah is already activated. Thus the unmarked pronominal אַתָּה functions anaphorically; it continues to focus attention upon the previously activated referent. This strengthens the argument for a close connection between the two sections, rather than the view that these are two separate sections.[66]

---

64   van der Merwe and Talstra, "Interface," 85.

65   While Rosenbaum proposes interrogative focus as a subset of focus in general, there is a typological reason that this is not the case. Primus notes that cross-linguistically the association of interrogatives with focus is not straightforward because interrogatives (*wh*-words) do not carry the main sentence stress, show limited word order variability and mark the interrogative sentence type, whereas focus constituents are not necessarily sentence type markers; they do carry the stress of the whole clause, and show more word order variation. Primus, "Word Order Typology," 873.

66   Carroll sees a close connection between the two sections, with the second vision being presented as clarification of the first. Carroll, *Jeremiah: A Commentary*, 105. On the other hand, Lundbom makes a clear distinction between the two. He notes that

However, Jeremiah 1.11e and 1.13e are instances of argument focus. The fronted entities in the responses מקל שקד אני ראה and סיר נפוח אני ראה are at the heart of the communication event. This is noted in Figure 4.9, where the perception spaces are the most deeply nested spaces in the cognitive network and access is restricted to the character's perspective. Apparently, even Yahweh must ask Jeremiah to report the content of his perception in this non-prototypical land-scape! In these clauses, Jeremiah, the embodied member of the adjacency pair, reports that he sees מקל שקד, an almond branch, at 1.11e and סיר נפוח, a boiling pot, at 1.13e. The significance of these observations will be taken up in the following section.

These sections are a continuation of the N² narrative level initiated at 1.4, with the first instance of the metapragmatic phrasal expression ויהי דבר־יהוה אלי, a *wayyiqtol-S* clause. The reported communication event is continued by *wayyiqtol-0* clauses in which Jeremiah is both narrator and reported speaker (1.11d and 1.13d), and by *wayyiqtol-S* clauses in which Yahweh is the reported speaker (1.12a and 1.14a). The perfective *wayyiqtol* forms move the reported discourse forward as a series of stepping stones. Importantly, as Figure 4.9 demonstrates, these clauses contain communication verbs so they contribute to the creation of subspaces, each of which contains a variety of verbal forms. Thus, Jeremiah 1.4-1.19 is neither straightforward **narrative speech**, nor wholly **discursive speech**, but rather a hybrid of the two that is well-modelled by the network model of cognitive construction.[67]

e.   Cognitive Construction

The containment schema indicated by the topical entity סיר נפוח struc-tures the *P* space in Jeremiah 1.13. This schema features:

- Boundary: in this case, the pot itself;

- Enclosed area or volume: here, the boiling contents of the pot; and

- Excluded area or volume: the area to which the liquid might go if the pot tips over.

This example also makes use of the force schema, which features physical and metaphorical causal interaction.

Jeremiah 1.4 and 1.11 are connected to the call, whereas Jeremiah 1.13 introduces a new revelation. Lundbom, *Jeremiah 1-20*, 240.

67   These terms are in bold type to emphasise the narrative-discursive opposition intro-duced by Schneider, as opposed literary genre. See chapter 2, section C.1.

f.   Conceptual Metaphor

Additionally, the conceptual metaphor ANGER IS THE HEAT OF A FLUID IN A CONTAINER structures Jeremiah 1.13-1.14. This conceptual metaphor occurs cross-culturally, with versions in Hungarian: *Anger was boiling inside of him*; Polish: *He is boiling with rage*; and English: *He was about to blow his stack*, to name a few.

The structure of the PRESSURISED CONTAINER metaphor for anger provides a set of mappings that account for the information in these verses:

- container with substance in it   the angry person's body

- the substance in the container   the anger

- the physical pressure within   the potentially dangerous force

- the cause of the pressure   the cause of the dangerous force

- the control of the pressure   the control of the force

- the inability to control the pressure   the inability to control the force[68]

First, the concrete object, the pot, maps with *the North* via the containment schema. The pot and *the North* each contain something – the pot contains the actual boiling liquid, while the North contains the abstract הרעה, *the evil*, mentioned in verse 14. Secondly, the pot is tipping and the boiling liquid is about to overflow and likewise, evil is about to break forth from the North. The force dynamics in the image are implicit, in that the heat source that is causing the pot to boil is the yet to be explored issue of disobedience. The people's disobedience causes the anger, which belongs to Yahweh. He is about to allow this emotion to overflow. The vehicle for the overflow is the foe from the North, who will become God's instrument of judgement upon Judah.

An additional characteristic of image schemas, such as the containment and path schemas, is that they are transformable. In other words, we tend to manipulate image schemata in our minds, which in this case allows us to finish the tilting job, allowing the boiling liquid to overflow as the pot ultimately tips over. Metaphorically, we are able to envision the evil flowing from the North as it moves towards us. Given our ability to move from multiplex, from many single figures (pixels) to mass (a single image) and back, it is not impossible to envision a single mass, the flowing evil, as a series of large armies whose faces become individuated, *Lord of the Rings* style, as they move into our immediate vicinity.

---

68   Kövecses, *Metaphor: A Practical Introduction*, 170.

The image of the almond branch in Jeremiah 1.11-1.12 acts as a topical frame without the benefit of a lengthy topical elaboration.[69] This is not the case for the boiling pot image in Jeremiah 1.13.[70] This image introduces the intensity and directionality of impending disaster. The topical frame, the image of evil flowing like boiling liquid from an overturned pot in 1.13, gives way to a topical elaboration in 1.14a. The *wayyiqtol-S* phrase וַיֹּאמֶר יְהוָה אֵלַי includes SAP 1, Yahweh, as subject and SAP 2, the first person speaker Jeremiah, as object. Within the quotation, an *X-yiqtol* clause, Yahweh, announces that evil will be poured upon all those dwelling in the land. The following *X-qotel* clause, כִּי הִנְנִי קֹרֵא לְכָל-מִשְׁפְּחוֹת מַמְלְכוֹת צָפוֹנָה, highlights the immediacy and the source of the coming disaster, in which Yahweh himself is the protagonist. Additional details accrue: the leaders will come and set their thrones at the very gates of Jerusalem, surrounding Jerusalem and the cities of Judah as well. These phrases provide spatial orientation for the discourse in Jeremiah 2.2ff, where the location of Jeremiah's oration becomes a subject of discussion.

This section demonstrates the way that conceptual metaphor uses information derived from human experience and makes this embodied perspective available for understanding abstract experiences and concepts. Additionally, the section describes how the Great Chain hierarchy becomes metaphorical when an entity occurs as a source domain for understanding an entity at a different level, i.e. a target domain. In the final example, the conceptual metaphor ANGER IS A HOT FLUID IN A CONTAINER comes into play when the single, human scale image of a boiling pot tilting away from the North zooms out to represent the larger than life threat of imminent judgment.

The examples in this chapter delineate some of the complex cognitive constructions that are represented by the text of Jeremiah 1.1-2.2. These are initiated by space building terms and constructions from the semantic fields of deixis; speech and perception; and epistemic modali-

---

69 Nonetheless, the image of the almond branch conveys a similar degree of compressed information. King thinks that the image is ambiguous, and that meaning has been lost to the word play between the terms שָׁקֵד, *almond*, and שֹׁקֵד, *watching*. However, the interplay between watching and the almond branch indicates that the watching is not haphazard, but rather that it follows a cycle as does the almond branch, which sprouts blossoms, leaves and fruit in a predictable cycle. Similarly, both the watching and the performing will follow a predictable pattern. Philip J. King, *Jeremiah: An Archeological Companion* (Louisville, Kentucky: Westminster/John Knox Press, 1993), 152.

70 Extra-textual information regarding culture and cultural artefacts in ancient Israel is available from a plethora of sources. Particularly relevant for this discussion are Oded Borowski, *Daily Life in Biblical Times* (Leiden: Brill, 2003); King, *Jeremiah: An Archeological Companion*, 152-153.

ty. Image schemata and frames structure the cognitive packets. Image schemata in Jeremiah 1.1-2.2 include the containment schema in 1.1-1.3; the force and containment schemata in 1.13; the path schema in 1.14; and the centre-periphery and force schemata in 1.15. These image schemata emerge as structuring devices throughout the remainder of Jeremiah 1.1-6.30. Quotation frames, such as the reported speech event between the LORD and Jeremiah at 1.4-2.2a, are also important structuring devices. The interlocutors discuss the situation at hand, what used to be, and what will be, and what the reactions of various people might be. Jeremiah and the LORD emerge as primary topical entities, and the details of Jeremiah's call are the subject of their conversation. The nations, the inhabitants of the land, the tribes of the kingdoms of the North, Jerusalem and the cities of Judah emerge as secondary entities. These entities are now part of the discourse, and are ready to be activated as primary entities as the discourse unfolds.

The conceptual metaphor ANGER IS A HOT FLUID IN AN ENCLOSED CONTAINER is the first of several conceptual metaphors that occur in Jeremiah 1.1-6.30. These metaphors, often structured by image schemata, provide information for literary metaphor and for narrative text.

5. Cognitive Structuring in Jeremiah 2.1-3.35

"The time has come", the Walrus said.
"To talk of many things..."

~ *Lewis Carroll*

Prose and poetry, those who listen and those who speak, reality and surreality: these are a few of the many things included in Jeremiah 1.1-6.30. This chapter will explore a few of the ways that cognitive approaches contribute to the discovery of unity within the text. The question at hand is, "What are the integrating features of the text?" Integration is a primary feature of human cognition, and the study of conceptual integration is the main point of conceptual blending theory.[1] The areas touched upon in this chapter include the integrative potential of frame knowledge (section A.2); the unifying effects of conceptual metaphor (section B.3); the creative use of counterfactual spaces (section C.2); virtual visual scanning (section D.2), image schemata and conceptual metaphor (section E), and the problem of identity (section F). Additionally, the area of space-builders in poetic text will be discussed (section F).

This chapter builds upon the discussion in Chapter 4, moving from section A.1, Jeremiah 1.1-2.1, to section A.2, Jeremiah 2.1-3.25. Two major cognitive constructions are indicated in Jeremiah 1.1-2.1. The first, Jeremiah 1.1-1.3, features the viewpoint of an unidentified narrator speaking to a general audience. It is a narrative section and has been tagged N[1]. The second, Jeremiah 1.4-2.1, is a discursive section in which the viewpoint belongs to the character Jeremiah. This section has been tagged N[2]. Jeremiah 1.4-2.1 comprises four speech domains, each of which is initiated by the space-building phrase ויהי דבר־יהוה אלי לאמר. The speech domains are linked to one another by the repetition of the clause ויהי דבר־יהוה אלי לאמר. Additionally, each speech domain acts as a base space for cognitive construction. Within the first three domains, embedded quotation spaces are opened by syntactic constructions containing the communication verb אמר (see Figure 4.9). The situation is somewhat different for the fourth domain, which is the subject of the present chapter.

---

1   Fauconnier and Turner, *The Way We Think*, 328.

A. Jeremiah 2.1-3.2: Speech Domain Four

The main concern of this chapter is the fourth speech domain, which begins at 2.1 and continues through 3.25. The fourth speech domain represents a point of departure from the previous domains. While reported interchanges between Jeremiah and Yahweh structure the first three domains, the fourth domain introduces an actant shift in: Jerusalem is activated as a new addressee and the voices of Jeremiah and Yahweh are amalgamated into the voice of a non-prototypical complex speaker, as demonstrated by the following diagram:

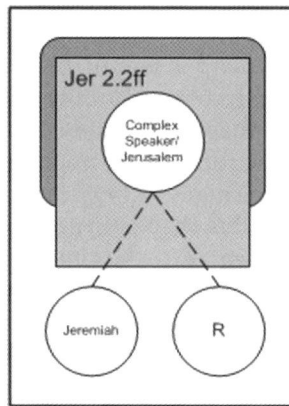

Figure 5.1 Viewing Arrangement for Jeremiah 2.2-3.25

As the diagram indicates, the complex speaker addresses the audience as a single voice. However, this single voice is mediated by two perspectives: that of Jeremiah, the very human prophet and that of Yahweh, the divine. This combination of speech act participants is tagged N^3.

1. Perspective

Tracking viewpoint through the text is important for determining perspective within a given section. Returning to the clause analysis, viewpoint is recorded in the MSC column. The tagging convention reflects viewpoint at two distinct levels: the text-level, in which the communication event takes place between the originator and reader; and the embedded level, in which the communication event takes place between various configurations of characters within the text. As the text-type column in the TD clauses analysis demonstrates, embedding is a recursive process, with each recursion representing an internal shift in perspective.[2] Three levels will be discussed here, although many sections of Jeremiah 1.1-6.30 contain multiple levels of embedding (see Figure 5.5).

The configuration of participants tagged N[1] operates at the text-level. The configuration of participants tagged N[2] operates at an intermediary level: the author has assigned the narrating voice to Jeremiah, who is also a character in the reported speech situation. Finally, the configuration of participants tagged N[3] operates at the embedded level, as the communication events occur between characters in the text. With regard to perspective, the N[2] tag indicates that the viewpoint belongs to Jeremiah as narrator. Likewise, the C[2] tag is used in embedded spaces to indicate that the viewpoint belongs to Jeremiah as character. The C[1] tag is used in embedded spaces to indicate that the viewpoint belongs to Yahweh, and the C[3] tag is used to indicate that the viewpoint belongs to the third interlocutor, Jerusalem.[3]

The N tag and the C tag not only indicate layers of interaction, but they contribute information regarding subjectivity and objectivity as well. The N tag represents the text-level situation of speaking, which involves the author and reader in the subjective position. The C tag represents the embedded text-internal situations of speaking, which involve characters within the text, and may be at various levels of embedding. These situations are in the objective position for the author and reader, who are maximally subjective at this level. Within an embedded space the characters involved in the embedded situation are in a maximally subjective position and the entities that populate the space opened by the conversation are in the objective position.

Since the author is responsible for assigning perspective to the narrator, it is possible to locate the author, the anonymous third person narrator or the identified first person narrator within the subjective

---

2   Parunak utilises the term *incipit* to describe text-level interaction, which he assigns to the writer and reader. The term encompasses phrases such as the metapragmatic phrasal expression ויהי דבר־יהוה אלי לאמר and the quotation frame ויאמר יהוה אל. Parunak also differentiates between communication events that involve Yahweh and Jeremiah, termed the *background* and *dispatch*, and those that involve Jeremiah and his addressees, termed the *body*. He assigns phrases such as כה אמר יהוה to the background and dispatch, and phrases such as כה אמר יהוה and נאם־יהוה to the body. Parunak, "Some Discourse Functions of Prophetic Quotation Formulas in Jeremiah," 498-499.

3   The use of the term *character* in discussing Yahweh is for heuristic purposes. However, as this is a technical term it need not be carried over into theological reflection.

position in the TD viewing arrangement diagram (see Figure 2.1). On the other hand, because there is a tendency for the reader to empathise with the characters, the reader rather easily makes a cognitive jump from the subjective position in the diagram into the objective position represented by the situations of speaking that occur within the text. This will be illustrated in the following section.

2. Conceptual Scoping and Achieving Human Scale

The cognitive construction reflected in the movement from N^1 through N^2 and on to N^3 indicates conceptual scoping in which the text-level perspective shifts from anonymous narrator to identified narrator who is simultaneously a character in the embedded situation of speaking. Finally, perspective is assigned to the characters within the embedded spaces.[4] Consequently, there is a shift from a coarsely grained view to a more finely grained view of the situation as well.[5] To use a cinemato-graphic metaphor, the shifts in perspective create a zooming-in effect. The first shift, from the narrative at N^1 to the reported speech in N^2, represents a shift from the narrator's perspective to the perspective of the narrator as character. Thus, at 1.4, Jeremiah replaces the unidentified narrator of 1.1-1.3 as the deictic centre, the point from which the verbal forms and spatial and temporal information are indexed. As a consequence, the access path for the following information is restricted to the character's perspective.[6] Additionally, the reported speech and quotation spaces in N^2 contain viewpoint markers such as description from the subject's belief space (1.6, *I do not know how to speak*), and im-

---

4   A shift in verbal forms accompanies the shift in perspective from an outside view to an inside view of the situation in the text. As noted in Chapter 4, impenetrability of a situation is indicated by perfective *wayyiqtol* and *qatal* forms, whereas penetrability of a situation is indicated by imperfective *yiqtol* and participle forms. As the level of embedding increases, so does the use of imperfective forms, which allow the reader to enter into the situation.

5   Croft and Cruse describe this construal operation as *quantitative scalar adjustment*, which is the result of adjusting the granularity of scalar dimensions. This may occur across both spatial and temporal boundaries. Croft and Cruse, *Cognitive Linguistics*, 52.

6   Werth describes levels of accessibility as follows: "… a participant has access to a participant, a character in the text world he or she has created and to a sub-character in a participant accessible sub-world, but not to a sub-character in a character accessible sub-world, or any entity more than two levels removed." While Werth is speaking with reference to truth evaluation and inference chaining in sub-worlds, his theory resembles the TD approach in that accessibility becomes limited with sucessive levels of embedding. Paul Werth, *Text Worlds: Representing Conceptual Space in Discourse* (London: Longman, 1999), 215.

plicit rather than explicit attribution to the subject's mental state (1.15, *Do not break down before them, or I will break you before them*).

The second shift, from N² to N³, takes place at 2.2d, where perspective is assessed from the embedded space. In 1.4-1.10, Yahweh confirms Jeremiah as a prophet to the nations, so he is authorised to speak on behalf of Yahweh, and now does so. The prophetic voice, which dominates Jeremiah 2.1-6.30, is the result of the amalgamation of the voices of Jeremiah and Yahweh into the voice of the complex speaker – a speaker with one voice, but two perspectives. Shifts in perspective occur often within this stretch of text. At times perspective is assigned directly to Yahweh by quotative frames, such as ויאמר יהוה אלי, or by the use of citation formulae, such as כה אמר יהוה. At other times, Jeremiah seems to be inserting his own words of lamentation. These instances are not overtly marked for the change in speaker, rather, there is an indicator in the shift in person, which "... must be deduced from the surrounding context."[7] However, the presence of the complex speaker unifies both voice and intention. Additional voices present themselves, as well, particularly in Jeremiah 4.5-6.30.[8] These are the subject of the chapter 6. Conceptual scoping is summarised in the following set of diagrams, which recapitulate the viewing arrangements introduced to this point in the cognitive network:

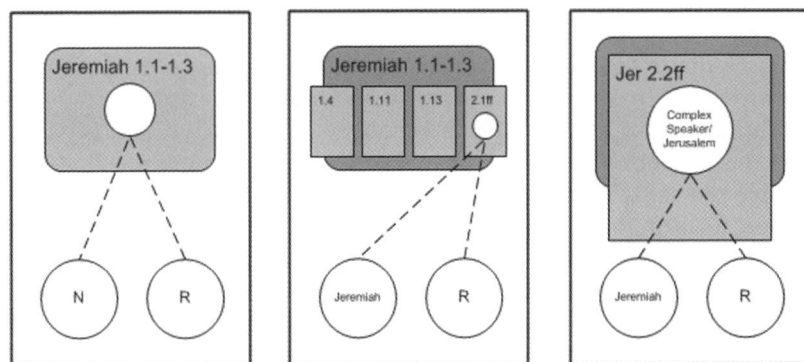

a. Narrator's P: N¹   b. Character's P: N²   c. Complex Speaker: N³

Figure 5.2 Summary of Viewing Arrangements in Jeremiah 1.1-3.25

---

7   Parunak, "Some Discourse Functions of Prophetic Quotation Formulas in Jeremiah," 502.

8   O'Conner describes this as a colloquy of voices. K. M. O'Connor, "Jeremiah," in *The Oxford Bible Commentary*, eds John Barton and John Muddiman (Oxford: OUP, 2000), 487-528 (487).

The use of quotative frames and the report of speech situations between human and divine in Jeremiah 1.1-2.2ff is an example of conversion to human scale. This construal of the situation is particularly effective because, according to Fauconnier, conversion to human scale is the overarching goal of conceptual integration. Fauconnier reasons, "Human beings are evolved and culturally supported to deal with reality at human scale – that is, through direct action and perception inside familiar frames, typically involving few participants and direct intentionality."[9] The inclination to deal with reality at human scale is an essential goal of integration, which is a primary topic in conceptual blending theory. Fauconnier notes:

> The impulse to achieve integrated blends is an overarching principle of human cognition… Since the essence of a conceptual integration network is to project from many different and sometimes clashing inputs into a single blended space, integration in that space is a considerable achievement, not something implicit in the inputs. Integration in the blended space allows its manipulation as a unit, makes it more memorable, and enables the thinker to run the blend without constant reference to the other spaces in the network. Integration helps bring the blend to human scale, and thereby also increase (sic) the possibility for further useful recruitments to the blend from a range of our knowledge that is already at that human scale.[10]

Conceptual blending theory describes how information from various input spaces contributes toward the formation of a blended space. Blending theory was introduced in chapter 3 as it applies to grammar. It will be discussed further in section B.4 as is applies to the interrelationship between conceptual metaphor and literary metaphor.

Conversion to human scale is a matter of perspective, and is based upon the animacy hierarchy. Consequently, this volume posits that it is possible to evaluate the perspective in a given situation based upon its relation to human scale. The perspective in situations that express a one-to-one correspondence to normal scale (such as two human beings involved in a conversation) might be termed *iconic*, while the perspective in situations moving away from a one-to-one correspondence to normal scale (such as a conversation between a human and an animal, or a human and the deity) might be termed *non-iconic*.[11]

---

9   Fauconnier and Turner, *The Way We Think*, 322.
10   Ibid., 328-329.
11   In this case, the term *iconic* is used as a descriptive, heuristic term rather than as a technical linguistic term. There is an affinity between this use of iconic and the term *prototypical*. However, neither formal theory is being invoked here.

iconic perspective   *non-iconic perspective*

Figure 5.3 Iconicity Scale

Factors used in determining the degree to which a situation is non-iconic include the degree to which entities and relations resemble their normal-scale counterparts.[12] In the case of Jeremiah 1.1-2.2ff, situations vacillate along the scale of iconicity. For example, by 2.2, three main interlocutors have been introduced: Jeremiah, Yahweh and Jerusalem as addressee. Because Jeremiah and Yahweh are conjoined as a complex speaker, a speaker with one voice, but two perspectives the interaction that follows in Jeremiah 2.3-6.30 occurs between the complex speaker and Jerusalem. Whereas the situation in 1.1-1.3 occurs toward the normal or iconic end of the scale, this situation is moving towards the non-iconic end of the scale. Jeremiah 1.1-6.30 vacillates between iconic and non-iconic representation of situations. Situations located at the non-iconic end of the scale include speech frames that include the complex speaker and sections that mention Israel and Daughter Zion. Situations located nearer the iconic end of the scale include Jeremiah's direct address to Jerusalem and sections that refer to the House of Israel and the House of Judah. However, due to the fact the Jeremiah and Yahweh share the voice of the complex speaker, the text of Jeremiah 1.4-6.30 never reaches the limits of the iconic end of the scale. It is conceptually significant that three entities from various points on the Extended Great Chain hierarchy are included in a common situation of speaking. When society and the divine participate in conversation, which is a human level activity, the originator is using an element from one level in the Great Chain to understand elements from other levels, thus creating an instantiation of cognitive metaphor. Thus, Jeremiah 1.1-2.2ff represents scoping to human scale: the originator of the text portrays society and the divine in non-iconic, human terms in order to create understanding of these abstract concepts. The following series of examples will elaborate upon these points.

---

12 Definiteness is another parameter that contributes to evaluation of iconicity. Regarding definiteness in BH, see Kirk Lowery, "Relative Definiteness and the Verbless Clause," in *The Verbless Clause in Biblical Hebrew: Linguistic Approaches*, ed. Cynthia L. Miller (Winona Lake, Indiana: Eisenbrauns, 1999), 251-272; E. J. van Wolde, "The Verbless Clause and Its Textual Function," in *The Verbless Clause in Biblical Hebrew* (Winona Lake, Ind: Eisenbrauns, 1999), 321-335.

B. Jeremiah 2.1-2.3: Transition to Complex Speaker

Jeremiah 2.1-2.3 is a pivotal section that functions both as a link between the previous discourse spaces and as the base space for additional cognitive construction.[13] This will be demonstrated by the
following TD analysis.

Clause Layout	JER
וַיְהִי דְבַר־יְהוָה אֵלַי	2.1a
לֵאמֹר	b
הָלֹךְ וְקָרָאתָ בְאָזְנֵי יְרוּשָׁלַם	2.2a
לֵאמֹר	b
כֹּה אָמַר יְהוָה	c
זָכַרְתִּי לָךְ חֶסֶד נְעוּרַיִךְ	d
אַהֲבַת כְּלוּלֹתָיִךְ	e
לֶכְתֵּךְ אַחֲרַי בַּמִּדְבָּר	f
בְּאֶרֶץ לֹא זְרוּעָה	g
קֹדֶשׁ יִשְׂרָאֵל לַיהוָה	2.3a
רֵאשִׁית תְּבוּאָתֹה	b
כָּל־אֹכְלָיו יֶאְשָׁמוּ	c
רָעָה תָּבֹא אֲלֵיהֶם	d
נְאֻם־יְהוָה	e

Figure 5.4 Jeremiah 2.1-2.3 Clause Layout

---

13 At this point, it becomes apparent that the cognitive construction in the final form of
the MT is at variance with that of the LXX. As Carroll notes, the LXX does not contain 2.1a, b, or 2.2a. Rather it reads "…and he said, Thus says Yahweh." Carroll
claims that "the formulaic introduction is typical of the late redaction of the tradition
(lacking in G) and reflects a concern with establishing the source of the speaker's
statements as well as indicating divine instructions for the speaker's movements."
Carroll, *Jeremiah: A Commentary*, 119.

JER	Type	Clause Tag	PNG	Stem/ Focus	MSC
2.1a	N	*Wayyiqtol-S*	3sgM	Pred	Base VP=N^2
b	N	Qetol			SB
2.2a	NQ	Qatol *W-Qatal*	2sgM	Pred	VP=C^2
b	NQ	Qetol			
c	NQQ	*X-Qatal*	3sgM	Pred	SB
d	NQQP	*Qatal*	1sg	Pred	VP=N^3 (C^1)
e	NQQP	Ellip			VP=C^1
f	NQQP	Qetol		(2sgF)	
g	NQQP	PreP	sgF		
2.3a	NQQP	NmCl		Sent	
b	NQQP	Ellip			
c	NQQP	*X-Yiqtol*	3plM	Sent	
d	NQQP	*X-Yiqtol*	3sgF	Sent	
e	N	Focus			VP=N^2

Figure 5.5 Jeremiah 2.1-2.3 Clause Analysis

In this diagram the terms C^1 and C^2 are introduced, where C indicates a character's viewpoint within a mental space and the superscript numeral indicates the identity of the character. For this diagram, C^1 indicates Yahweh and C^2 indicates Jeremiah. The term SB indicates the space building term or construction that opens the following mental space.

1.   Syntax, Semantics and Information Structure

a.   Jeremiah 2.1a-2.2c

The clause hierarchy layout for the series of verbal forms in 2.1a-2.2c is as follows:

2.1   a) N $\boxed{wayyiqtol\text{-}S}$ +
      b) N   qetol לֵאמֹר = metapragmatic expression
2.2   a) NQ   qatol הָלֹךְ, $\boxed{w\text{-}qatal}$ קְרָא +
      b) NQ   qetol לֵאמֹר = marked construction
      c) NQQ $\boxed{x\text{-}qatal}$ – single verb, אָמֹר =
                                    unmarked

The three main clauses in Jeremiah 2.1-2.2 form a hierarchy at the syntactic, semantic and pragmatic levels. Syntactically, the main clause hierarchy is *wayyiqtol, W-qatal* and *X-qatal*. The term לֵאמֹר in the first two clauses functions as a grammaticalized complementiser. The term introduces complement clauses that fully join within the main clause.[14] At 2.2a the infinitive absolute joins with the *qatal* form at an equal level due to parataxis.[15] The constituent order in the four clauses is VSO; V/VO; X-VSO, indicating predicate focus in each. This is consistent with providing background information.

The syntactic constructions in Jeremiah 2.1, 2.2 and 2.2c contribute to the discourse pragmatics of the hierarchy. This argument is based upon Miller's discussion of markedness in quotative frames.[16] Miller proposes that three types of quotative frames may be hierarchically ordered with respect to markedness.[17] The first opposition is between single verb frames, such as 2.2c, and complex (multiple verb) frames, in

---

14   An infinitive clause connects directly to the preceding clause. van der Merwe and Talstra, "Interface," 87.

15   There is no hierarchical downgrading between the two verbal forms. Lehmann, "Towards a Typology of Clause Linkage," 184.

16   See chapter 2, section C.2 for a discussion of markedness and focus types. The basic idea regarding markedness is that "markedness is concerned with the distinction between what is neutral, natural, or expected" and "what departs from the neutral along some specific parameter." What is neutral, natural and expected is termed unmarked, while what departs from neutral is termed marked. Additionally, it has been demonstrated that "markedness asymmetries have been shown to hold not only for binary systems, but also for larger sets of elements, yielding markedness hierarchies." H. Bussman, Dictionary, 294. This understanding of markedness underlies Miller's linguistic analysis of reported speech as well.

17   Miller, *Representation*.

which the matrix verb is mediated by a finite form of אמר. The first are unmarked and the second is marked. [18] The second opposition is between two types of complex frames. In this opposition, a multiple verb frame mediated by a finite form of אמר is unmarked, whereas a frame without a finite form of אמר but containing לאמר, such as 2.1 or 2.2, is marked. Significantly, unmarked multiple verb frames often represent a prototypical dialogic situation, while לאמר frames "allow for the the indexing of non-dialogic features within the frame, within the quotation, or within the adjacency pair."[19]

Jeremiah 2.1a-b contains the expression ויה דבר־יהוה אלי לאמר. Word order for this clause is VSO, indicating predicate focus. The sentence answers the question "What did דבר־יהוה do?" The question presupposes that something occurred involving the activated topical entity, דבר־יהוה. This clause is a metapragmatic phrasal expression that indexes a marked, non-dialogic quotation. This speech situation reflects elements at odds with a prototypical communication event: the speech participants are neither face-to-face, nor in the same physical location. While this expression opens another speech domain, this domain is structured differently than the previous three domains. The communication situations in the previous three speech domains (1.4; 1.11 and 1.13) exhibit dialogic turn-taking, while this expression gives way to a second לאמר frame at 2.2.

Jeremiah 2.2a-b, הלך וקראת באזני ירושלם לאמר, contains a second לאמר quotative frame. This statement indexes a marked, non-dialogic quotation in which Jerusalem is identified as the addressee for the following information. Word order in this clause is V/VO, indicating predicate focus.[20] The sentence answers the question "What was J to do?"

---

18   Miller explains that the opposition between marked and unmarked terms is privative, rather than equipollent, stating "A privative opposition involves an unmarked member, which includes all of the range of a phenomenon, and a marked member, which specifies a subset of the phenomenon…by contrast, an equipollent opposition involves two members that are opposites. Neither member is more central than the other; the presence of one member signals the opposite of the other member. An equipollent opposition, then, is symmetrical. By contrast, a privative opposition is asymmetrical, and most oppositions in language are privative." Ibid., 427.

19   "Within the frame, the speakers may be choral, unidentified, props, or displaced… the addressees may be unspecified or unidentified. Within the quotation non-dialogic features include quotations that are semi-direct, retold, iterative, hypothetical, or fabricated. In addition, the quotation introduced with lemor may exhibit pronominal reference indicating that the principal and the animator are distributed between two individuals." Ibid., 394.

20   In this case, the infinitive absolute acts as an imperative form (it is asyndetic and begins its clause), which increases the force of the statement. For the imperative function of the infinitive absolute, see J. H. Hospers, "Some Remarks About the So-Called Imperative Use of the Infinitive Absolute (Infinitivus Pro Imperativo) in Clas-

This question presupposes that the activated topical entity, the implied *you*, will do something, presumably in response to the direct instruction to do so.

Jeremiah 2.2c consists of the citation formula כה אמר יהוה. This phrase is unmarked, thus the quotation may or may not be prototypically dialogic. Word order for this clause is X-VS, again indicating predicate focus. In this clause, X represents the particle כה, which functions as a cataphoric discourse marker directing the reader to the following quotation. Taken together, the three clauses are instantiations of Miller's markedness hierarchy, and occur in decreasing order of markedness, as follows:

2.1a. metapragmatic phrasal expression + לאמר: marked in 2nd opposition

2.2a. קרא + לאמר: marked in 1st opposition

2.2c. conjugated אמר: unmarked in 1st opposition

Significantly, the identity of the subject shifts in each clause, disrupting the coherence of the passage.[21] In the first clause, the explicit subject is דבר־יהוה. The speaker in this clause is Jeremiah as narrator, and the addressee is the assumed reader. In the second clause the subject is the implied "you", Jeremiah. The implied speaker is Yahweh and the implied "you", Jeremiah, is the addressee. In the third clause, the explicit subject is Yahweh, who is the speaker. Meanwhile Jeremiah continues as addressee. All three are primary topical entities, and all three are discourse activated in 1.1-1.19.

---

sical Hebrew," in *Studies in Hebrew and Aramaic Syntax*, ed. K. Jongeling (Leiden: Brill, 1991); Waltke and O'Connor, *An Introduction to Biblical Hebrew Syntax*, § 35.35.31.

21   According to Givon, coherence is determined by an amalgamation of participant (topic) continuity, temporal continuity, spatial continuity and action (theme continuity). This is reflected in Khan's definition of a discourse span as a "stretch of text with some kind of uniformity". With regard to kinds of uniformity, Khan distinguishes between *topic-span* and *theme-span*. A topic span is a span of discourse delineated by topic continuity. A topic span may function at the level of a primary topic, and may also incorporate a secondary topic span, based upon the presence of a secondary topic. A theme span is based upon a series of actions based upon a single semantic domain. This understanding of coherence is supported by the cognitive grammar definitions of *thing* and *relation*. Coherence, discourse span and the differentiation between *thing* and *relation* all may be viewed as a direct result of the manner in which the human brain processes various inputs: the Werneke's area of the brain is responsible for "assigning to and retrieving meaning (concepts) from signs that refer to discrete entities." On the other hand, the Broca's area is responsible for "concepts referring to types of situations and actions." T. Givon, "Beyond Foreground and Background," in *Coherence and Grounding in Discourse*, ed. R. S. Tomlin (Amsterdam: John Benjamins, 1987); Khan, *Studies*, xxxv; Raible, "Language Universals and Language Typology," 13.

The introduction of Jerusalem as the future addressee is an important addition at this point. The prepositional phrase in 2.2a mentioned Jeremiah, which activated the entity for the following discourse section. Additionally, the complex speaker is discourse-activated as well. Prior to this point, Jeremiah and Yahweh were in dialogue with one another: now, together, they address Jerusalem.

b.   Jeremiah 2.2d-2.3d

Jeremiah 2.2d-2.3e is a syntactically complex NQQP space. There are only three conjugated verb forms in nine clauses, one *qatal* form at 2.2d and two *X-yiqtol* forms at 2.3c and 2.3d. In this instance the complex speaker exhibits the viewpoint of the explicit speaker, Yahweh. He addresses his audience directly, using the f/s pronominal suffix four times within three clauses (2.2d-f). As noted previously, Jeremiah 2.2a establishes Jerusalem as the addressee to whom Jeremiah is to deliver this speech on behalf of Yahweh. However, the mention of Israel in 2.3a is the first indication that the identity of the addressees may not be as clear-cut as would first appear. This raises the question of identity, which is the subject of section E below.

The final element in this section is the term נאם־יהוה. While various scholars have proposed no less than eight functions for this term, Parunak's argument that it is a focus marker is persuasive.[22] Parunak notes that the phrase indicates "a highly local highlighting of a clause or phrase that merits the recipients' special attention."[23] In this case, the term highlights the unfortunate consequences for any who would harm Israel in the early days of the nation. This sets up a positive situation that provides the background for the great contrast to come.

2.   Cognitive Construction

At Jeremiah 2.1, three distinct quotative frames act as space-builders for the fourth speech domain. The first, Jeremiah 2.1, is a repetition of the metapragmatic phrasal expression ויהי דבר־יהוה אלי לאמר, which functions as a link to the previous three speech domains. The second, Jeremiah 2.2a, simultaneously introduces the following quotation and iden-

---

22   For a full explanation of focus particles, see Ekkehard König, *The Meaning of Focus Particles: A Comparative Perspective*, Theoretical Linguistics (London: Routledge, 1991).

23   Parunak, "Some Discourse Functions of Prophetic Quotation Formulas in Jeremiah," 571.

tifies the three main interlocutors for the following section: Yahweh, Jeremiah and Jerusalem. In Jeremiah 2.2a, is Yahweh the implied speaker, while Jeremiah is the direct addressee and Jerusalem is activated as Jeremiah's future addressee. Notably, the interlocutors make their appearance in the text in order of importance indicated by the animacy hierarchy: SAP 1, SAP 2 and SAP 3; or C^1, C^2 and C^3. The three entities occur together within a speech act situation, introducing this as an instantiation of conceptual metaphor as well (see section B, above). Finally, the third quotative frame, Jeremiah 2.2c, introduces the quotation that Jeremiah is intended to present to Jerusalem. Cumulatively, the three statements contribute to the identification of Jeremiah and Yahweh as a complex speaker at 2.2d. At this point Jeremiah is to begin speaking for Yahweh in his address to Jerusalem. As a result, Jeremiah's words carry a force beyond that of an ordinary human. Although Jeremiah remains very human, his speech now carries the force of divine speech. In this way, the unified speaking voices contribute to the unity of the section, and to the book as a whole.

Jeremiah 2.1-2.3 is an example of scoping to human scale. All three speech-act participants, Jeremiah, Jerusalem and Yahweh, appear at human scale, highlighting the non-iconic nature of this section of text. In this way, the speech-act frame contributes to the unity of the section. The fourth speech domain appears against the backdrop of Jeremiah 1.1-1.3 in the following diagram:

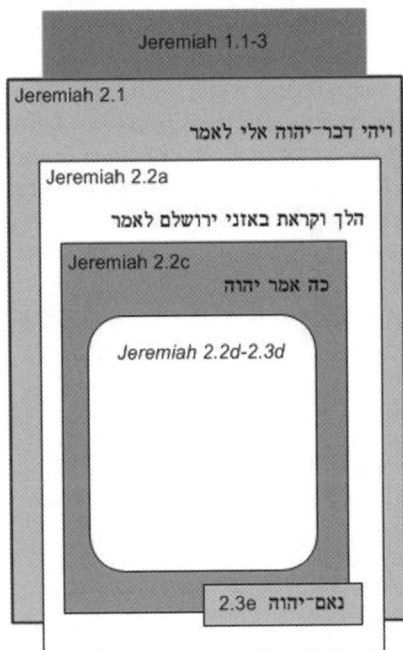

Figure 5.6 Cognitive Construction in Jeremiah 2.1-2.3

3. Conceptual Metaphor

The phrase זכרתי לך חסד נעוריך initiates the *P* space at Jeremiah 2.2d. The phrase contains the mental-states predicate זכרתי, and the first person reference invokes the perspective of the speaker, Yahweh. Since the embedded space belongs to the character, Yahweh, the reader has access to the internal thought world of the divine. This insider view includes his fond remembrance of the relationship he shared with his people at the inception of the nation (2.2d), the holy status of the nation, Israel, and his protective stance towards the nation (2.3a-d). Two significant conceptual networks or blended spaces structure this section: the Bride, and First Fruits. An examination of these spaces will demonstrate their relationship between literary metaphor and cognitive construction.

4.   Literary Metaphor and Conceptual Metaphor

Fauconnier and Turner's recent work in the area of conceptual blending theory brings clarity to the crucial differences between literary metaphor and conceptual metaphor. According to conceptual blending theory, the literary metaphors in Jeremiah 2.2c-2.3 represent conceptual networks or many-space blends. Such blends incorporate information from the source and target inputs of one or more conceptual metaphors, as well as information from frames, ICMs and image schemata. Thus, the relationship between a literary metaphor and a conceptual metaphor is not one to one, but rather, one to many. Likewise, a single conceptual metaphor may structure various literary metaphors, bringing a covert unity to a passage. For example, the literary metaphors in Jeremiah 2.2-2.3, the Bride and First Fruits, share the conceptual metaphor SOCIETY IS A PERSON. In each instance, the source domain, HUMAN, gives clarity to the target domain, SOCIETY. The two uses differ only in gender, a feature that sets up two ways of discussing the same society.[24] Importantly, society in both guises is held responsible for unfaithfulness.

The Bride blend comprises a pair of conceptual metaphors: SOCIETY IS A PERSON and LOVE IS A JOURNEY. First Fruits comprises three cognitive metaphors: SOCIETY IS A PERSON; PEOPLE ARE PLANTS; and SOCIAL ORGANISATIONS ARE PLANTS. These conceptual metaphors exert a controlling influence upon Jeremiah 2.2-6.30 and provide the conceptual background for several literary metaphors both within this section and throughout the remainder of the book.[25] Thus, these conceptual metaphors act as a unifying factor for this section of text.

For Kövecses the SOCIETY IS A PERSON and SOCIAL ORGANISATIONS ARE PLANTS metaphors are instantiations of ABSTRACT COMPLEX SYSTEMS metaphors. Abstract complex systems are entities that occur above the level of humans in the Extended Great Chain: society, the cosmos and

---

24   This covert unity undergirds O'Connor's assertion that the marriage metaphor is an organisational, or root metaphor in the book of Jeremiah. As an organisational metaphor, the marriage metaphor allows Jeremiah to address society either as a female, i.e. Judah and Jerusalem; or as a male, i.e. Israel. She notes the differences in grammatical form that characterise the different sections: f/s suffixes are present at 2.2; 2.17-25; and 2.33-3.5, while m/s and m/p suffixes are present at 2.3; 2.4-16; and 2.26-32. O'Connor, "Jeremiah," 491. The bifurcation between female and male representations of society is problematic for feminist interpretation. See A. R. Diamond and K. M. O'Connor, "Unfaithful Passions: Coding Women Coding Men in Jeremiah 2 - 3 (4.2)," in *Troubling Jeremiah*, eds A. R. Diamond et al. (Sheffield: Sheffield Academic Press, 1999), 123-145.

25   See Jeremiah 2.14-15; 2.20-21; 3.1-2; 3.6-11; 4.30-31; 5.10; 6.2; 6.9; 6.14. Some of these examples will be discussed in the following sections.

God. Additionally, abstract complex systems are characterised as "abstract configurations of entities," such as the mind, economic systems, social organisations, relationships and society. Four main metaphors result:

1. An abstract complex system is the human body;

2. an abstract complex system is a building;

3. an abstract complex system is a machine; and

4. an abstract complex system is a plant.

Kövecses notes that the complex systems elicit four major concerns:

1. Do they function effectively?

2. Are they long-lasting and stable?

3. Are they developing as they should?

4. Are they in appropriate condition? [26]

The society is a person metaphor is a manifestation of the metaphor that refers in particular to the body of the person. The metaphor has a double focus: first upon the appropriateness of the condition of the abstract system, and secondly upon the structure of the abstract system. The focus on condition contributes to the simple metaphor an appropriate condition is a healty condition and its converse, an inappropriate condition is an unhealty condition. The second focus contributes to the simple metaphor the structure of an abstract complex system is the physical structure of the human body.[27] Thus, the SOCIETY IS A PERSON metaphor presents material relevant to the condition of the society. The focus of the SOCIAL ORGANISATIONS ARE PLANTS metaphor is upon the growth and development of the social organisation. The choice of metaphor reflects the originator's concern both with the condition of society and with its growth and development. There is a strong connection between the choice of these metaphors and Jeremiah's commission to pluck up and to pull down; to destroy and to over throw; and to build and to plant.

a.   The Bride

Jeremiah 2.2d-g is a deceptively simple statement on the part of Yahweh. However, the four short phrases evoke a tremendous amount of information that is foundational for the following sections of text.

---

26   Kövecses, *Metaphor: A Practical Introduction*, 127.

27   The second metaphor occurs frequently in the New Testament writings. For example, see I Corinthians 12.12-27.

Jeremiah 2.2d-g

זכרתי לך חסד נעוריך
אהבת כלולתיך
לכתך אחרי במדבר
בארץ לא זרועה

The Bride is a blended space, or cognitive network comprising the source and target inputs found in the SOCIETY IS A PERSON conceptual metaphor and the source and target domains found in the LOVE IS A JOURNEY conceptual metaphor. It involves conceptual blending of several input spaces, rather than the two-space model involved in a single conceptual metaphor. Elements from the SOCIETY IS A PERSON metaphor allow for the conceptualisation of the entire society as an individual person. This is an instance of scoping to human scale, and it allows the reader to conceptualise the whole of society as a singular bride. Society, the bride, is now available as a participant in the LOVE IS A JOURNEY metaphor. Basic mappings are available for the LOVE IS A JOURNEY metaphor.[28] These include:

Source: journey		*Target*: love
the travellers	>	the lovers
the vehicle	>	the love relationship
the journey	>	events in the relationship
the distance covered	>	the progress made
the obstacles encountered	>	difficulties experienced
decisions about direction	>	choices about what to do
the destination of the journey	>	goal of the relationship

Jeremiah 2.2d-g includes the lovers as travellers and the initial stage of travel in the wilderness as the journey, which may allude to the Exodus period. There is no mention of events in the relationship, progress, difficulties, choices or goal; only the first flush of married love. However, the journey metaphor is well entrenched as frame knowledge, based upon the path schema. The path schema involves physical or metaphorical movement from place to place and normally comprises a starting point, a goal and intermediate points.[29] Thus, a mention of a single part of the journey will activate the entire frame. In this case, the initial phase of the journey is in view, setting up an expectation that the re-

---

28 Kövecses, *Metaphor: A Practical Introduction*, 6-7.
29 Johnson, *The Body in the Mind: The Bodily Basis of Meaning, Imagination, and Reason*, 115.

mainder of the journey is to follow. The journey from Egypt to Canaan is an instantiation of the path schema that recurs when recounting the events in the life of the nation, Israel. This is often paired with the idea that being *in* or *out* of Canaan is a measure of God's approval of his people, which is an instantiation of the containment schema. These two schemata act as covert unifying devices, both in their original contexts and in the contexts in which they later appear.

b.   First Fruits

Jeremiah 2.3 presents Israel as the first fruits of the harvest of Yahweh. Again, the originator compresses a tremendous amount of information into a few short comments.

Jeremiah 2.3

קדש ישראל ליהוה
ראשית תבואתה
כל־אכליו יאשמו
רעה תבא אליהם

First Fruits is a blended space, comprising the source and target domains of three conceptual metaphors: SOCIETY IS A PERSON; PEOPLE ARE PLANTS; and SOCIAL ORGANISATIONS ARE PLANTS.[30] Israel appears in the singular, again scoping the entire society to human scale via the SOCIETY IS A PERSON metaphor. Once this move is accomplished, Israel may be mapped as a person within the target domain in the PEOPLE ARE PLANTS metaphor. The characteristics of plants are then available as the source domain for understanding humans. The source domains in each of the first two metaphors each utilise an entity that is a single step lower on the Extended Great Chain than the entity utilised in the target domain.

The third metaphor, SOCIAL ORGANISATIONS ARE PLANTS, uses an entity in the source domain (plants) that is two steps lower than the entity in the target domain (society). Basic mappings for the SOCIAL ORGANISATIONS ARE PLANTS metaphor are:

---

30   For a full discussion see Kövecses, *Metaphor: A Practical Introduction*, 8-9.

Source: plant		*Target*: social organisations
The whole plant	>	the entire organisation
A part of the plant	>	a part of the organisation
Growth of the plant	>	growth of organisation
Removing a part of the plant	>	reducing organisation
The root of the plant	>	origin of the organisation
The flowering	>	the most successful stage
The fruits or crops	>	beneficial consequences

Jeremiah 2.3 introduces only the idea of the first fruits, the fruit or crops that map to the *beneficial consequences*. Israel was holy and set apart, and due to this relationship, Israel enjoyed the protection of Yahweh. The conceptual metaphors used in the Bride and the First Fruits blends recur throughout Jeremiah 2.1-6.30 and provide the conceptual backdrop for much of this section of text. The conceptual backdrop has been set for what follows, and what follows is a contrast, indeed. The same pair of metaphors recurs at 2.20-2.21, but from a very negative perspective: the bride has become a loose woman, and the choice vine which Yahweh had planted has become wild. Other references to the settled nation as a vine occur at Jeremiah 5.10 (feminine reference) and Jeremiah 6.9 (masculine reference to Israel) [31]

5.   The Addressees and the Problem of Identity

One issue to be resolved with regard to the addressees is the problem of identity (see full discussion on page 178). While the MT is fairly clear that Jeremiah is to address Jerusalem, the presence of references to Israel and Jacob has caused some to posit that Jeremiah's earliest preaching included addresses to the North.[32] For example, Albertz notes that terms referring to Israel, the House of Israel, the Israelites and the House of Jacob are prevalent in Jeremiah 2.4-4.2, whereas terms referring to Jerusalem, Zion, the Daughter of Zion, Judah and the

---

31   Robert Carroll observes that the force of the images in this section, including the images of loyalty, love, fruitfulness and protection, is derived from the contrast with the following material, which includes references to disloyalty, misplaced love, fruitlessness and lack of protection. Carroll, *Jeremiah: A Commentary*, 119.

32   This situation also militates against utilising the computation of cumulative referential density tool that was so effective in analysing the frequency and distribution of entities in Jeremiah 1.1-2.2 (see Figure 4.8).

House of Judah are prevalent in Jeremiah 4.3-6.30. Regarding this division, Albertz states:

> Nur die Teilsammlung 2.4-4.2 (ohne 3.6-18) gehört die Frühzeit Jeremias (627-609) an. Es handelt sich um Unheils- und Heilsprophetie an die Bewohner des ehemaligen Nordreichs...4.3-6.30 is eine Sammlung von Unheilsworten gegen Juda an der Zeit nach 609, wahrscheinlich bis zur Aufzeichnung der Urrolle 605/4.[33]

Albertz concludes that this division resolves a series of terminological, functional and chronological problems in Jeremiah 2-6. Given the composite nature of the book of Jeremiah, it is entirely possible that the two sections represent early disaster and salvation preaching to former inhabitants of the North that was repeated to the inhabitants of Judah later.

However, given the previous discussion of perspective in Jeremiah 2.1ff, it becomes apparent that in the final form of the text, both sections of material function as the words of the complex speaker to Jerusalem, who appears as the addressee in 2.2a. In this section the perspective belongs to Yahweh. Thus, while it is entirely possible that Jeremiah may have addressed some of the remnant of the Northern Kingdom, the text-space of the MT supports Jerusalem as the main addressee. The issue of addressee identity plays an important role in the following discussion.

C. Jeremiah 2.4-2.9: Visual Scanning

1. Scoping from Human Scale

While the examples discussed above presented speech frames and conceptual metaphors that involve scoping *to* human scale, the virtual visual scanning in Jeremiah 2.10 provides an example of scoping *from* human scale. Scoping from human scale requires both a localised human experiencer as an anchor point and identifiable points along a physical and/or metaphorical trajectory. In the case of Jeremiah 2.10, establishing the identity of the localised human experiencer is of primary importance. The references to Cyprus and Kedar may be calculated accurately only when this is understood. Again, this is a matter of perspective. In order to identify the localised human experiencer in

---

33 Rainer Albertz, „Jer. 2-6 und die Frühzeitverkündigung Jeremias," *ZAW* 94 (1982), 47.

Jeremiah 2.10, it first is necessary to account for participant reference and perspective in Jeremiah 2.4-2.9.

The terminological difficulties mentioned in section B.5 above are evident in the phrase שמעו דבר־יהוה בית יעקב וכל־משפחות בית ישראל, Jeremiah 2.4, in which the term דבר־יהוה links the present space to Jeremiah 1.2a. Two questions now arise. First, to whom does the perspective in this clause belong? Second, how are the references to the house of Jacob and the house of Israel to be reconciled with the identity of the addressee as Jerusalem in Jeremiah 2.2a? Since this section is a continuation of N³, examining the configuration of participants in the mental spaces construction tagged N³ clarifies the issue of perspective within the clause. Participants in N³ include Jeremiah and Yahweh as complex-speaker and Jerusalem as addressee (see Figure 5.1). Since the section is also at the NQQ level of embedding, it is possible to account for the verb שמעו as a shift in perspective for the complex speaker. Within the previous section, the explicit perspective belongs to Yahweh, while in the present section the implicit perspective belongs to Jeremiah. Likewise, according to the argument above, when reading the text in its present form the addressee is Jerusalem. Jeremiah addresses the people directly in this instance, so it is possible to construe the situation as more iconic. This is because the individuated addressees and Jeremiah appear within a human scale situation of speaking. (However, since there is a complex speaker involved, the situation is not at the far end of the scale.)

A second feature of Jeremiah 2.4-2.9 also depends upon the localised human experiencer as an anchor point, this time as an anchor point along a time scale. The time scale is an instantiation of the path schema, which includes a path and points along the path. The earliest point on the time scale is Jeremiah 2.5b, מה־מצאו אבותיכם בי עול. This rhetorical question is significant on several counts. Linguistically, it makes the subject *your fathers* discourse-active for the following section of text. It does so by anchoring the term *fathers* to the present addressees by the m/p suffix attached to the noun.[34] Stylistically, it is the first in a series of rhetorical questions that act as a unifying feature for Jeremiah 2.4-16.[35] Theologically, the expected answer is "nothing," which implies that Yahweh had not given the ancestors any reason to distance themselves, nor to run after worthless things. Yahweh declares himself blameless. The time scale moves from past to present in Jeremiah 2.7a, וָאָבִיא אֶתְכֶם אֶל־אֶרֶץ הַכַּרְמֶל, where the 2/pl addressees are the object of the sentence. Finally, the time scale moves from present to future in Jeremiah 2.9, where Yahweh states his intention to contend with both the present addressees and with their children's children.

2. Counterfactuals

A pair of un-asked rhetorical questions introduces the reasons for this contention. The embedding in the first, Jeremiah 2.6a, וְלֹא אָמְרוּ אַיֵּה יְהוָה, belongs to the ancestors. The embedding in the second, Jeremiah 2.8a, הַכֹּהֲנִים לֹא אָמְרוּ אַיֵּה יְהוָה, belongs to the priests, who are a subgroup of the current addressees. The failure to ask the

---

34 This follows the second of Langacker's general principles of structure building, which include:

1) The basic units of structure building are relationships rather than things;

2) When structure is added, it is usually anchored to what has already been built, by virtue of conceptual overlap;

3) Even when covert, the ground is the ultimate anchor for building connected structures; and

4) In a sequence of clauses, the subject has a special status as a point of attachment to what has already been constructed and as a point of access to what is currently being constructed.

Langacker, "Discourse in Cognitive Grammar," 171-173.

35 Carroll views the series of rhetorical questions as the unifying feature in this section of text. O'Connor widens the issue of unity to include "… the unifying effects of root metaphors in poetry and prose, narrative devices, symbolic meanings of events and dates." O'Connor quotes Biddle, who notes that unity comes from the dominance of the divine voice across the book and from the central role given to Jeremiah. These views are compatible with the TD approach. As previously explained, the concern of this volume is to gain an understanding of the text of MT Jeremiah 1.1-6.30 through a cognitively based text analysis. This analysis includes an expanded description of the literary metaphors found in the book by including an explanation of literary metaphor as a conceptual blending process that incorporates conceptual metaphor with knowledge derived from frames, schemas and cognitive models. It also allows for the conceptualisation of Jeremiah and Yahweh as a complex speaker. Mark Biddle, *Polyphony and Symphony in Prophetic Literature: Rereading Jeremiah 7-20* (Macon: Macon University Press, 1996); Carroll, *Jeremiah: A Commentary*, 122; O'Connor, "Jeremiah," 489.

question may be described as a non-event. Other negative statements occur in Jeremiah 2.8: those who handle the law לֹא יְדָעוּנִי; the rulers transgress against; Yahweh and the prophets, who both prophesy by Baal and go after worthless things. While these are negative statements, only the failure to ask "Where is Yahweh?" is a non-event, which is something that should have happened, but did not. Taken together, the subgroups in Jeremiah 2.8 managed to do things they should not have done and *not* to do things they should have done. None is more significant for this discussion than the non-event of the un-asked question,"Where is Yahweh?"

Jeremiah 2.6 and 2.8 claim that the ancestors and the priests did not utter the statement *Where is Yahweh?* Additionally, the ancestors did not ask after Yahweh *who brought us up from Egypt, who led us in the wilderness*, which is an instantiation of the path schema. The situation is different for the present addressees, as Yahweh states, *"I brought you into a plentiful land to eat its fruits and good things, but when you entered you defiled my land,"* which is an instantiation of the containment schema. The unasked rhetorical question, *Where is Yahweh?*, is a conceptual blend that involves the generation of a counterfactual space. To this point in the volume, the described mental spaces network has included a series of interconnected single spaces. However, Fauconnier states, "we use 'counterfactual' to mean that one space has forced incompatibility with another."[36] Therefore, counterfactual constructions are more complex. The description of a counterfactual blend requires a pair of spaces as inputs, and a blended space as well. For Jeremiah 2.6, the actual space, Input 1, contains: a) the ancestors and b) the unasked question. The presence of this non-event results in c) Yahweh's displeasure. This generates Input 2, a counterfactual space that contains: a) the ancestors, b) the event, the asked question, and c) the absence of contention. As a result, the blended space contains the negated possibility that: a) the ancestors, b) might choose to ask the question, and as a consequence, c) Yahweh's displeasure would cease.

---

36 Fauconnier and Turner, *The Way We Think*, 230.

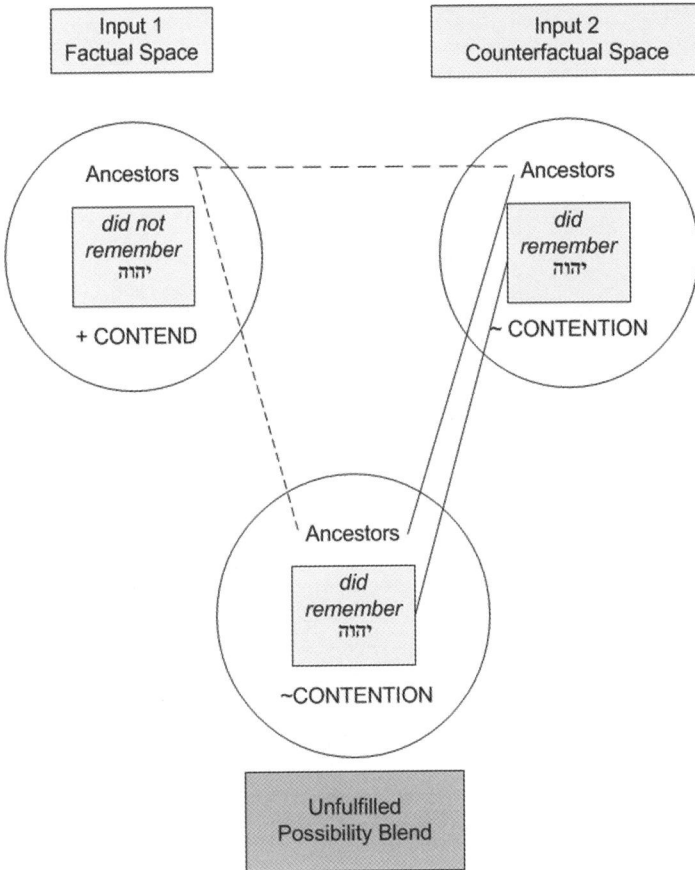

Figure 5.7   Counterfactual 1: Unfufilled Possibility

For Jeremiah 2.8, the actual space, Input 1, contains a) the addressees, b) the non-event of the unasked question, and c) Yahweh's displeasure.[37] This generates Input 2, a counterfactual space that contains a) the addressees, b) the asked question, but c) no contention. As a result, the blended space contains a) the possibility that the addressees might b) choose to ask the question, thus, c) Yahweh's displeasure would cease.

---

37   For a discussion of non-things and non-events in conceptual blending theory, see Ibid., 241-247.

Input 1
Factual Space

Input 2
Counterfactual Space

YOU

Priests
did not ask
יהוה

+ CONTEND

YOU

did
ask
יהוי

~ CONTENTION

YOU

did
ask
יהוה

~CONTENTION

POSSIBILITY
BLEND

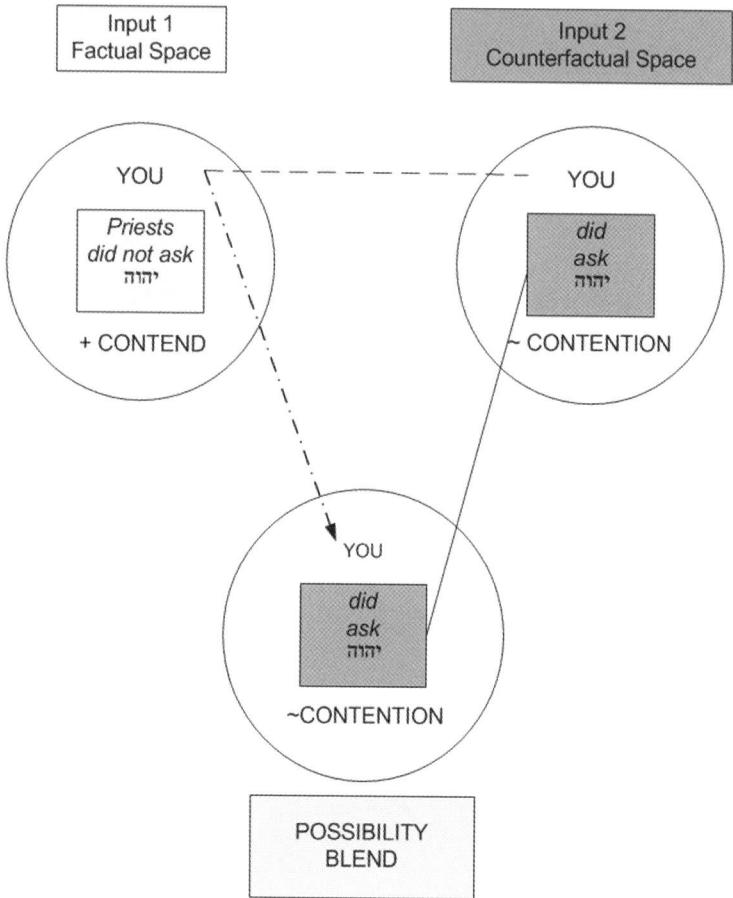

Figure 5.8   Counterfactual 2: Possibility Blend

It now becomes important to establish the significance of the non-event represented by the clause *"Where is Yahweh?"*. Given the references to the land of Egypt (path schema) in Jeremiah 2.6, and the arrival into the plentiful land (containment schema) in Jeremiah 2.8, it is possible to see elements of deuteronomistic thought within these poetic sections. For example, Deuteronomy 6.12 states *"… take care that you do not forget the* LORD, *who brought you out of the land of Egypt, out of the house of slavery"* (NRSV). The description of non-event, forgetting Yahweh, and the event of serving other gods, occurs in many other places as well. Among them are Deuteronomy 8.11-20, which discusses the impor- tance of *not forgetting* to follow Yahweh's commandments, ordinances and statutes and the threat of destruction if they do so, and Deuteronomy 11.13, which discusses the promise of rain and the threat of it being withheld should the people serve other gods. The significance of the un-asked question is its status as a non-event. Not-asking is synonymous with forgetting. The ancestors forgot Yahweh, and the addressees were in the throes of the same *non-event*.

D. Jeremiah 2.10: Visual Scanning

Jeremiah 2.10 follows upon Yahweh's accusations toward the addressees and toward their children's children in 2.9. The addressees are the reference point on a timescale of misbehaviour that began with the ancestors in the wilderness and will continue unless checked. This is in contrast with the idyllic remembrances in 2.2-2.3, a contrast that grows in the following sections of text as attention becomes more and more focused upon the present situation. The clause analysis of Jeremiah 2.10 follows.

Clause Layout	JER
כִּי עִבְרוּ אִיֵּי כִתִּיִּים וּרְאוּ	2.10a
וְקֵדָר שִׁלְחוּ וְהִתְבּוֹנְנוּ מְאֹד	b
וּרְאוּ הֵן הָיְתָה כָּזֹאת	c
הַהֵימִיר גּוֹי אֱלֹהִים	2.11a
וְהֵמָּה לֹא אֱלֹהִים	b
וְעַמִּי הֵמִיר כְּבוֹדוֹ	c
בְּלוֹא יוֹעִיל	d
שֹׁמּוּ שָׁמַיִם עַל־זֹאת	2.12a
וְשַׂעֲרוּ חָרְבוּ מְאֹד	b
נְאֻם־יְהוָה	c

Figure 5.9 Jeremiah 2.10 Clause Layout

JER	Type	Clause Tag	PNG	Stem/Focus	MSC
2.10a	NQQ	X-Impv W-Impv	2plM 2plM	Qal Qal	N³ VP=C²
b	NQQ	W-Impv W-Impv	2plM 2plM	Qal Htpol	
c	NQQ	*W-Impv* *X-Qatal*	2plM 3sgF	Qal Qal	
2.11a	NQQ	*X-Qatal*	3sgM	Hiphil	VP=C¹
b	NQQ	*W-NmCl*			
c	NQQ	*W-S-Qatal*	3sgM	Hiphil	
d	NQQ	*X-Yiqtol*	3sgM	Hiphil	
2.12a	NQQ	Impv	2plM	Qal	
b	NQQ	W-Impv Impv	2plM	Qal Qal	
c	N	NmCl	*Focus*		VP=C²

Figure 5.10   Jeremiah 2.10 Clause Analysis

1.   Syntax, Semantics and Information Structure

The five-fold series of imperative verbs is an outstanding feature in this section. The string of imperatives in Jeremiah 2.10 begins with the term כִּי in Jeremiah 2.10a. This term functions at the text level, connecting this section with the accusations in 2.9.[38] An imperative verb expresses predicate focus. Additionally, attention is upon the addressee rather than speaker. The identity of the speaker must be inferred from the situation of speaking. Because imperative verbs indicate deontic modality, establishing the speaker's identity is of first importance. In this case, the voice is that of the complex speaker. Perspective was assigned to Yahweh in Jeremiah 2.9. However, the mention of the area names וְקֵדָר and כִתִּיִּים may indicate a shift to Jeremiah's perspective for these

---

38 Aejmelaeus describes this function of the term כִּי as an argumentative coordinator. The following series of imperatives are part of a contention frame that begins with the phrase לָכֵן עֹד אָרִיב אִתְּכֶם at 2.9. Anneli Aejmelaeus, "Function and Interpretation of 'Ki' in Biblical Hebrew," *JBL* 105 (1986), 205; Follingstad, "Deictic Viewpoint."

clauses. The force of these verbs is strengthened because, although the words come from Jeremiah's mouth, they originate with the divine.

2. Cognitive Construction

The instructions to cross over to כתיים and to send to קדר are instantiations of the path schema. Jerusalem, the addressee in the text-level situation, provides an anchor point for two paths. The other anchor points for the conceptual trajectories, or paths, are כתיים in northern Arabia on the one hand, and קדר, the islands and coastline of the Mediterranean, on the other. This results in virtual visual scanning of the environment. A second set of perceptual instructions accompanies the instructions to cross over and to send. Not only are the addressees to scan the environment, but also to וראו and והתבוננו, to see and to understand. The first use of the imperative וראו indicates physical perception, but the use of the term והתבוננו, hithpolel of the √בין, indicates the the second use of וראו in Jeremiah 2.10c, וראו הן היתה כזאת, is a metaphorically based extension of its meaning.[39] In this text, the speaker takes the hearers on a virtual tour of the surrounding area in order to establish the basis for the following accusation. This begins with the rhetorical question ההימיר גוי אלהים והמה לא אלהים at 2.11a-b. Virtual visual scanning is an effective rhetorical device, in part because of the manner in which cognitive construction takes place. Damasio speaks of recalled images within the mind. Such images might have their origination in actual perceptual events, or they might take shape during the planning stages of an activity.[40] Never-the-less, the images are available for cognitive activity. Such are the vivid images drawn by Moses to prepare the Israelites for entry into the land. Other examples in Jeremiah 1.1-60 include: 2.18-2.19; 2.23-2.25; 3.2a-d; 3.6ff; 5.1; and 6.1.

E. Jeremiah 2.14-2.15: Image Schemata and Metaphor

At Jeremiah 2.13, the preceding section ends with the declaration of two evils associated with the the people. The first, "… they have forsaken me," is the opposite of the faithful following in Jeremiah 2.2. The second, "… they have dug out cisterns for themselves," implies inade-

---

39   Viberg states "the verbs of perception have a tendency to extend their meaning into the neighboring field of cognition and to cover meanings such as 'know' and 'think'." Viberg, "Verbs of Perception," 1304.

40   Antonio R Damasio, *Descartes' Error* (New York: HarperCollins, 2000), 96-97.

quate self-sufficiency. They have exchanged the un-containable for containers that cannot contain anything. This is transparently an instantiation of the containment schema.

Jeremiah 2.14-15 continues the N³ level, in which the voice of the complex speaker gives way to the perspective of the character Yahweh, who directly addresses the hearers. See the following clause analysis:

Clause Layout	JER
הַעֶבֶד יִשְׂרָאֵל	2.14a
אִם־יְלִיד בַּיִת הוּא	b
מַדּוּעַ הָיָה לָבַז	c
עָלָיו יִשְׁאֲגוּ כְפִרִים	2.15a
נָתְנוּ קוֹלָם	b
וַיָּשִׁיתוּ אַרְצוֹ לְשַׁמָּה	c
עָרָיו *נִצְּתָה **נִצְּתוּ מִבְּלִי יֹשֵׁב	d

Figure 5.11   Jeremiah 2.14-2.15 Clause Layout

JER	Type	Clause Tag	PNG	Stem/ Focus	MSC
2.14a	NQQ	NmCl		interrog	VP=C²
b	NQQ	X-NmCl			
c	NQQ	X-Qatal	3sgM	Qal	
2.15a	NQQ	X-Yiqtol	3plM	Qal	
b	NQQ	Qatal	3pl	Qal	
c	NQQN	Wayyiqtol-0	3plM	Qal	
d	NQQN	X-Qatal	3sgF/ 3pl	Niphal	

Figure 5.12   Jeremiah 2.14-2.15 Clause Analysis

1.   Syntax, Semantics and Information Structure

Jeremiah 2.14 consists of three rhetorical questions: two interrogative nominal clauses and an *X-qatal* clause, in which the *X* is an interrogative particle. The addressees are asked to consider the status of Israel. Jeremiah 2.15a is an *X-yiqtol* clause. The *X* represents the fronted prepositional phrase עליו. Since Israel is a discourse-active topical entity, this clause exhibits argument focus.[41] There is a degree of emphasis here and an increase in the force dynamics of the section.

2.   Cognitive Construction

This short section is rich in image schematic information. The visual image of a group of lions roaring against Israel includes both the path schema, with lions on one side and Israel as a human figure on the other, and the force schema. The force schema is described as physical or metaphorical causal interaction and includes:

- Source and target of the force;

- Direction and intensity of the force;

- Path of motion of the source/target; and

- Sequence of causation[42]

The force schema first appears in the image of the boiling pot in Jeremiah 1.13, and it reappears more and more frequently within Jeremiah 2.1-6.30.

This section also contains an instantiation of the containment schema. As demonstrated in the discussion of Jeremiah1.1-1.3 in chapter 4, section A, geographical features such as the land may be described as a type of container. In this case, the cities are empty of inhabitants. The empty container reappears more and more frequently within Jeremiah 2.1-6.30.

Two conceptual metaphors contribute towards the literary metaphors in Jeremiah 2.14 and 2.15. The first, SOCIETY IS A PERSON, stands behind the term Israel as it did in Jeremiah 2.3. In this case, Israel is compared to a servant who could become the plunder of war. The second, PEOPLE ARE ANIMALS, occurs when the enemies are described as lions, a one-step demotion on the Extended Great Chain. The descrip-

---

41   In other words, it is not fronted for topicalisation.

42   Johnson, *The Body in the Mind: The Bodily Basis of Meaning, Imagination, and Reason*, 42-44.

tion of the enemies as animals also recurs throughout the following section of text.

F. Jeremiah 3.6-3.11/12: Who is "Me"?: The Problem of Identity and the Access Principle[43]

Jeremiah 3.6a, ויאמר יהוה אלי בימי יאשיהו המלך, raises the issue of identity that was touched upon in section B.5, above. At first glance, the sentence appears to be no more than an easily recognisable prophetic citation formula. However, upon closer inspection, one discovers that there is a problem of identity. Just who is the addressee referred to by the first person pronoun, *me*? While both Yahweh and Josiah are mentioned by name, the identity of the first person speaker remains underspecified. Additionally, the speaker's identity is not discernible from the immediately preceding text. This is an important issue on two counts: some view Jeremiah 3.6-11 as a redactional addition, and the section is at the heart of the prose-poetry debate. A key feature of MST, the *Access Principle*, is helpful for confronting the problem of identity.

As previously discussed, MST describes the way that mental spaces, or cognitive packets, are opened, structured and linked in the communication process. Many grammatical devices contribute to this process. Space-builders open new spaces or shift focus to an existing space. Frames, schemas, presuppositional structures such as clefting, tenses and moods, and names and descriptions are used to structure spaces. Grammatical devices such as *transspatial operators*, i.e. the copulative verb *to be*, link spaces.[44] Linking is also a function of the *Access Principle*.

The Access Principle is basic to cognitive construction. As Fauconnier explains, "… an expression that names or describes an element in one mental space can be used to access a counterpart of that element in another mental space." Described in somewhat more technical terms:

> If two elements a and b are linked by a connector F (b=F(a)), then element b can be identified by naming, describing, or pointing to its counterpart a. When this indirect identification procedure is used, we say that the ele-

---

43 See section 2.C.3, for the TD analysis of this section.

44 The Greek predicate nominative construction utilises the copulative verb εἰμί as a transspatial operator, and such constructions are marked in that both arguments are in the nominative case. This construction is used frequently in the book of John, specifically in Jesus' numerous statements of self-identification, such as, Ἐγώ εἰμι ὁ ἄρτος τῆς ζωῆς.

ment named or described, a, is the trigger, and that the element identified, b, is the target.[45]

Fauconnier and Sweetser offer the following example of the type of ambiguity that may be addressed by the indirect identification procedure outlined by the access principle:

In 1952, the man with the gray hair headed the CIA.

This statement raises the question of *when* the man had gray hair. Was it in 1952 or the present? The phrase *the man with the gray hair* may describe an element in the base space. When a new space is set up by the time margin *in 1952*, the element *the man with the gray hair* has a counterpart in the base space. That counterpart might have different properties, such as being young and brown-haired. The *Access Principle* will allow discussion of the counterpart and what he was doing in 1952 through a description of the initial element, the man with the gray hair.[46]

In the same way, the *Access Principle* will allow for indirect identification of the ambiguous *me* in Jeremiah 3.6a by referencing the cognitive structure of the text. By maneuvering between several spaces, it is possible to trace the complex cognitive construction that underlies the presupposition that the speaker, *me*, is Jeremiah.[47] Jeremiah 3.6a opens with the phrase ויאמר יהוה אלי. This phrase is followed by the time margin בימי יאשיהו המלך, *in the days of Josiah the king*. The phrase ויאמר יהוה אלי appears 15 times in the book of Jeremiah, and at this point in the discourse it is well on its way to becoming entrenched.[48] The verb of speaking, ויאמר, indicates that the sentence is an instance of reported speech, with Yahweh as the initiating speaker and the first pair part of an adjacency pair. The underspecified *me*, indicated by the 1sg pronominal suffix, is the second part of the adjacency pair. The sentence serves to introduce material summarised by the following question: הראית אשר עשתה משבה ישראל *Have you seen what Turnable Israel has done?*

---

45   Fauconnier, *Mappings*, 41.

46   Fauconnier and Sweetser, *Spaces, Worlds, and Grammar*, 9-10.

47   The NET Bible disambiguates the identity of the speaker by inserting a vocative into the sentence; *When Josiah was king of Judah, Yahweh said to me, "Jeremiah, you have no doubt seen what wayward Israel did."* www.netbible.com. This translation presents two problems: the addition of the vocative, Jeremiah, and the dilution of the marked force in the following statement. That clause, here presented as a statement, is an interrogative construction in the MT.

48   Of these, 13 instances have a 1sg pronominal suffix (1.7; 1.9; 1.12; 1.14; 3.6; 3.11; 11.6; 11.9; 13.6; 14.11; 14.14; 15.1; 24.3) and two have a 3sM pronominal suffix (9.12; 15.11). Parunak, "Some Discourse Functions of Prophetic Quotation Formulas in Jeremiah," 499.

The TD diagram introduced in Chapter 2 is a mental spaces mapping, and a simplified form of the diagram explains how the *Access Principle* can assist in discovering the identity of *me*.

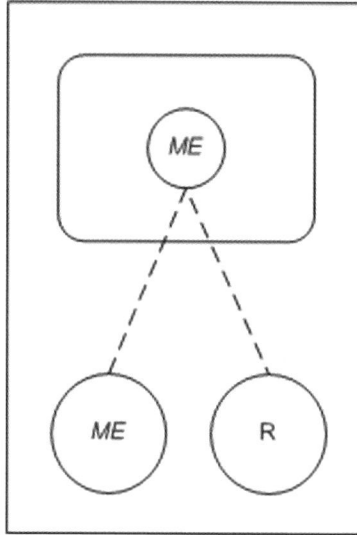

Figure 5.13 The Problem of Identity in Jeremiah 3.6

In this diagram, the phrase אלי יהוה ויאמר, *Yahweh said to me*, is located in the current focus space in the onstage region at the top of the diagram. In this case, the term *me* is identified as the *trigger*. The ambiguous entity, *me*, may be described as the one who communicated directly with Yahweh in the days of Josiah. The term *me* also occupies the originator space at the bottom left of the diagram, because the phrase is presented as first person reported speech.[49] This space is part of the base space for the communication situation that holds between author and reader of the text. In this instance, *me* is identified as the *target*. It is now possible for the reader to discover something about the speaker in the base space by referencing his counterpart in the new space, M, specifically, that the current speaker at text level is also the speaker who communicated with Yahweh in the days of Josiah. Simply stated, the reported speaker is also the reporting speaker. This situation reflects

---

49 Langacker notes, "It is also possible for a facet of the ground to go onstage as the specific focus of attention. i.e. as the expression's profile. This is the case with forms like I, you, here, now." Langacker, "Context, Cognition, and Semantics: A Unified Dynamic Approach."184.

the metapragmatics of reported speech, which is a governing feature of the Jeremiah text. The identity of *me* is someone who had communicated directly with Yahweh in the days of Josiah. By backtracking to Jeremiah 1.1-1.3, it is possible to discover that Jeremiah is the one to whom the word of Yahweh came in the thirteenth year of the reign of Josiah. This relationship develops in 1.4-1.19, a section that consists of reported communication between Yahweh and Jeremiah. It contains four repetitions of the phrase ויאמר יהוה אלי (1.7; 1.9; 1.12; 1.14), which gives further evidence that, *in the text*, Jeremiah is both the reported speaker and the reporting speaker at 3.6a.

Reading the text from a literary perspective strengthens this line of reasoning, as it allows one to ask questions regarding the identity of the speaker at a given point in the text. Van Wolde summarises various possibilities, which include either the narrator as speaker or the character as speaker. The narrator might speak directly to the reader, as a narrative aside; or from his or her own perspective as a story-teller; or indirectly from the perspective of the character. When the character speaks, he or she might speak directly, in which case the quotation is placed in quotation marks, or indirectly.[50] Given this set of options, in Jeremiah 3.6a the narrator is speaking indirectly from the perspective of the character Jeremiah.

This leads to a second instance of the problem of identity: what is the relationship between the character Jeremiah in the text and the historical Jeremiah outside of the text? Are they one and the same? If so, the relationship between the time margin (the days of Josiah) and the speaker (Jeremiah) provides evidence for historical arguments. Looking at the text from an historical perspective, the narrator might be identified as Jeremiah himself. Alternatively, he might be Jeremiah's scribe Baruch, in which case it would be natural for him to document in the first person on Jeremiah's behalf. However, the narrator might be a clever redactor making use of the entrenced phrase ויאמר יהוה אלי and a previously introduced time margin for Jeremiah's reception of the word of Yahweh, in order to insert a section of narrative within the otherwise poetic section of Jeremiah 3.1-3.13.[51]

---

50   Wolde, *Ruth and Naomi*, 146.

51   While historical and redactional issues are not at the forefront of this volume, the findings of the cognitive approach intersect with such concerns at a number of levels. The identity of the speaker and the date of the speech event are two important points of intersection. Reading from a literary perspective allows for a holistic understanding of the text itself, but does not contribute to these issues, whereas analysing the cross-space connections that hold between the cognitive construction cued by the text and those cued by external sources is both desirable and necessary for developing a full understanding of the text. Regarding external sources, Biddle docu-

This short example demonstrates that even the identity of presupposed elements is the product of complex cognitive construction, and that such construction draws from sources such as encyclopedic background knowledge and linguistic constructions that have become entrenched in previous discourse. Establishing and maintaining identity is essential for textual coherence.

G. Jeremiah 3.19-20: Space-building in Poetic Text

The poetic text in Jeremiah 3.19-20 is largely discursive, and also contains several space-building terms. These terms are boxed in the following diagram:

---

ments three strands of interpretation in his study of the redaction history of Jeremiah 2.1-4.2. The first approach differentiates between verse oracle and prose expansion in ordering material chronologically, from Jeremiah's earliest preaching to the composition of the scroll in Jeremiah 36. This approach makes an early appearance in Duhm's 1901 commentary, and Mowinckel's source-critical analysis expanded on Duhm's approach. Mowinckel detected four sources in the Jeremiah text: A, the poetry in chapters 1-25; B, a prose biography; C, collections of sermons; and D, the collection of OANs, with source A being considered authentic by virtue of style. Scholars such as Hitzig, Graf, Ewald, Duhm, Cornhill, Giesbrecht, Mowinckel, Volz, Rudolph and Reitzchels utilise the chronological approach. The second approach examines the text from a rhetorical perspective, looking for rhetorical devices and structures that contribute to the contours of the text. Scholars that take this approach include Lundbom and Holladay. Finally, some scholars, such as Robert Carroll, criticise various chronological conclusions and the reliability of the presuppositions underlying the existence of the *Urrolle*. Mark Biddle, "A Redaction History of Jeremiah 2:1-4:2." (Doctoral Thesis, University of Zürich 1988, Theologischer Verlag, 1989), 1-27. McKane relies upon criteria such as adjacency and contiguity when he determines that exegesis and comment upon the poetry in 3.1-3.5 and 3.12-3.13 generated the prose section in Jeremiah 3.6-11. He cites the use of the divorce theme in 3.1 and the use of the term מְשֻׁבָה יִשְׂרָאֵל at 3.6 and 3.13. William McKane, "Relations between Poetry and Prose in the Book of Jeremiah with Special Reference to Jeremiah iii 6-11 and xii 14-17," in *A Prophet to the Nations: Essays in Jeremiah Studies*, eds L. G. Perdue and B. W. Kovacs (Winona Lake, Ind: Eisenbrauns, 1984), 269-284 (277-278). Sweeney views 3.6-3.11 as redactional. He notes that this material is used to establish an analogy between Israel and Judah, specifically that "the anticipation of Judah's punishment and expectation of Judah's repentance…are based on Israel's experience in 2.2-4.2." Marvin Sweeney, "Structure and Redaction in Jeremiah 2-6," in *Troubling Jeremiah*, ed. A. R. Diamond (Sheffield: Sheffield Academic Press, 1999), 214.

Clause Layout	JER
וְאָנֹכִי אָמַ֫רְתִּי	3.19a
אֵיךְ אֲשִׁיתֵךְ בַּבָּנִים	b
וְאֶתֶּן־לָךְ אֶ֫רֶץ חֶמְדָּה נַחֲלַת צְבִי צִבְא֣וֹת גּוֹיִם	c
וָאֹמַר	d
אָבִי *תִּקְרְאוּ־ **תִּקְרְאִי־לִי	e
וּמֵאַחֲרַי לֹא *תָשׁ֫וּבוּ **תָשׁ֫וּבִי	f
אָכֵן בָּגְדָה אִשָּׁה מֵרֵעָהּ	3.20a
כֵּן בְּגַדְתֶּם בִּי בֵּית יִשְׂרָאֵל	b
נְאֻם־יְהֹוָה	c

Figure 5.14   Space-building in Poetic Text: Clause Layout

JER	Type	Clause Tag	PNG	Stem/Focus	MSC
3.19a	NQ	W-S-Qatal	1sg	Qal	SB
b	NQQP	X-Yiqtol	1sg (2sgF)	Qal	VP=C¹
c	NQQP	W-Yiqtol	1sg	Qal	
d	NQN	Wayyiqtol-0	1sg	Qal	SB
e	NQNQP	X-Yiqtol	2plM (2sgF)	Qal	VP=C¹
f	NQNQ	W-X-Yiqtol	2plM (2sgF)	Qal	
3.20a	NQ	X-Qatal	3sgF	Qal	
b	NQ	X-Qatal	2plM	Qal	
c	NQ	Focus			

Figure 5.15   Space-building in Poetic Text: Clause Analysis

1.   Syntax, Semantics and Information Structure

a.   Jeremiah 3.19a ואנכי אמרתי

This *X-qatal* clause exhibits Subject-Verb word order, and opens a new mental space due to the presence of the term אמרתי. The fronted term ואנכי indicates *argument focus*. In other words the argument (entity) that is fronted is the element that turns the *presupposed proposition* in the clause into a piece of information. In this case, the presupposed proposition is that *"I" spoke*. The answer to the question *"Who spoke?"* is reinforced by the fronted term, the explicit subject ואנכי. The fronted, explicit subject is emphasised, which in turn increases the force dynamics in the section. This first person clause indexes information from the perspective of the speaker, Yahweh. The reader is brought together with Yahweh in the subjective position within the character space. The object of their shared perception is Yahweh's rumination regarding *you*, the ones whom Yahweh desires to treat as offspring. The adverb איך in 19.b is followed by a *yiqtol* verbal form. If the *yiqtol* form is viewed as conveying *imperfective* aspect, this combination reflects a distinctly modal nuance, which is confirmed by the first person perspective in the prior clause. The reader essentially peers over the shoulder of Yahweh as he remembers his fond hopes for Israel, *you* in the interchange. This interchange contains an interesting array of participant referents.

b.   Jeremiah 3.19d ואמר

This *wayyiqtol-0* clause contains no explicit subject. By default it is a *predicate focus clause*, as *wayyiqtol* verbal forms are obligatorily fronted. The clause answers the question *"What did X do?"* The first person speaker is Yahweh, and in this case the term ואמר acts as the mental state predicate *I thought*, which opens a subspace within a previously opened space.

2.   Verbs of Speaking and Cognitive Extension:
The Function of אמר

Several of the previous examples contain a form of √אמר. The text-level deictic sentence in Jeremiah 1.4 consists of the metapragmatic phrasal expression ויהי דבר־יהוה אלי לאמר. In this sentence, לאמר is used as a complementiser, which connects the sentence to what follows. In Jeremiah 1.1-10, conjugated forms of the term אמר are used to open quotation spaces, which are nearly as easy to recognise as their highly marked English counterparts. The quotation spaces are new mental spaces that could potentially contain a new *ground*, complete with new spatio-temporal parameters and new characters. The new characters might speak, thus introducing the possibility of new deictic centres. Finally, in Jeremiah 3.7a, 3.19a and 3.19e, the idiomatic use of the term אמר opens epistemic modality spaces in which the reader is privileged to enter into the thought world of Yahweh himself.

Thus, different forms from the same root are used to construe a situation of speaking from differing perspectives: that of the narrator himself at 1.1-1.3; that of the narrator as character at 1.4, 1.11, 1.13 and 2.1; that of characters in a conversational setting at 1.6 and 1.7; and that of the internal thought world of a character at 3.7a, 3.19a and 3.19e. When the term is used from the narrator's perspective, the mental spaces cued by the construction are large speech domains. Subspaces are opened within these domains by uses of the term from the character's perspective. These spaces connect directly to the base space set up in Jeremiah 1.1-1.3. Finally, the term is used to access the thought world of a character. The subspaces opened in this manner exhibit access that is restricted to the character's space, in that it may only connect directly to the space in which it is generated. However, due to the *transitivity of containment* principle, such spaces are incorporated into the network as a whole. Thus, if the space that generates the restricted access space has direct connections to the base space, the restricted access space "comes along for the ride." Clearly, the construal operations involved in establishing the varying perspectives contribute to the high level of interest found in BH prophetic text.

Conclusion: Conceptual Integration of *Many Things*

This chapter has explored the integrating features of frame knowledge, conceptual metaphor, conterfactual blending and the cross-genre nature of cognitive construction through a series of examples drawn from Jeremiah 2.1-3.25. Initially, Jeremiah 1.4-2.1 was used to discuss the conceptual integration of elements from various points on the Extended Great Chain via scoping to human scale within speech frames (section A.1). This was followed by an analysis of the development of the complex-speaker (section A.2). Literary metaphor was explained as a many-space conceptual blend, comprising conceptual metaphor, ICMs, image schemas and background knowledge of the world. It was discovered that material in Jeremiah 2.1-3.25 is characterised by the containment and path schemas, and by the SOCIETY IS A PERSON conceptual metaphor. Complex systems metaphors such as SOCIETY IS A PERSON and SOCIETY IS A PLANT act as unifying devices throughout Jeremiah 1.4-6.30 (section B.4). The problem of identity was taken up and explained via the *Access Principle*, which allows for the identification of the speaker in 3.6a as Jeremiah (section B.5). Finally, the cross-genre nature of mental space building was discussed (section G). The network model is well suited for this task because the model is neutral with regard to the genre of a text. Narrative texts, poetic texts, legal texts and prophetic texts all contain space-builders that act as prompts for mental-spaces constructions. Thus, conceptual theories allow for the integration of seemingly disparate elements within the text of Jeremiah 1.1-6.30.

6. Cognitive Structuring in Jeremiah 4.1-6.30

Ierusalem, Ierusalem,
convertere ad Dominum Deum tuum

~ Tallis, De Lamentatione

This chapter explores the final set of examples taken from Jeremiah 1.1-6.30. The examples are from section B, Jeremiah 4.1-4.31, and section C, Jeremiah 5.1-6.30. Each of these sections is a continuation of the cognitive network that begins at Jeremiah 1.1. The previous two chapters examine the formation of the cognitive network through space-building terms and constructions, cognitive connections and structuring devices such as frame knowledge, image schemata and conceptual metaphor. In this chapter, the analysis of the final two sections of text uses the same set of features. While chapters 4 and 5 delve into the formation and structuring of text-level cognitive spaces, the focus of the present chapter is an examination of linguistic construal operations and structuring devices that operate at the sentence and paragraph level of the text in order to discover small-scale effects that contribute to the unity of the larger whole.

Section B, Jeremiah 4.1-4.31, differs from the previous narrative section as it consists mainly of discursive (D) text.[1] Jeremiah 4.1-4.9 is discursive with embedded quotation. Jeremiah 4.10 is narrative with embedded quotation, and the remainder of the section, Jeremiah 4.11-4.31, is narrative with embedded discursive text. Section C, Jeremiah 5.1-6.30, is largely quotation, with some embedded quotation. Unlike the narrative sections in Jeremiah 1.1-3.25, which regularly exhibit three or more levels of embedding, sections B and C rarely move beyond two levels. Text-type contributes to establishing perspective, as demonstrated in chapters 4 and 5.

---

1   Categories include: N, narrative text starting from *wayyiqtol*; Q, discursive text starting from quotation; D, discursive text starting from *yiqtol* in narrative text; and P, perception starting from verbum sentiendi. The fourth category is a cognitive addition proposed in this volume. For the first three categories see E. Talstra, "A Hierarchy of Clauses in Biblical Hebrew Narrative," in Narrative Syntax and the Hebrew Bible, ed. E. J. van Wolde (Leiden: Brill, 1997), 106.

The discussion in chapter 5 details the shift in perspective in Jeremiah 1.1-3.25 as it moves from narrator, to narrator as character, and finally to character. Sections B and C continue the process of scoping to human scale that began in Jeremiah 1.1-3.25. In these sections, the characters are fully engaged with one another within the objective portion of the viewing arrangement. Significantly, the reader now perceives the situation from within the text itself. Although the voice of the complex speaker is still perceptible, other voices and perspectives also occur within Jeremiah 4.1-6.30.

Frame knowledge derived from metapragmatic reported speech diminishes in sections B and C. Text level citation formulae all but disappear in these sections, demonstrating that the identities of the primary interlocutors: יְהוָֹה‎, Jeremiah and Jerusalem are now well entrenched. The containment, force, path and centre-periphery image schemata are prevalent in this stretch of text, providing covert unity for these sections. The force schema appears more often than in section A, with the ever-increasing announcements of impending doom. The path schema occurs in further examples of the LOVE IS A JOURNEY metaphor, although now unfaithfulness hampers the journey. With Jerusalem as a centre point, the centre-periphery schema provides the conceptual base for understanding the overarching shift in perceptual scoping in Jeremiah 1.1-6.30. As in section A, the SOCIETY IS A PERSON and SOCIETY IS A PLANT conceptual metaphors are prevalent in sections B and C. These features also contribute to the unity of Jeremiah 1.1-6.30.

A. Jeremiah 4.1-4.31: Discursive Text and Perspective

Jeremiah 4.1-4.31 represents a shift from the narrative text-type to the discursive text-type.[2] This section contains only two isolated *wayyiqtol*

---

2 Schneider's differentiation between narrative and discursive text is explained in chapter 2, section C.1. Niccacci provides added information from a text-linguistics perspective. He notes that the *wayyiqtol* forms are used for the main level of communication in narrative text, and a shift away from the main level is indicated by a shift to a secondary verbal form, such as W-X-*qatal*, W-X-*yiqtol*, W-*qatal* or W-*nominal clause*. Primary level forms can stand alone, while secondary level must rely upon a sentence at the primary level. On the other hand, discursive text is more complex. He notes that discursive text uses all three temporal axes, while narrative uses only the past: the simple nominal clause indicates the present; *yiqtol*, W-*qatal*, imperatives and volitives indicate the future; *qatal* indicates the past. In discursive text, *qatal* in the first position in a sentence begins the main line, which is often continued by a W-*qatal string*. *Yiqtol* provides the main line for the future. Niccacci, 'Essential Hebrew Syntax', 111-117. In this volume discursive text is differentiated from quoted speech. The first is written as direct discourse, while the second is written as reported direct

clauses (4.10a; 4.16d), but imperative and cohortative forms abound. Jeremiah 4.1 begins with an *X-yiqtol* clause, which, according to Schneider, is the leading verbal form for discursive text. Unlike narrative text, which creates distance between the reader and the text, discursive text often features first and second person interaction that draws the reader into the text.³

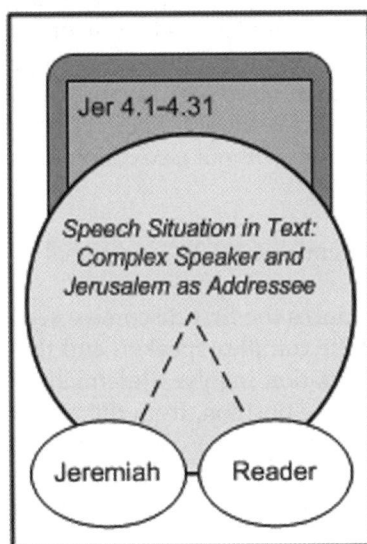

Figure 6.1 Viewing Arrangement for Jeremiah 4.1 – 4.31

---

discourse. The two indicate distinctly different speech domains: direct discourse involves the originator and (original) reader directly, while reported direct discourse is indexed from a character's perspective.

3   In an article discovered by the present writer only after the first chapters of this volume were written, Van Wolde develops this use of Schneider's categories in her analysis of narrative text. She notes that verbal forms, including temporal and locative terms, are used to "identify the person (narrator or character) who determines the perspective by which the reader is guided." She goes on to describe other BH terms that affect perspective, and her list is quite similar to the list of space building terms discussed in chapter 4 of this volume. While the two lists were compiled independently, the present writer owes her use of idea of the character as a guide through the text to another of van Wolde's volumes, *Ruth and Naomi*. The present writer's focus upon perspective derives from readings in cognitive grammar and cognitive linguistics. E. J. van Wolde, "Who Guides Whom? Embeddedness and Perspective in Biblical Hebrew Narrative and in I Kings 3.16-28," *JBL* 114 (1995), 624; Wolde, *Ruth and Naomi*.

As the viewing arrangement diagram for Jeremiah 4.1-4.31 demonstrates, this section continues the process of scoping to human scale
that began in Jeremiah 1-3, with the successive moves from N¹ to N²
and finally to N³ (see Figure 5.2). Both Jeremiah, as the covert guide
through the text, and the reader now appear as if partially encom-
passed by the situation in the text. This arrangement is termed D¹. For
the first time, the situation appears as if it is larger than the human
observer. This correlates with the metaphor of linguistic situations as
material entities. In this case, the fluid imperfective forms subsume the
solid bodies of the human observers, creating a view from within the
situation. By way of contrast, the solid perfective forms in the narrative
sections create a view from without (see chapter 3, section D.4).

1.   Jeremiah 4.1-4.2: Conditional Space

Jeremiah 4.1-4.2 introduces the first discursive section, D¹. The voice in
this section is that of the complex speaker, and the perspective belongs
to יְהֹוָי. The speech situation involves Jeremiah, יְהֹוָי and Israel, all of
whom are in the objective position, from the reader's viewpoint. Additionally, Jeremiah is present as the covert guide through the text. The
reader is in a less subjective position than in previous sections, due to
the empathy created by the discursive text-type.

a.   Jeremiah 4.1-4.2 Clause Layout and Analysis

Clause Layout	JER
אִם־תָּשׁוּב יִשְׂרָאֵל	4.1a
נְאֻם־יְהוָה	b
אֵלַי תָּשׁוּב	c
וְאִם־תָּסִיר שִׁקּוּצֶיךָ מִפָּנַי	d
וְלֹא תָנוּד	e
וְנִשְׁבַּעְתָּ חַי־יְהוָה בֶּאֱמֶת	4.2a
בְּמִשְׁפָּט וּבִצְדָקָה	b
וְהִתְבָּרְכוּ בוֹ גּוֹיִם	c
וּבוֹ יִתְהַלָּלוּ	d

JER	Type	Clause Tag	PNG	Stem Focus	MSC
4.1a	D	*X-Yiqtol*	2sgM	Qal	D¹
b	D	*Focus*			C¹
c	D	*X-Yiqtol*	2sgM	ARG	
d	D	*W-X-Yiqtol*	2sgM	Hiphil	
e	D	*W-X-Yiqtol*	2sgM	Qal	
4.2a	D	*W-Qatal*	2sgM	Niphal	
b	D	*Ellip*			
c	D	*W-Qatal*	3pl	Hith	
d	D	*W-X-Yiqtol*	3plM	Hith	

b. Syntax, Semantics and Information Structure

There are several sets of boxed terms in the clause analysis. The first group consists of the conditional particle, אִם, which appears at 4.1a and again at 4.1d.[4] In these clauses, Yahweh presents a series of conditions to the addressees. Next, there are two suffixed prepositions: אֵלַי appears at 4.1c and מִפְּנַי occurs at 4.1d. These terms set up trajectors for the path schema, with Yahweh as the focal point for each. Finally, there is a group of prepositional phrases, each including the preposition בְּ and an abstract noun: בֶּאֱמֶת, בְּמִשְׁפָּט and בִּצְדָקָה. Additionally, the *hithpael* verbal forms in 4.2c, √בְרך, and 4.2d, √הלל, are of interest.

The set of clauses at 4.1a-c form a chiasm, with the focus particle נְאֻם־יְהוָה in the centre, calling attention to the surrounding phrases.

אִם־תָּשׁוּב יִשְׂרָאֵל   a

נְאֻם־יְהוָה   b

אֵלַי תָּשׁוּב   c

Clause 4.1a exhibits VS constituent order, thus it is an example of predicate focus. Asking the diagnostic question, *what will Israel do*, reveals

---

4   For a full treatment of the particle אִם, see C. van Leeuwen, "Die Partikel 'Im'," in *Syntax and Meaning: Studies in Hebrew Syntax and Biblical Exegesis*, ed. C. J. Labuschagne, OS 18 (Leiden: Brill, 1973).

one difficulty that occurs when assessing the imperfective forms. Are the imperfective forms, in fact, modal forms?[5] *What might Israel do* is probably a more useful question to ask. The answer, *return*, is one of the many uses of the root שוב in the book of Jeremiah.[6] Clause 4.1c exhibits OV order, as it contains the fronted term אלי, which makes this an example of argument focus.[7] Since the speaker is already discourse-active, and no contrast is implied, the term אלי is emphasised. The emphasis contributes force to the clause. The return requested is not the simple about face familiar to every military private. Rather, it is the heart cry of a betrayed lover unwilling to release an unfaithful spouse.

The hithpael verbal forms in 4.2c, √ברך, and 4.2d, √הלל, present a choice of two interpretations, or, as Mandelblit observes, "two alternative blending characterizations."[8] She notes that for MH verbs, the difference between reflexive hitpa'el verbs and middle hitpa'el verbs has to do with causal force. For reflexive verbs, the causal force is separate from the affected entity, while for middle verbs, the causal force is internal to the affected entity. For BH verbs, the hithpa'el form represents the middle voice, and such verbs may be either reflexive or reciprocal.[9] Again, it is a matter of causal force. The conditions laid out in the previous clauses indicate that the causal force is external to the affected entity: Israel's return is the external causal force that will affect the nations. Thus, a reflexive nuance seems to be represented here,   nations shall be blessed by him. This raises the question of the status of the nations. The internal logic of this section seems to suggest that if the

---

5   Joosten proposes that BH has both an indicative system and a modal system. Jan Joosten, "The Indicative System of the Biblical Hebrew Verb and Its Literary Exploitation," in *Narrative Syntax and the Hebrew Bible*, ed. E. J. Van Wolde (Leiden: Brill, 1997), 57-58. Cook introduces another category, contingent modality, to the discussion. Contingent modality is indicated when the speaker's view of the situation in a subordinate clause is contingent upon the actuality of the statement to which it is subordinated. Cook, "Grammaticalization," 127.

6   Carroll notes that the language of turning is part of the rhetoric of the Yahweh-alone party, who believed that to turn to Yahweh meant both turning away from the false cults and consolidating worship in the Jerusalem temple. The latter included the consolidation of power as well. Carroll, *Jeremiah: A Commentary*, 156. Holladay associates the language of turning with the idea of covenant in William Lee Holladay, *The Root Šûbh in the Old Testament with Particular Reference to Its Usages in Covenantal Contexts* (Leiden: E.J. Brill, 1958).

7   Other examples of fronted self-referential terms occur in Jeremiah 1.1 – 6.30. Jeremiah 1.18a is a *casus pendens*, and indicates contrastive focus; Jeremiah 2.13b exhibits OV order; Jeremiah 2.21a is in SVO order, with a fronted pronoun as explicit subject. Each of these appears to indicate argument focus, with Yahweh as the entity in focus.

8   Mandelblit, "Grammatical Marking," 232.

9   Arnold and Choi, *A Guide to Biblical Hebrew Syntax*, 194.

addressee (Israel in the first instance and Jerusalem as the current addressee in the text in the second) would return to Yahweh, this would
cause the nations to reap benefits from him.[10]

c. Cognitive Construction

As observed in chapters 4 and 5, cognitive construction in Jeremiah 1.1-
3.25 comprises several speech domains. The speech domains themselves comprise various embedded spaces opened by space-builders
from the semantic fields of speech, perception, cognition, and deontic
and epistemic modality. Frames, idealised cognitive models and image
schemata structure the spaces.

Jeremiah 4.1 is a continuation of the fourth speech domain. The metapragmatic structuring of "speech reporting speech" that characterises
Jeremiah 1.4-2.1 has given way to reported speech in Jeremiah 2.2-3.25.
New cognitive construction is in process, as Jeremiah 4.1 represents
both a shift in verbal forms and a shift in space-building terms. Jeremiah 4.1 begins with the statement אִם־תָּשׁוּב יִשְׂרָאֵל, in which the conditional particle אִם appears to be acting as a space-builder. If this is the
case, the new space, M, might be termed a conditional space.[11] The
group of clauses at 4.1a-4.1c functions as a topical frame, introducing
the invitation of Yahweh to *return to me*. The four clauses at 4.1d-4.2b
act as a topical elaboration upon the idea of *return to me*. 4.1d is a
second conditional clause that describes a feature of the return. Three
conditions contribute to the situation: if the addressees remove their
abominations *from before me*, if they do not waver, and if they swear
חַי־יהוה, *as the Lord lives*, then the nations will be blessed by him, and
will boast in him. Carroll notes that the abominations are the idols of
the false cults, and that turning back to Yahweh requires the putting
away of false gods. He sees this as an indication of the type of worship
advocated by theYahweh-alone party.[12]

Several image schemata are present in this section. The first person
suffix on the terms אֵלַי and מִפָּנַי indicates that the speaker, Yahweh, is a
point of reference both for the path schema and for the centre-

---

10 It is somehow doubtful that Israel/Jerusalem would be motivated to change their
    ways for the benefit of the nations in the face of imminent judgement. Carroll ex-
    plains that this section represents a late stage of the royal ideology of the temple,
    and that the association of the nations with the cultic reformation of Israel is unusual
    for the tradition. Carroll, *Jeremiah: A Commentary*, 136.

11 A conditional space differs from a hypothetical space in that it creates an opportuni-
    ty both to reason and to choose a course of action, whereas a hypothetical space
    creates an opportunity to reason, but does not always entail a change in action

12 Carroll, *Jeremiah: A Commentary*, 156.

periphery schema, since he is the point to whom the addressees are to return, and the point from whom the addressees are to remove their abominations. Not only are the addressees to swear חי־יהוה, but they are to do so באמת, במשפט and ובצדקה. The preposition ב in these three phrases indicates the containment schema. In this case, the three terms are abstract nouns, thus the swearing is to take place within the abstract confines of truth, justice and righteousness. The return to Yahweh and the removal of the abominations from before Yahweh appear to be abstractions as well.

There is no overt reference to the Jerusalem temple; rather the overt reference is to Yahweh himself. In Fauconnier's terms, this is due to the monumental disconnection between the Jerusalem temple as *material anchor*, and the peoples' *complex projections* regarding the deity.[13] The practices of the people have altered the symbolic structure of the temple and the worship of Yahweh. For the Israelites, worship was to be a light-splitting prism that allowed the people to perceive their God more fully. However, just as a prism held at the wrong angle turns beauty to fire, so unfaithfulness in worship has turned the beauty of relationship with the divine into the destructive fire of judgement.[14]

2.   Jeremiah 4.11-4.18 (4.19-4.21): Centre-Periphery

The centre-periphery image schema is prevalent throughout Jeremiah 1.1-6.30. The centre-periphery schema includes a physical or metaphorical core or edge and degrees of distance from the core. The structure of an apple, an individual's perceptual sphere and an individual's social sphere are some examples of the centre-periphery schema.[15] With regard to physical location, reference to the gates of Jerusalem and the cities of Judah in 1.14 is one of the first instances of the centre-periphery schema in MT Jeremiah. In this case, Jerusalem is at the centre, and the cities of Judah at various points around the periphery. With regard to metaphorical location, Jeremiah 1.12 introduces the idea of Jeremiah himself as a fortified city, ready to withstand attack. Finally, with re-

---

13   The temple in Jerusalem is an example of a "material anchor for spiritual and personal integration networks." The temple, like a cathedral, is "a material anchor for communing with the relatively inaccessible world of the divine." Fauconnier and Turner, *The Way We Think*, 206-207.

14   Responsibility for the coming judgement is attributed to the people and their unfaithfulness. This contributes to the argument that the Jeremiah text has elements of a theodicy. See Jeremiah 2.17; 2.19; 4.4; 4.18; and 5.25.

15   Johnson, *The Body in the Mind: The Bodily Basis of Meaning, Imagination, and Reason*, 124-125.

gard to abstract location, there are the many instances in which the people are urged to return to Yahweh, who provides the centre point for his people. Jerusalem, Jeremiah and Yahweh are three key entities in the text and they often provide a focal point for the centre-periphery schema both individually and as a group. Significantly, Yahweh is presented without reference to the Temple. Thus, the location under discussion is abstract rather than physical.

In the current section, Jeremiah 4.9-4.10 reinstates the narrative level with an exchange between Yahweh and Jeremiah. Jeremiah 4.9.a begins with the clause וְהָיָה בַיּוֹם־הַהוּא נְאֻם־יְהוָה, in which the focus particle נְאֻם־יְהוָה draws attention to the undifferentiated phrase *on that day*. This phrase forms a parallelism with the phrase, בָּעֵת הַהִיא, *at that time*, in Jeremiah 4.11.[16] Jeremiah's response to the pronouncement of doom at 4.10a is an instantiation of metapragmatic reported speech.

וָאֹמַר	a
אֲהָהּ אֲדֹנָי יְהוִה אָכֵן הַשֵּׁא הִשֵּׁאתָ לָעָם הַזֶּה וְלִירוּשָׁלִַם לֵאמֹר	b
שָׁלוֹם יִהְיֶה לָכֶם וְנָגְעָה חֶרֶב עַד־הַנָּפֶשׁ	c

However, the text in 4.11-4.31 is discursive, which results in ND as the baseline text level for the remainder of the section.

---

16   This combination of the preposition בְּ, which indicates the containment schema, and the deictic terms הוּא and הִיא, is rather unsettling from a cognitive perspective. The phrases *on that day* and *at that time* do not give actual temporal information; rather, the deictic terms select a day and a time at which certain activities will take place. The reader now knows that the leaders of the society will be overwhelmed, and that a hot wind is on its way towards Jerusalem and the inhabitants of the city. However, they do not know precisely when this will occur.

a.   Jeremiah 4.11-4.18 Clause Layout and Analysis

Clause Layout	JER
בָּעֵת הַהִיא יֵאָמֵר לָעָם־הַזֶּה וְלִירוּשָׁלַם	4.11a
רוּחַ צַח שְׁפָיִים בַּמִּדְבָּר דֶּרֶךְ בַּת־עַמִּי	b
לוֹא לִזְרוֹת וְלוֹא לְהָבַר	c
רוּחַ מָלֵא מֵאֵלֶּה יָבוֹא לִי	4.12a
עַתָּה גַם־אֲנִי אֲדַבֵּר מִשְׁפָּטִים אוֹתָם	b
הִנֵּה כַּעֲנָנִים יַעֲלֶה	4.13a
וְכַסּוּפָה מַרְכְּבוֹתָיו	b
קַלּוּ מִנְּשָׁרִים סוּסָיו	c
אוֹי לָנוּ כִּי שֻׁדָּדְנוּ	d
כַּבְּסִי מֵרָעָה לִבֵּךְ יְרוּשָׁלַם	4.14a
לְמַעַן תִּוָּשֵׁעִי	b
עַד־מָתַי תָּלִין בְּקִרְבֵּךְ מַחְשְׁבוֹת אוֹנֵךְ	c
כִּי קוֹל מַגִּיד מִדָּן	4.15a
וּמַשְׁמִיעַ אָוֶן מֵהַר אֶפְרָיִם	b
הַזְכִּירוּ לַגּוֹיִם הִנֵּה	4.16a
הַשְׁמִיעוּ עַל־יְרוּשָׁלַם	b
נֹצְרִים בָּאִים מֵאֶרֶץ הַמֶּרְחָק	c
וַיִּתְּנוּ עַל־עָרֵי יְהוּדָה קוֹלָם	d
כְּשֹׁמְרֵי שָׂדַי הָיוּ עָלֶיהָ מִסָּבִיב	4.17a
כִּי־אֹתִי מָרָתָה	b
נְאֻם־יְהוָה	c
דַּרְכֵּךְ וּמַעֲלָלַיִךְ עָשׂוֹ אֵלֶּה לָךְ	4.18a
זֹאת רָעָתֵךְ כִּי מָר כִּי נָגַע עַד־לִבֵּךְ	b

JER	Type	Clause Tag	PNG	Stem	MSC
4.11a	ND	*X-Yiqtol*	3sgM	Niphal	ND[1]
b	NDQ	NmCl			C[1]
c	NDQ	X-Qetol X-Qetol		Qal/ Hiph	C[1]
4.12a	NDQ	*X-Yiqtol*	3sgM	Qal	C[1]
b	NDQ	*X-Yiqtol*	1sg	Piel	C[1]
4.13a	NDQ	*X-Yiqtol*	3sgM	Qal	C[3]
b	NDQ	W-NP			C[3]
c	NDQ	*Qatal*	3pl	Qal	C[3]
d	ND	*X-Qatal*	1pl	Pual	C[3]
4.14a	ND	Impv	sgF	Piel	C[1]
b	ND	*X-Yiqtol*	2sgf	Niphal	C[1]
c	ND	*X-Yiqtol*	3sfF	Qal	C[1]
4.15a	ND	X-Qotel	sgM	Hiphil	C[1]
b	ND	W-Qotel	sgM	Hiphil	C[1]
4.16a	ND	Impv	plM	Hiphil	C[1]
b	ND	Impv	plM	Hiphil	C[1]
c	ND	Qotel	plM	Qal	C[1]
d	NN	*Wayyiqtol-0*	3plM	Qal	C[1]
4.17a	ND	*X-Qatal*	3pl	Qal	C[1]
b	ND	*X-Qatal*	3sgF	Qal	C[1]
c	ND	*Focus*			C[1]
4.18a	ND	S-Qatol		Qal	C[1]
b	ND	NmCl *X-Qatal*	3sgM	Qal	C[1]

b.   Syntax, Semantics and Information Structure

Several syntactic and semantic features in Jeremiah 4.11-4.13 affect the information structure of the passage and affect cognitive structuring as well. This discussion concerns the boxed terms in the above analysis. (The first phrase, Jeremiah 4.11a בעת ההיא, is explained in the cognitive construction section.)

Jeremiah 4.14a כבסי מרעה לבך ירושלם contains the imperative כבסי, *wash*. Word order in this sentence is V-PreP-O-Vocative. The imperative verb contributes force to the clause. The directive *wash your heart* contributes to the SOCIETY IS A PERSON conceptual metaphor that structures the following section. However, perhaps the most important information in the sentence is לבך, *your heart* (sgF), spoken with regard to Jerusalem as the area in need of cleansing. The term reoccurs at 4.18, which summarises this section in four terse clauses.

> דרכך ומעלליך עשו אלה לך   a
>
> זאת רעתך כי מר כי נגע עד־לבך   b

Word order for the first clause is SVO. The double, fronted subject consists of the terms דרכך ומעלליך, each of which contains a 2sgF possessive suffix. The deictic term אלה, which refers back to the besiegers surrounding Jerusalem, follows the infinitive absolute verbal form in the first clause (see 4.16c-4.17b). The second, nominal clause consists of the deictic term זאת and the noun רעתך, which also has a 2sgF possessive suffix.[17] The third clause, כי מר, functions as an interjection.

The final clause, כי נגע עד־לבך, *it has reached as far as your heart*, is a turning point within the larger section. This clause contains one of three instances of the term נגע in Jeremiah 1.1-6.30. The first, וישלח יהוה את־ידו ויגע על־פי, *and Yahweh sent out (extended) his hand and touched my mouth*, is at 1.9b. The second and more ominous instance, ונגעה חרב עד־הנפש, *the sword reaches the soul,* is at 4.10f (NRSV has *throat*). These clauses refer metaphorically to the haptic sense, or sense of touch. In 1.9b, Jeremiah receives authorisation as a prophet when Yahweh reaches out his hand and touches Jeremiah's mouth. In 4.10f, the figure of a sword held to the throat is menacing in the extreme – it gives the metonymically perceived swordsman the power of life and death over the victim, in this case Jerusalem. Thus, when the judgement of Yahweh reaches Jerusalem's heart at 4.18d, there is no longer any opportunity to change.

---

17   Regarding BH nominal clauses, see Andersen, *The Hebrew Verbless Clause in the Penta-teuch*; Miller, *C. Miller, Verbless*.

c. Cognitive Construction

Jeremiah 4.11-4.18 contains several terms that function as small-scale space-builders. These include the prepositional phrase בעת ההיא at 4.11a, which describes a future quotation between 4.11b-4.13c and the imperative כבסי at 4.14a. As previously mentioned, the phrase בעת ההיא invokes the containment schema for time, but the phrase contains a deictic term without a specified referent. Thus, the phrase *at that time* is actually indeterminate with regard to calendar time. Rather, it specifies the certainty of the promised event: *this people* and Jerusalem will indeed hear about the hot wind that is to come. The following quotation space presents the details of the event. The phrase רוח צח שפיים במדבר דרך בת־עמי invokes both the path schema and the centre-periphery schema. The hot wind is to come from the שפיים במדבר.

Somewhat ironically, the term שפיים seems to associate the direction of the destructive wind with the place where the addressees were unfaithful to יהוה (Jeremiah 3.2a) and the place from which Israel's weeping was heard (Jeremiah 3.21). In both instances the location is indeterminate. This is as indicated by the rhetorical question איפה לא *שגלת **שכבת, *Where have you not been unfaithful*, which follows the instruction שאי־עיניך על־שפים וראי, *lift up your eyes to the bare heights and see*, at Jeremiah 3.2a.[18] There is some discussion about whether the term שפים indicates bare heights or paths.[19] However, for this argument it is more important to note that the the term שפים indicates a location at a distance from Jerusalem, which provides the centre point for the centre-periphery schema. In conceptual metaphor terms, CLOSE TO CENTRE IS GOOD and FAR FROM CENTRE IS BAD. This conceptual metaphor is fundamental to the arrangement of the wilderness tabernacle, and seems to contribute to the rhetoric of the Yahweh-alone part as well.[20]

---

18 Both K, שגלת, *been ravished*, and Q, שכבת, *lain with* are fairly explicit terms. Carroll notes that שגלת is an obscene term. Carroll, *Jeremiah: A Commentary*, 141.

19 In his 1906 article, Joüon challenges the accepted translation of the term שפים as *bare heights* or *bare slopes* by proposing the terms *trodden paths* or *tracks*. Gelston agrees that *tracks* is a likely but not necessary translation. On the other hand, Ellinger argues convincingly that *bare heights* or *bare slopes* is the correct option. K. Ellinger, "Der Sinn des Hebräischen Wortes 'SFY'," *ZAW* 83 (1971); A. Gelston, "Some Notes on Second Isaiah," *VT* 21 (1971); Paul Joüon, "Le Sens Du Mot Hébreu 'SFY'," *Journal Asiatique* (1906).

20 Directionality and the centre-periphery schema are also instantiated in present-day worship. In certain Christian traditions, places of worship are situated so that the worshippers face east during parts of the liturgy, but face the centre of the building at other times. Muslims face east to pray. Not only do worshippers in Armenia face

Returning to Jeremiah 4.12a, the description of the hot wind as being too strong for winnowing invokes the force schema. The hot wind sweeping down upon the people of Jerusalem is moving along the same trajectory as the contents of the boiling pot in Jeremiah 1.13, and with a similar degree of hot, fluid, undifferentiated force.

At 4.14a and 4.18d, the term לבך invokes the centre-periphery image schema, which derives from embodied human experience in which bodies have both a core, containing the vital elements of life, and a periphery, i.e. the extremities. If Jerusalem would follow the imperative כבסי מרעה לבך at 4.14a, there is a chance that she might be saved. The rhetorical question at 4.14c עד־מתי תלין בקרבך מחשבות אונך, *How long will your evil thoughts lodge within you*, indicates the magnitude of Jerusalem's difficulty. The final clause, כי נגע עד־לבך, announces that it is too late. The ways and doings of the people have brought them to the point of no return.

The answering cry in Jeremiah 4.19 reflects the anguish of the city under attack.

מעי מעי   a

*אחולה **אוחילה קירות לבי   b

המה־לי לבי לא אחריש   c

In Jeremiah 4.19, the identity of the speaker is not clear. While the first person reference might seem to point to Jeremiah as speaker, and his perspective is certainly prevalent in the complex speaker's voice, there is a strong possibility that the speaker is society as a whole. The reason for this has to do with the SOCIETY IS A PERSON conceptual metaphor that runs through Jeremiah 4.14-4.18. If the perspective of יהוה dominates these verses, it is likely that the response at 4.19 would be that of the now besieged third interlocutor, Jerusalem. The description of battle continues through 4.20. Jeremiah 4.21 contains a comment upon the state of the people as foolish and lacking knowledge, given from the perspective of יהוה.

3.   Jeremiah 4.23-4.26: De-creation

Jeremiah 4.23-4.26 presents a series of post-battle impressions, which are nearly apocalyptic in scope. At Jeremiah 4.23-4.28 the first person

---

east when approaching tha altar, but they back out of the church so as not to turn their backs to the altar. See Mary Douglas, *Purity and Danger: An Analysis of Concepts of Pollution and Taboo* (London: Routledge, 2003).

verbal form רָאִיתִי and the particle וְהִנֵּה indicate a shift in perspective to Jeremiah as character.[21] The shift to Jeremiah's perspective seems to indicate an iconic situation, presented at human scale. However, a second glance reveals that this is not the case.

a. Jeremiah 4.23-4.26 (27) Clause Layout and Analysis

Clause Layout	JER
רָאִיתִי אֶת־הָאָרֶץ	4.23a
וְהִנֵּה־תֹהוּ וָבֹהוּ	b
וְאֶל־הַשָּׁמַיִם וְאֵין אוֹרָם	c
רָאִיתִי הֶהָרִים	4.24a
וְהִנֵּה רֹעֲשִׁים	b
וְכָל־הַגְּבָעוֹת הִתְקַלְקָלוּ	c
רָאִיתִי	4.25a
וְהִנֵּה אֵין הָאָדָם	b
וְכָל־עוֹף הַשָּׁמַיִם נָדָדוּ	c
רָאִיתִי	4.26a
וְהִנֵּה הַכַּרְמֶל הַמִּדְבָּר	b
וְכָל־עָרָיו נִתְּצוּ מִפְּנֵי יְהוָה מִפְּנֵי חֲרוֹן אַפּוֹ	c
כִּי־כֹה אָמַר יְהוָה	4.27a

---

21 Van Wolde notes that the particle הִנֵּה indicates "embedded direct observation" and assigns the following information to the character's perspective. Wolde, "Guides," 634. See Follingstad, "C. Follingstad, Deictic Viewpoint"; C. J. Labuschagne, "The Particles 'hn' and 'hinneh'," in Syntax and Meaning: Studies in Hebrew Syntax and Biblical Exegesis, ed. C. J. Labuschagne, OS 18 (Leiden: Brill, 1973).

JER	Type	Clause Tag	PNG	Stem Focus	MSC
4.23a	ND	*Qatal*	1sg	Qal	ND[1]
b	ND	W-X-NmCl			C[2]
c	ND	W-X-NmCl			C[2]
4.24a	ND	*Qatal*	1sg	Qal	C[2]
b	ND	W-X-Qotel	plM		C[2]
c	ND	*W-S-Qatal*	3pl	Hithpp	C[2]
4.25a	ND	*Qatal*	1sg	Qal	C[2]
b	ND	W-X-NmCl			C[2]
c	ND	*W-S-Qatal*	3pl	Qal	C[2]
4.26a	ND	*Qatal*	1sg	Qal	C[2]
b	ND	W-X-NmCl			C[2]
c	ND	*W-S-Qatal*	3pl	Niphal	C[2]
4.27a	*ND*	*X-Qatal*	3sg	Qal	C[2]
b	NDQ	*X-Yiqtol*	3sgF	Qal	C[2]

b. Syntax, Semantics and Information Structure

The syntax, semantics and information structure of Jeremiah 4.23-4.26 contribute force and clarity to the section. The repeated use of the first person *verbum sentiendi* ראיתי and the sentence-focus particle והנה in Jeremiah 4.23-4.26 indicates character perspective.[22] At this point, the voice of the complex speaker seems to give way to that of Jeremiah as character. He appears on stage alone, a solitary figure whose eyes wander through a scene of incredible destruction.

---

22   For *verbum sentiendi* see chapter 3.

Jeremiah 4.23-4.26 contains a noteworthy series of verbal forms. There are seven *qatal* and *X-qatal* forms that indicate the main level of the text. One *qotel* form and four nominal clauses indicate the embedded level in the text.[23] Leading tense *wayyiqtol* and *yiqtol* forms are lacking altogether, thus the clauses are at nearly the same level of embedding.[24] This gives the section a repetitive terseness, which is a characteristic of Hebrew poetry. Constituent order of the main clauses in Jeremiah 4.23a and 4.24a is VO, and in 4.25 and 4.26 it is simply V. The verbal form in all four clauses is the first person רָאִיתִי, a *qatal* form indicating the main level of the text.

Jeremiah 4.23a is an example of sentence focus. It contains two direct objects, the earth and the heavens. These entities are made discourse-active for further elaboration in the clause that follows each: the earth appears to be וְהִנֵּה־תֹהוּ וָבֹהוּ, and in the heavens וְאֵין אוֹרָם, *there was no light*.[25] Both phrases are reminiscent of the creation language in the first chapter of Genesis, but the negation evokes a sense of decreation.

Jeremiah 4.24a is also an example of sentence focus. In this case, the direct object is הֶהָרִים. *The mountains* are the activated entity elaborated upon in the following phrase. The complement clause וְכָל־הַגְּבָעוֹת הִתְקַלְקָלוּ, *and all the hills moved to and fro*, makes the hills discourse active as well. The verb form הִתְקַלְקָלוּ is onomatopoeic and creates dynamism in the clause. The word pair הֶהָרִים and גְּבָעוֹת also appears in Psalm 114.4, הֶהָרִים רָקְדוּ כְאֵילִים גְּבָעוֹת כִּבְנֵי־צֹאן, *the mountains skipped like rams, the hills like lambs*, which is part of a psalm describing the exodus from Egypt.[26]

---

23   The approach taken in this thesis indicates that there is a continuum of embedding rather than a strict bifurcation between main level and secondary level verbal forms. This reflects the influence of MST as explained in chapters 4 and 5: when new mental spaces are opened, there might be a shift in ground that includes a shift in the temporal axis or a shift from narrator to character perspective. Either or both of these may include a shift in the group of verbal forms included in the text. Since the formation of mental spaces is a recursive process, many layers of embedding may occur in a given stretch of text.

24   Niccacci notes that in discursive text a chain of *W-qatal* forms acts in much the same way as a chain of *wayyiqtol* forms does in narrative. Since both *wayyiqtol* and *qatal* forms are perfective, "solid" forms according to Janda's metaphor, this is an accurate observation from a cognitive grammar point of view. Niccacci, "Essential Hebrew Syntax," 119.

25   Activating new entities by placing them in the object position illustrates Langacker's fifth principle of structure building. He notes that the object grammatical position is commonly used to introduce new participants. Langacker, "Discourse in Cognitive Grammar," 173.

26   This point deserves further study.

Jeremiah 4.25a is also an example of sentence focus; however, in this case there is no direct object used to activate a new entity. This is because, as the reporting observer points out in 4.25b וְהִנֵּה אֵין הָאָדָם, *there was no one*, even the birds had flown away. Jeremiah 4.26a continues this pattern. There is no direct object, but the reporting observer notes in a terse appositional phrase that הַכַּרְמֶל הַמִּדְבָּר, *the fruitful land is the desert*, at 4.26b. Additionally, 4.26c states וְכָל־עָרָיו נִתְּצוּ, *all the cities were laid waste*. While the three previous verses are each contain two parallel lines, 4.26 contains a third: מִפְּנֵי יְהוָה מִפְּנֵי חֲרוֹן אַפּוֹ, *before Yahweh and before his fierce anger*.

c. Cognitive Construction

The observing character is an important factor in determining how the cognitive network in this section is opened, structured and linked, as the section is highly dependent upon that character's perception of the situation. This volume identifies the speaking character as Jeremiah, although it has been argued that this section is a later insertion.[27] Two features stand out. First, as discussed above, there is the four-fold repetition of the terms רָאִיתִי and וְהִנֵּה, which draws the reader into the observed situation through shared gaze. Secondly, the language of de-creation utilises negative terms to create a sense of vacuous destruction. The land changes from fruitfulness to desert in a single appositional phrase at 4.26b and the description of destroyed cities follows at 4.26b. De-creation, un-planting and un-building occur due to חֲרוֹן אַפּוֹ, *his burning anger*, which is the consequence of the peoples' unfaithfulness.

The phrase חֲרוֹן אַפּוֹ is an indicator of the ANGER IS A HOT FLUID IN AN ENCLOSED CONTAINER conceptual metaphor because the combination of the terms חָרוֹן, burning anger, and אַפּוֹ, *his nose* evoke the "underlying conceptual metonymy" BODY HEAT STANDS FOR ANGER. Embodied experience give rise to the metonymy, for anger causes physiological changes: the face grows hot and there is an internal sense of pressure.[28] De-creation, un-planting and un-building are credited to Yahweh by the ANGER IS A HOT FLUID metaphor. Consequently, Yahweh is portrayed in embodied terms even though he has no physical body. This situation is evocative of the first instantiation of the ANGER IS A HOT FLUID IN AN ENCLOSED CONTAINER metaphor, the boiling pot at Jeremiah 1.13-1.14

---

27 Carroll notes that Giesebrecht, Volz and Hyatt question Jeremianic authorship. Carroll, *Jeremiah: A Commentary*, 168.
28 Kövecses, *Metaphor: A Practical Introduction*, 171.

B. Jeremiah 5.1-6.30: Embedded Quotation and Perspective

Section C, Jeremiah 5.1-6.30, is a stretch of embedded quotation that begins with the series of four imperative verbs at Jeremiah 5.1. This marks the final shift in perspective within Jeremiah 1.1-6.30, and the section tag is Q. As previously mentioned, there are seldom more than two layers of embedding in this section. Because quotation is firmly associated with a speaking character, this section pulls the reader even further into the situation of speaking within the text.

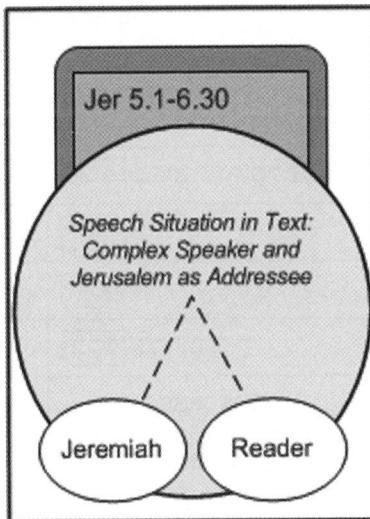

Figure 6.2 Viewing Arrangement for Jeremiah 5.1-6.30

The viewing arrangement diagram for Jeremiah 5.1-6.30 shows that the situation in the text has become even larger in proportion to the observers, who are now well involved in the text (contrast Figure 6.1). The separate ground that surrounds each observer is nearly subsumed by the ground represented by the situation in the text.

The following array of examples has been chosen to illustrate the syntax, semantics and information structure at the paragraph and sentence level. The examples provide a chance to perform a small-scale TD analysis, which brings the discussion from text level cognitive construction to a close-up look at some of the structuring devices that operate all the way through the text.

1. Jeremiah 5.1-5.14: Image Schemata and Cognitive Metaphor

The following four examples have been taken from Jeremiah 5.1-5.14. The examples talk about the situation at hand from the perspective of various speech participants. Jeremiah 5.1-5.2 is an example of visual scanning. Jeremiah 5.3-5.6 and Jeremiah 5.8-5.9 are examples of the PEOPLE ARE ANIMALS conceptual metaphor. Jeremiah 5.10 is an example of the SOCIETY IS A PLANT conceptual metaphor. Jeremiah 5.11-5.14 draws upon the imagery of anger and fire in announcing imminent judgement.

a. Jeremiah 5.1-5.2 Clause Layout and Analysis: Visual Scanning

Clause Layout	JER
שׁוֹטְטוּ בְּחוּצוֹת יְרוּשָׁלַם	5.1a
וּרְאוּ־נָא	b
וּדְעוּ	c
וּבַקְשׁוּ בִרְחוֹבוֹתֶיהָ	d
אִם־תִּמְצְאוּ אִישׁ	e
אִם־יֵשׁ עֹשֶׂה מִשְׁפָּט	f
מְבַקֵּשׁ אֱמוּנָה	g
וְאֶסְלַח לָהּ	h
וְאִם חַי־יְהוָֹה יֹאמֵרוּ	5.2a
לָכֵן לַשֶּׁקֶר יִשָּׁבֵעוּ	b

JER	Type	Clause Tag	PNG	Stem Focus	MSC
5.1a	Q	Impv	plM	Polel	C¹
b	Q	W-Impv	plM	Qal	
c	Q	W-Impv	plM	Qal	
d	Q	W-Impv	plM	Piel	
e	Q	X-Yiqtol	2plM	Qal	
f	Q	X-Qotel	sgM	Qal	
g	Q	Qotel	sgM	Piel	
h	Q	W-Yiqtol	1sg	Qal	
5.2a	Q	W-X-NP-Yiqtol	3plM		
b	Q	X-Yiqtol	3plM	Niphal	

Syntax, Semantics and Information Structure

As noted in the chart above, Jeremiah 5.1 contains a string of four plM
imperative forms from √שוט, √ראה, √ידע and √בקש. Similar strings of
imperative forms occur throughout Jeremiah 1.1-6.30.[29] Aside from the
polel form of √שוט, *hurry to and fro*, the remaining imperatives are taken
from the semantic fields of perception and cognition. The speaker urges
the addressees to *look*, to *know*, to *seek*, and in the other examples, to
understand and to *hear*. In Jeremiah 2.10, 2.19, and 2.23 the addressees
are urged to take note of their own unfaithful behaviour. In Jeremiah
6.18-6.19, יהוה enjoins the nations, the congregation and the earth to
hear and to know about the disaster that he is sending upon the un-
hearing people. However, in Jeremiah 5.1, the addressees are instructed
to go out into the streets of Jerusalem in search of even one person who
does justice and seeks truth. If they are successful, there is a possibility
that the city may be pardoned.

---

29 Noteworthy examples include Jeremiah 2.10, with imperatives from √בין and
√ראה; Jeremiah 2.19, from √ידע and √ראה; Jeremiah, 2.23, from √ראה and
√ידע; and Jeremiah 6.18-19, from √ידע and √שמע.

The series of clauses in Jeremiah 5.1a-h demonstrates a variety of clause connections. The imperatives in 5.1a-d join at an equal level. This is an example of parataxis. Jeremiah 5.1e, an X-*yiqtol* clause, joins at an unequal level. However, it exhibits interlacing because both the main clause and the complement clause share the same subject.[30] Jeremiah 5.1f and g are coordinating clauses that describe the object of the search. Jeremiah 5.1h returns to the same level as 5.1e.

Cognitive Construction: De-centring the Centre

The string of imperative forms in Jeremiah 5.1 contributes to the sense of urgency conveyed in this section. Conceptually, the reader engages in a virtual visual scanning of the streets of the city. The combination of imperative form and perception and cognition terms results in an increase in dynamic tension in this section. Jeremiah 5.1-5.2 connects the lack of even a single just person in Jerusalem, with the characteristically dishonest repetition of the oath חי־יהוה by the inhabitants of the city. The seekers will not be successful in their search. The centre itself is de-centred, with an accompanying sense of disequilibrium.

---

30 As Lehmann proposes, clauses may be interlaced on a continuum from complete disjunction to maximal identity. This is an intriguing train of thought, in that interlacing of clauses depends upon both syntax and semantics, which complements the cognitive grammar approach. Lehmann's approach is a promising one for further developing the idea of main-line and secondary-line verbs proposed by Schneider and explained by Talstra and Niccacci. See Niccacci, "Essential Hebrew Syntax."

b. Jeremiah 5.3-5.6 and 5.7-5.8 Clause Layout and Analysis:
    PEOPLE ARE ANIMALS

Clause Layout	JER
עַל־כֵּן הִכָּם אַרְיֵה מִיַּעַר	5.6a
זְאֵב עֲרָבוֹת יְשָׁדְדֵם	b
נָמֵר שֹׁקֵד עַל־עָרֵיהֶם	c
כָּל־הַיּוֹצֵא מֵהֵנָּה יִטָּרֵף	d
כִּי רַבּוּ פִּשְׁעֵיהֶם	e
עָצְמוּ *מְשֻׁבוֹתֵיהֶם **מְשׁוּבוֹתֵיהֶם	f
אֵי לָזֹאת *אֶסְלוֹחַ־ **אֶסְלַח־לָךְ	5.7a
בָּנַיִךְ עֲזָבוּנִי	b
וַיִּשָּׁבְעוּ בְּלֹא אֱלֹהִים	c
וָאַשְׂבִּעַ אוֹתָם	d
וַיִּנְאָפוּ	e
וּבֵית זוֹנָה יִתְגֹּדָדוּ	f
סוּסִים מְיֻזָּנִים מַשְׁכִּים הָיוּ	5.8a
אִישׁ אֶל־אֵשֶׁת רֵעֵהוּ יִצְהָלוּ	b
הַעַל־אֵלֶּה לוֹא־אֶפְקֹד	5.9a
נְאֻם־יְהוָֹה	b
וְאִם בְּגוֹי אֲשֶׁר־כָּזֶה	c

JER	Type	Clause Tag	PNG	Stem/Focus	MSC
5.6a	QQ	*X-Qatal*	3sgM (3plM)	Hiphil	C[1]
b	QQ	*S-Yiqtol*	3sgM (3plM)	Qal	
c	QQ	S-Qotel	sgM	Qal	
d	QQ	*S-Yiqtol*	3sgM	Niphal	
e	QQ	*X-Qatal*	3pl	Qal	
f	QQ	*Qatal*	3pl	Qal	
5.7a	Q	*X-Yiqtol*	1sg	Qal	
b	Q	*S-Qatal*	3pl (1cs)	Qal	
c	QN	*Wayyiqtol-0*	3plM	Niphal	
d	QN	*Wayyiqtol-0*	1sg	Hiphil	
e	QN	*Wayyiqtol-0*	3plM	Qal	
f	QND	*W-X-Yiqtol*	3plM	Hithpo	
5.8a	QND	*S-Qatal*	3pl	Qal	
b	QND	*S-Yiqtol*	3plM	Qal	
5.9a	Q	*X-Yiqtol*	1sg	Qal	
b	Q	Focus			
c	Q	W-X-NmCl			

Syntax, Semantics and Information Structure

Jeremiah 5.3 asks the rhetorical question, יהוה עיניך הלוא לאמונה, *O LORD, do your eyes not look for truth?* This clause appears to meet the criteria for Khan's extraposed construction: the extraposed nominal is not connected to a preposition or object marker and the grammatical relation is signalled by the resumptive pronoun on the term עֵינֶיךָ.[31] According to Khan, this structure is used "to signal the boundaries of spans of discourse."[32] In this case, the rhetorical question appears to be a bridge between Jeremiah 5.1-2 and the following discourse, which is concerned with the peoples' refusal to change their ways. From poor to rich, all of the people had broken away from Yahweh.

Jeremiah 5.6 describes the consequences. The word order in Jeremiah 5.6a is X-V(O)S. The object suffix stands before the subject, which is the last element in the clause. The term אַרְיֵה מִיַּעַר, *a lion from the forest*, is activated (topicalised) for the discourse, but the sentence itself exhibits predicate focus. The word order in Jeremiah 5.6b is SV(O). Since this is the first occurrence of the term זְאֵב עֲרָבוֹת, *wolf from the desert*, the subject is fronted for topicalisation rather than for argument focus. This is also the case in Jeremiah 5.6c, where the word order is SV and the term נָמֵר, *a leopard*, is fronted for topicalisation. Jeremiah 5.6d also exhibits SV word order. However, because the phrase כָּל־הַיּוֹצֵא מֵהֵנָּה, *all who go out from them*, is connected anaphorically to the previous section, this is an example of argument focus. This indicates emphasis, a feature that is reinforced by the *niphal* verb יִטָּרֵף, *be torn in pieces*. The following כִּי clause reiterates the enormity of the transgressions and apostasies of the people.

The allusion to the people as horses at Jeremiah 5.8 demonstrates the same word order pattern: both 5.8a and 5.8b are SV. Again, since the subjects are already discourse-active, these are examples of fronting for argument focus. The people themselve are described in distinctly unflattering terms.

Cognitive Construction

Since Jeremiah 5.1 is an extraposed clause that signals the boundaries of a discourse span, it is possible to propose that the extraposed clause is a type of space-builder. If so, it is an example of a syntactic construction acting as a space-builder, in contrast to the previously introduced space-builders that depend upon both syntax and semantics. This merits further study.

Jeremiah 5.6a-c introduces a series of wild animals bent on destroying the people: a lion from the forest, a wolf from the desert and a leopard. Clearly a single lion, wolf or leopard would be unable to wreak havoc upon a city full of people. These animals are presented as non-iconic entities, thus this is an instantiation of conceptual metaphor. In

31   Khan, *Studies*, xxvi.
32   Ibid., 83.

this case, humans, who exhibit higher order attributes and behaviour, are demoted on the Great Chain to the level of animals, who exhibit instinctual attributes and behaviour.[33] Kövecses notes that the HUMAN IS ANIMAL METAPHOR gives rise to the OBJECTIONABLE HUMAN BEHA- VIOUR IS ANIMAL BEHAVIOUR metaphor. In this case, the objectionable behaviour is vividly presented as killing, destroying and being torn in pieces. These clauses demonstrate the high degree of force engendered by the transgressions and apostasies of the people. This contributes to the rising force dynamics in this section, which concludes with two rhetorical questions at Jeremiah 5.9.

c.   Jeremiah 5.10: SOCIETY IS A PLANT

Clause Layout	JER
עֲלוּ בְשָׁרוֹתֶיהָ	5.10a
וְשַׁחֵתוּ	b
וְכָלָה אַל־תַּעֲשׂוּ	c
הָסִירוּ נְטִישׁוֹתֶיהָ	d
כִּי לוֹא לַיהוָה הֵמָּה	e

JER	Type	Clause Tag	PNG	Stem/Focus	MSC
5.10a	Q	Impv	plM	Qal	C¹
b	Q	W-Impv	plM	Piel	
c	Q	W-X-Yiqtol	2plM	Qal	
d	Q	Impv	plM	Hiphil	
e	Q	X-NmCl			

33 Kövecses, *Metaphor: A Practical Introduction*, 126.

Syntax, Semantics and Information Structure

Jerermiah 5.10 contains a string of plM imperative forms, instructing the addressees to *go up through her vine rows*, to *destroy* and to *strip away her branches*. In this example, the entities בשרותיה and נטישותיה indicate an agrarian setting, in which the workers are to clear the vineyard of unproductive growth.[34] The addressees are unidentified.

Cognitive Construction

This is an instantiation of the SOCIAL ORGANISATIONS ARE PLANTS metaphor (see chapter 5, section B.4). Clearly, in this case, the plant is not flourishing and is about to be thoroughly pruned, although perhaps *unplanted* would be a more accurate understanding. This section connects back to Jeremiah 2.21, the degenerate vine, and forward to the grape-gatherer image at Jeremiah 6.9. All of these examples stand in stark relief against the backdrop of the First Fruits example in Jeremiah 2.3.

d.   Jeremiah 5.14 Clause Layout and Analysis:
Anger, Fire and Judgement

Clause Layout	JER
לָכֵן כֹּה־אָמַר יְהוָה אֱלֹהֵי צְבָאוֹת	5.14a
יַעַן דַּבֶּרְכֶם אֶת־הַדָּבָר הַזֶּה	b
הִנְנִי נֹתֵן דְּבָרַי בְּפִיךָ לְאֵשׁ	c
וְהָעָם הַזֶּה עֵצִים	d
וַאֲכָלָתַם	e

---

34   While the second term indicates branches or shoots, the meaning of the first term is unclear. Carroll mentions two possibilities: "among its walls" or "her (vine) rows." For a discussion of possibilities, see Carroll, *Jeremiah: A Commentary*, 181.

JER	Type	Clause Tag	PNG	Stem/Focus	MSC
5.14a	Q	X-Qatal	3sgM	Qal	SB C²
b	QQ	X-Qetol	(2plM)	Piel	C¹
c	QQ	X-Qotel	sgM	Qal	C¹
d	QQ	NmCl			C¹
e	QQ	W-Qatal	3sgF (3plM)	Qal	C¹

Syntax, Semantics and Information Structure

Jeremiah 5.11-5.13 is a precursor to 5.14. The speaker in this section is Yahweh, and Jeremiah is the addressee. In Jeremiah 5.11, Yahweh remarks upon the utter faithlessness of the house of Israel and the house of Judah; in 5.12, he accuses them of speaking falsely by claiming that he would do nothing and in 5.13, the prophets are described as empty containers: the word is not in them.

Jeremiah 5.14a is an expanded citation formula that opens a new quotation space. The addressee appears to be Jeremiah. There are no *wayyiqtol* or *yiqtol* clauses in this section, which is highly discursive. 5.14b begins with the adverbial particle יַעַן, *because*.[35] This clause sums up the reason for the following action: *because they have spoken this word*. The *X-qotel* clause at 5.14c contains the sentence focus particle, הִנְנִי, which brings the entire sentence into focus. The *qotel* form brings a sense of immediacy to the siuation, נֹתֵן דְּבָרַי בְּפִיךָ לְאֵשׁ, *I am now making my words in your mouth a fire*. This clause is identical to the clause in 1.9, with the addition of the phrase לְאֵשׁ. The addition of the term *fire* in the description of Jeremiah's words from Yahweh demonstrates these words are not of the *building and planting variety*. The people are to become wood, and the words will devour them.

Cognitive Construction

This section contains a previously introduced space-building construction, the citation formula לָכֵן כֹּה־אָמַר יְהוָה אֱלֹהֵי צְבָאוֹת. This citation formula is unmarked so the following quotation may or may not be

35 For an exposition of this particle, see M. J. Mulder, "Die Partikel 'Yaan'," in *Syntax and Meaning: Studies in Hebrew Syntax and Biblical Exegesis*, ed. C. J. Labuschagne, OS 18 (Leiden: Brill, 1973).

prototypically dialogic. The quotation belongs to Yahweh as character, and there is no recorded response by Jeremiah. Thus, the situation is non-prototypical. Jeremiah 5.14 seems to be a hinge between 5.12-5.13 on the one hand, and 5.15-5.19 on the other.[36] Terms from the אכל√ occur both in 5.14, where a single use of the term describes the action of the fire upon the people, and in 5.19, where four occurences of the term describe the action of the invaders upon the house of Israel. Thus, situations that include this term set up a distant parallelism between 5.14 and 5.19.[37]

Jeremiah 5.14-5.19 includes several instances of the containment schema. Jeremiah's mouth is full of fiery words, in contrast to the prophets mentioned in 5.13, who themselves are empty of words. The unidentified nation in Jeremiah 5.16-5.19 is so successful in warfare that אשפתו כקבר פתוח, *their quiver is like an open tomb*. The results of the invasion are devastating: the foreign nation shall systematically empty the land of sustenance, people, animals, plants, and will destroy the fortified cities. The promise of destruction by the sword follows the four-fold repetition of terms derived from the אכל√. Not only will the destruction include the un-planting of the society as described in the previous example, but it will include un-building as well.

2.   Jeremiah 6.1-6.30: Image Schemata and Cognitive Metaphor

Jeremiah 6.30 is replete with poetry that is structured by image schemata and cognitive metaphor. This section will examine several sets of examples taken from Jeremiah 6.1-30. The first set of examples is taken from taken from Jeremiah 6.1-6.15. These verses are also text-type Q, with a limited amount of embedding. Several image schemata and conceptual metaphors structure Jeremiah 6.1-6.7: the centre-periphery and path schemata at 6.1; the SOCIETY IS A PLANT metaphor at 6.2; the force schema and the PEOPLE ARE ANIMALS metaphor at 6.3 and THE CITY IS A PERSON metaphor at 6.6. Two important conceptual metaphors structure Jeremiah 6.8-6.12: the SOCIETY IS A PLANT metaphor at 6.9 and ANGER IS A BOILING LIQUID metaphor at 6.11. An example of visual scanning opens Jeremiah 6.16-6.21. These examples are representative rather than comprehensive.

---

36   Commentators are not in agreement regarding the division of the larger section. For McKane, the verse belongs in 5.12-5.14, while Lundbom includes it in 5.14-5.19. Lundbom, *Jeremiah 1-20*; McKane, *A Critical and Exegetical Commentary on Jeremiah*.

37   Berlin, *Dynamics*, xx.

a.   Jeremiah 6.1-6.7 Clause Layout and Analysis

Clause Layout	JER
הָעִזוּ בְּנֵי בִנְיָמִן מִקֶּרֶב יְרוּשָׁלַם	6.1a
וּבִתְקוֹעַ תִּקְעוּ שׁוֹפָר	b
וְעַל־בֵּית הַכֶּרֶם שְׂאוּ מַשְׂאֵת	c
כִּי רָעָה נִשְׁקְפָה מִצָּפוֹן וְשֶׁבֶר גָּדוֹל	d
הַנָּוָה וְהַמְעֻנָּגָה דָּמִיתִי בַת־צִיּוֹן	6.2a
אֵלֶיהָ יָבֹאוּ רֹעִים וְעֶדְרֵיהֶם	6.3a
תָּקְעוּ עָלֶיהָ אֹהָלִים סָבִיב	b
רָעוּ אִישׁ אֶת־יָדוֹ	c
קַדְּשׁוּ עָלֶיהָ מִלְחָמָה	6.4a
קוּמוּ וְנַעֲלֶה בַצָּהֳרָיִם	b
אוֹי לָנוּ כִּי־פָנָה הַיּוֹם	c
כִּי יִנָּטוּ צִלְלֵי־עָרֶב	d
קוּמוּ	6.5a
וְנַעֲלֶה בַלָּיְלָה	b
וְנַשְׁחִיתָה אַרְמְנוֹתֶיהָ	c
כִּי כֹה אָמַר יְהוָה צְבָאוֹת	6.6a
כִּרְתוּ עֵצָה	b
וְשִׁפְכוּ עַל־יְרוּשָׁלַם סֹלְלָה	c
הִיא הָעִיר הָפְקַד	d
כֻּלָּהּ עֹשֶׁק בְּקִרְבָּהּ	e

JER	Type	Clause Tag	PNG	Stem/	MSC
6.1a	Q	Impv	plM	Hiphil	C²
b	Q	W-X-Impv	plM	Qal	
c	Q	W-X-Impv	plM	Qal	
d	Q	X-Qatal	3sgF	Niphal	
6.2a	Q	X-W-Qatal	1s	Qal	C¹
6.3a	Q	X-Yiqtol	3plM	Qal	
b	Q	Qatal	3pl	Qal	
c	Q	Qatal	3pl	Qal	
6.4a	Q	Impv	plM	Piel	C⁴
b	Q	Impv/ Cohortative	plM 1pl	Qal Qal	
c	Q	X-Qatal	3sgM	Qal	
d	Q	X-Yiqtol	3plM	Niphal	
6.5a	Q	Impv	plM	Qal	
b	Q	W-Cohortative	1pl	Qal	
c	Q	W-Cohortative	1pl	Hiphil	
6.6a	Q	X-Qatal	3sgM	Qal	SB C²
b	QQ	Impv	plM	Qal	C¹
c	QQ	W-Impv	plM	Qal	
d	QQ	X-Qatal	3sgM	Hoph	
e	QQ	NmCl			

Syntax, Semantics, Information Structure and Cognitive Construction

In this section, four verses contribute to cognitive structuring: Jeremiah 6.1; 6.2; 6.3; and 6.6. Jeremiah 6.1 is structured by the centre-periphery image schema. In a string of three plM imperatives the addressees are instructed to flee for safety, to blow a trumpet and to raise a signal. The centre-periphery schema is indicated by the complex preposition מִקֶּרֶב, *from the midst* (of Jerusalem). Jerusalem also provides the end-point for the path schema, as indicated by the phrase מִצָּפוֹן, *from the north*, which indicates the beginning point from which evil will come.[38] Word order for Jeremiah 6.1a is unmarked. However, 6.1b-c exhibit marked word order, due to the fronting of the locative terms וּבִתְקוֹעַ and וְעַל־בֵּית הַכֶּרֶם. Even though these terms appear here for the first time in the discourse, it seems that they are fronted for argument focus. This, in combination with the force of the imperative verb forms, results in sentence focus: all of the information is new, and all is important for "turning the proposition into an assertion."[39]

When the term נָוָה is read as pasture, Jeremiah 6.2 provides a further example of the SOCIETY IS A PLANT conceptual metaphor.[40] Word order for this sentence is OVO. Talstra's data-base proposes that it actually consists of two phrases, an OV phrase, and a second O phrase plus an ellipsis. In either case, the focus is upon the addressees.

Jeremiah 6.3 is an instantiation of the force schema and the PEOPLE ARE ANIMALS metaphor:

אֵלֶיהָ יָבֹאוּ רֹעִים וְעֶדְרֵיהֶם   a

תָּקְעוּ עָלֶיהָ אֹהָלִים סָבִיב   b

רָעוּ אִישׁ אֶת־יָדוֹ   c

Jeremiah 6.3a is an *X-yiqtol* clause in which the X represents the fronted prepositional phrase אֵלֶיהָ, *against her*. The fronting indicates argument focus and sets up the centre-point for the centre-periphery schema. This phrase also occurs in Jeremiah 6.4a. In each case, the phrase sets up an atemporal relationship between the affected entity, *her*, and the actants in the sentence, the shepherds and their flocks. The preposition *against* indicates that a degree of force is involved. Jeremiah 6.3b contains the prepositional phrase עָלֶיהָ, again setting up an atemporal relationship between the affected entity, *her*, and the actants in the sentence. In this instance, the actants are setting up their tents, which indicate that the shepherds and their flocks are actually humans, rather than animals.

---

38   The ambiguity of the term צָפוֹן leads to difficulty from the historical-critical perspective. However, by viewing the term with the path and centre-periphery image schemata in mind, it is possible to understand how the figure plays upon the undifferentiated nature of the coming evil. Other uses of the term occur in Jeremiah at 1.13; 1.14; 1.15; 3.12; 3.18; 4.6; 6.1 and 6.22.

39   Lambrecht, *Information Structure*, xx.

40   This term is difficult, and has been interpreted as "delicately bred" or "beautiful meadow." Carroll, *Jeremiah: A Commentary*, 191.

This instance of conceptual metaphor functions as a shift on the Great Chain, with human beings protrayed as animals. In general, the image of shepherds and flocks is tranquil. However, in this instance, there is a sinister undertone, as the shepherds and flocks are now in position *against* Daughter Zion. This is realised in Jeremiah 6.4a, which presents an overt call for a holy war.[41] Again, there is reference to un-building.

Jeremiah 6.6a-e presents the city of Jerusalem as a person:

כי כה אמר יהוה צבאות	a
כרתו עצה	b
ושפכו על־ירושלם סללה	c
הִיא העיר הפקד	d
כלה עשק בקרבה	e

This section contains the unmarked citation formula כה אמר יהוה צבאות, which is preceded by the particle כי. The citation formula indicates that perspective belongs to Yahweh. The particle כי might be either anaphoric, linking the section to what precedes, or cataphoric, introducing the reason for the following section. The reference to the city as a person is the result of the term הִיא in Jeremiah 6.6d, and the sgF suffix on the term בקרבה in Jeremiah 6.6e. Further references confirm this assessment, such as the sgF references at Jeremiah 6.7.b, רעתה, *her wickedness* and 6.7c, בה, *in her*, and the vocative, ירושלם, at 6.8a. These references compress both location and society to human scale. Additionally, they create instantiation of the centre-periphery schema.

b. Jeremiah 6.9-6.11

In Jeremiah 6.9-11, two verses are important for cognitive construction: Jeremiah 6.9 and Jeremiah 6.11

---

41 According to Carroll, the theme of fleeing in Jeremiah 6.1 indicates prophetic proclamation of holy war, as does the presence of holy war terminology. Carroll, *Jeremiah: A Commentary*, 191-192. Given the present-day situation, one must be exceptionally careful when interpreting texts such as this. It would be irresponsible to draw a literal application from such passages.

Clause Layout	JER
כֹּה אָמַר יְהוָה צְבָאוֹת	6.9a
עוֹלֵל יְעוֹלְלוּ כַגֶּפֶן שְׁאֵרִית יִשְׂרָאֵל	b
הָשֵׁב יָדְךָ כְּבוֹצֵר עַל־סַלְסִלּוֹת	c

JER	Type	Clause Tag	PNG	Stem/Focus	MSC
6.9a	Q	X-Qatal	3sgM	Qal	SB C²
b	QQ	Qatol-Yiqtol	3plM	Poel	C¹
c	QQ	Impv	sgM	Hiphil	

Jeremiah 6.9: Syntax, Semantics, Information Structure and Cognitive Construction

Jeremiah 6.9 begins with an unmarked citation formula that acts as a low-level space-builder. The voice is that of the narrator, who identifies the following speaker as Yahweh. At Jeremiah 6.9b the *qatol-yiqtol* combination עוֹלֵל יְעוֹלְלוּ creates an intensifying effect even though the verbs are not imperative in form. The phrase כַגֶּפֶן, *as a vine*, in combination with the phrase שְׁאֵרִית יִשְׂרָאֵל, creates an instantiation of the SOCIETY IS A PLANT metaphor. In this case, the source domain PLANT provides rich information for understanding the target domain, SOCIETY. The entire phrase evokes frame knowledge based upon agricultural practices. This in turn provides information regarding roles: the addressees are to take the role of vineyard workers. The imperative clause at Jeremiah 6.9, הָשֵׁב יָדְךָ כְּבוֹצֵר עַל־סַלְסִלּוֹת, is slightly problematic, as it changes from the plural of the first two clauses to the singular. The instruction to *pass your hand again like a grape gatherer* indicates the force dynamics of the passage: the remnant of Israel has been harvested and now is to be gleaned. Jeremiah 6.10 indicates a shift in voice, from Yahweh to Jeremiah. While there is no overt indication that this is so, Jeremiah has been in conversation with Yahweh in the previous sections of Jeremiah 1.1-6.30.

וְ‫אֵת חֲמַת יְהוָה‬ מָלֵאתִי	6.11a
נִלְאֵיתִי הָכִיל	b
‫שְׁפֹךְ‬ עַל־עוֹלָל בַּחוּץ	c
וְעַל סוֹד בַּחוּרִים יַחְדָּו	d
כִּי־גַם־אִישׁ עִם־אִשָּׁה יִלָּכֵדוּ	e
זָקֵן עִם־מְלֵא יָמִים	f

6.11a	Q	W-X-Qatal	1sg	Qal	C²
b	Q	Qatal Qetol	1sg	Niphal Hiphil	C¹
c	Q	Impv	sgM	Qal	
d	Q	Ellip			
e	Q	X-Yiqtol	3plM	Niphal	
f	Q	Ellip			

Jeremiah 6.11: Syntax, Semantics, Information Structure and Cognitive Construction

Jeremiah 6.11a, ‫ואת חמת יהוה מלאתי‬, is an example of OV order, with the object entity, ‫חמת יהוה‬, fronted for argument focus. Because the voice in this section is that of the complex speaker, and because the reference is in the first person, it appears that the perspective in this phrase belongs to Jeremiah. This is a prime example of the ANGER IS A HOT LIQUID IN A CONTAINER metaphor. Jeremiah's body is the container, but the boiling liquid is the anger of Yahweh. In response to Jeremiah's complaint that he is weary of holding it in, of maintaining control over this potentially dangerous emotion, Yahweh instructs him to pour it out. The boiling pot overturns upon all of the inhabitants of the land. There is no turning back as the judgement of Yahweh is decanted upon his people. Yet, as Jeremiah 6.13-6.18 demonstrates, Yahweh is not capricious in his judgement. The people themselves, from the greatest to the least, are equally guilty in their unfaithfulness, which exonerates Yahweh.

c.   Jeremiah 6.16 Clause Layout and Analysis

Clause Layout	JER
כֹּה אָמַר יְהוָה	6.16a
עִמְדוּ עַל־דְּרָכִים	b
וּרְאוּ	c
וְשַׁאֲלוּ לִנְתִבוֹת עוֹלָם	d
אֵי־זֶה דֶרֶךְ הַטּוֹב וּלְכוּ־בָהּ	e
וּמִצְאוּ מַרְגּוֹעַ לְנַפְשְׁכֶם	f
וַיֹּאמְרוּ	g
לֹא נֵלֵךְ	h

JER	Type	Clause Tag	PNG	Stem/Focus	MSC
6.16a	Q	X-Qatal	3sgM	Qal	SB C²
b	QQ	Impv	plM	Qal	C¹
c	QQ	W-Impv	plM	Qal	
d	QQ	W-Impv	plM	Qal	
e	QQ	X-W-Impv	plM	Qal	
f	QQ	W-Impv	plM	Qal	
g	QN	Wayyiqyol-0	3plM	Qal	
h	QNQ	X-Yiqtol	1pl	Qal	

Syntax, Semantics, Information Structure and Cognitive Construction

Jeremiah 6.16 contains a final example of the centre-periphery image schema. This verse begins with the unmarked citation formula,

כֹּה אָמַר יְהֹוָה, which assigns voice to the complex speaker and perspective to Yahweh. The following series of pIM imperative forms instructs the addressees to *stand at the crossroads*, to *look* and to *ask for the ancient paths*. This series of instructions evokes the centre-periphery image schema, with the addressees at the centre. They are to engage in a virtual visual scan of the conceptual environment in order to find and choose the good way. Even though the addressees are able to envision the good way, they refuse to walk in it.

d. Jeremiah 6.27-6.30 Clause Layout and Analysis:
The Refiner

Clause Layout	JER
בָּחוֹן נְתַתִּיךָ בְעַמִּי מִבְצָר	6.27a
וְתֵדַע	b
וּבָחַנְתָּ אֶת־דַּרְכָּם	c
כֻּלָּם סָרֵי סוֹרְרִים	6.28a
הֹלְכֵי רָכִיל נְחֹשֶׁת וּבַרְזֶל	b
וּבַרְזֶל כֻּלָּם מַשְׁחִיתִים הֵמָּה	c
נָחַר מַפֻּחַ	6.29a
*מֵאִשְׁתַּם **מֵאֵשׁ **תַּם עֹפָרֶת	b
לַשָּׁוְא צָרַף צָרוֹף	c
וְרָעִים לֹא נִתָּקוּ	d
כֶּסֶף נִמְאָס	6.30a
קָרְאוּ לָהֶם	b
כִּי־מָאַס יְהֹוָה בָּהֶם	c

JER	Type	Clause Tag	PNG	Stem/ Focus	MSC
6.27a	Q	X-Qatal	1sg	Qal	C¹
b	Q	W-Yiqtol	2sgM	Qal	
c	Q	W-Qatal	2sgM	Qal	
6.28a	Q	Qotel Qotel	plM PlM	Qal	
b	Q	Qotel	plM	Qal	
c	Q	Qotel	plM	Hiphil	
6.29a	Q	Qatal	3sgM	Niphal	
b	Q	X-Qatal	3sgM	Qal	
c	Q	X-Qatal Qatol	3sgM	Qal	
d	Q	W-X-n-Qatal	3pl	Qal	
6.30a	Q	X-Qotel	sgM	Niphal	
b	Q	Qatal	3pl	Qal	
c	Q	X-Qatal	3sM	Qal	

Jeremiah 6.27-6.30 introduces frame knowledge from the area of metallurgy. According to Fauconnier, a mental space will often be organised by a conceptual frame. Elements in a frame may include scales, force dynamics, image schemas and vital relations such as change, identity, time, space, analogy, disanalogy and uniqueness, among others.[42] The shift to the metallurgical frame reintroduces the naturally occuring elements in relation to Jeremiah, who at 1.18 was declared to be an iron pillar and a bronze wall. In this case, Jeremiah is identified as an assayer of metal.

---

42   Fauconnier and Turner, *The Way We Think*, 93ff.

Syntax, Semantics and Information Structure

Jeremiah 6.27-6.30 is quotation, with no embedding. Jeremiah 6.27a contains the fronted term בָּחוֹן, *assayer*. Since this is the first time the term is used, fronting occurs for topicalisation rather than for argument focus or emphasis. The verbal forms in this section consist of various *qatal, yiqtol* and participle forms.

Cognitive Construction

The inclusion of metallurgical frame knowledge in Jeremiah 6.27 is significant for two reasons. First, the speech participants are Jeremiah and YHWH, as was the case in 1.1-2.1. The people are referred to in the third person plural. This representation of the situation mutes the once active voice of the third interlocutor, Jerusalem. Secondly, the imagery drawn from metallurgy demonstrates the presence of an underlying use of the Great Chain metaphor. Society, who until this point had been demoted only to human level in the animacy hierarchy, has been demoted to a natural physical thing. The individuals are now compared to valuable but inanimate bronze, iron and silver. The addressees are now unable to participate in the conversation. They have become the subject of an overheard conversation.

The Contribution of Frames, Image Schemata and Conceptual Metaphor

In this chapter, several smaller examples of MT Jeremiah have been examined using the TD approach. The analysis demonstrates that frames, image schemata and conceptual metaphor regularly structure the smaller examples. Space-builders are present, but function at a lower level than the metapragmatic speech frames in the first two chapters of Jeremiah.

a.   Image Schemata

Four types of image schemata are prevalent within Jeremiah 1.1-6.30. The centre-periphery schema is used to structure physical and metaphorical space; the path schema is an instantiation of scale; the container metaphor structures situations on the basis of containment, being in or out, being full or empty, and by the content of the container; and the force schema is evoked for understanding dynamicity in situations. While other schemata are no doubt present in this text, these four predominate.

The following chart summarises instances of the four schemata:

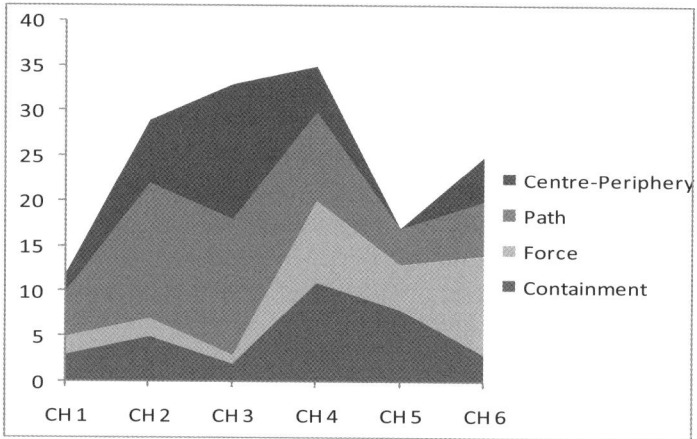

Figure 6.3   Summary of Image Schemata in Jeremiah 1.1-6.30

This chart provides an overview of four conceptual patterns that occur within the text. A few observations are pertinent to the discussion. The path schema occurs with great regularity and peaks in chapter 3. This is due to the extended discussion in Jeremiah 3.6-3.10, which some think is a redactional insertion. The centre-periphery schema is also prevalent, and also peaks in chapter 3 for the same reason. In chapter 3, Yahweh is the centre point in 11 out of 14 occurrences in the section as a whole. The containment schema peaks in chapter 4, due in part to the repeated use of the terms Judah and Jerusalem. Not surprisingly, the force schema exhibits an upward trend, particularly in chapters 4 and 6, where references to incursion and judgement appear more and more frequently. While exegesis is not a matter of statistics, the distribution of these image schemata is useful for gaining a global perspective of the text, which may be tested through more detailed exegetical methods. For a more detailed view of the data, see the chart at the end of the chapter.

b. Conceptual Metaphor

Conceptual metaphor plays a large role in establishing literary meta-phor. Yet, conceptual metaphor also occurs in other types of text as well, such as in speech frames shared by Jeremiah and Yahweh, which play on the Great Chain metaphor. Two conceptual metaphors are par-ticularly prevalent throughout Jeremiah 1.1-6.30. The SOCIETY IS A PER-SON and SOCIETY IS A PLANT metaphors provide the conceptual basis for understanding the relationship between the divine and his people, as mediated by the very human figure of Jeremiah. The SOCIETY AS A PER-SON metaphor occurs 12 times in Jeremiah 4.1-6.30: at 4.1; 4.14; 4.17; 4.18; 4.30; 4.31; 5.12; 6.2; 6.6; 6.9; 6.11; and 6.22. The SOCIETY IS A PLANT METAPHOR occurs at 5.10 and 6.9. This section also includes the PEOPLE ARE ANIMALS metaphor at 5.6 and 5.8.

These conceptual metaphors provide covert unity throughout the text and encourage the formation of literary metaphors that describe the state of the people and the manner in which their worship patterns affect their relationship with the divine. The state of these abstract sys-tems is scoped to human scale through the use of conceptual metaphor for the purposes of reasoning and persuasion. Information in Jeremiah 4.1-6.30 is presented from the perspective of the characters in the text: aspects of the reader's perception and cognition are conditioned by those of the observing characters. In this way, prophetic text com-presses aspects of the relationship between society and the divine to human scale, making it more understandable and accessible to the reader. The descriptions of de-creation, un-planting, un-building and de-centring, the destruction coming from the north, and the anger of YHWH indicate a society that has reflected upon dreadful circums-tances in an effort to reconcile the faithfulness of God with great socio-political and religious upheaval.

This chapter has described the manner in which the originators of MT Jeremiah used language to talk about what might have been, what happened, what might have happened and what should have hap-pened, using the full range of BH clause structures. [43] The variety of BH space-building terms expanded due to the addition of the extraposed construction. While syntax and semantics provide the basis for the ap-proach used in this volume, Jeremiah 4.1-6.30 clearly demonstrates that even the most competently arranged computer database is not yet ca-pable of performing the types of complex conceptual blending proces-ses that occur nearly effortlessly within the human mind.

---

43   Fauconnier and Sweetser, *Spaces, Worlds, and Grammar*, 9.

c.   A Summary of abstract complex system Metaphors and Image Schemata in Jeremiah 1.1-6.30

In the following chart, overlapping instantiations of conceptual metaphor and image schemata are shaded.

SOCIETY IS A PERSON, SOCIETY IS A PLANT					
containment		*force*		*path*	*centre-periphery*
		1.1			
		1.9			
		1.13	1.13	1.13	
				1.14	
					1.15
			1.19		
2.2 Bride/F				2.2	
	2.3 First Fruits/M				
				2.4	
		2.6		2.6	
		2.7		2.7	
				2.10	
		2.13			
2.14 Israel/M					
2.16 You/F					
				2.18	
				2.18	
2.20 Unfaithful/F					
	2.21 Vine/F	2.21			
2.22 Wash self/F					
				2.23	
				2.25?	
2.26 Thief/M					
				2.27	
				2.28	
			2.29		
			2.29		

SOCIETY IS A PERSON, SOCIETY IS A PLANT				
containment	force		path	centre-periphery
2.33 Unfaithful/F				
			3.1	
			3.1	
3.1 Unfaithful/F				
3.6-3.11			3.6	
Faithless Israel/F			3.6	
Faithless Judah/F			3.6	
			3.8	
Faithless Is/M			3.12	
			3.13	
			3.14	
			3.14	
	3.19			
3.20 Faithless/F			3.20	
			3.21	
			3.22	
	3.24			
4.1 Israel/M			4.1	4.1
			4.1	4.1
	4.3			
	4.5	4.5	4.5	
	4.7		4.7	
	4.9	4.9		
	4.11	4.11	4.11	
		4.13		
4.14 Jerusalem/F		4.14		4.14
4.17 Her/F			4.17	4.17
4.18 Your Heart/F		4.18	4.18	4.18
4.19 My heart			4.19	4.19
	4.23		4.23	
	4.24		4.24	
	4.25		4.25	

SOCIETY IS A PERSON, SOCIETY IS A PLANT					
containment		force		path	centre-periphery
		4.26		4.26	
		4.27			
4.30 O, desolate/F					
4.31 Daughter Zion					
		5.1		5.1	5.1
			5.3	5.3	
			5.6		
	5.10 Vine/F	5.10		5.10	
		5.14	5.14		
				5.15	
		5.16			
		5.17			
		5.20x2			
		5.22			
			6.1	6.1	6.1
6.2 Daughter Zion	pasture				
			6.4		
			6.5		
6.6 Jerusalem/F			6.6		6.6
6.9 Israel/M	6.9 Vine/F			6.9	
6.11 Anger=Heat		6.11	6.11		
		6.12	6.12		
				6.16	6.16
6.22 Daughter Zion			6.22	6.22	
			6.23		
			6.26		
		6.27			

7. Conclusions

In response to the difficulties presented by BH prophetic text, this volume has proposed a TD approach. This approach is text-centred, panchronic and integrative. Since text is a form of human communication, insight into the cognitive processes involved in human communication offer points of connection between the originators and readers of the text. Cognitive linguistics, cognitive grammar, and cognitive science inform the TD approach. Conceptual blending acts as the integrative principle for this approach.

Chapter 1: Text Dynamics: An Integrative Approach

This chapter contains a discussion of recent linguistic, literary and technological approaches to BH Text. The TD analysis of Jeremiah 1.1-6.30 incorporates findings from these studies (see chapters 4-6). The theoretical shift that underlies the movement from sentence level methodology to discourse level methodology is important for the holistic TD approach. However, the methodological shift engendered by computerised text processing is of immediate concern for text analyst, translator, and exegete alike.

TD theory and methodology address the multi-genred and highly discursive nature of BH prophetic text. The primary contribution of the TD approach is the re-conceptualisation of the relationship between originator, text and reader (see figure 1.3). The re-conceptualisation is experientially oriented, as it is based upon visual perception. The re-conceptualisation requires a suspension of judgement regarding the time line and it this conceptual shift allows for a principled analysis of the links between originator and reader.

The diagram in Figure 1.3 demonstrates that grammar, context and culture create partial links between originator and reader. Because humans possess similar neural networks, embodied experience provides an important analogical connection between originator and reader. The TD approach seeks to highlight this connection by including recent research in the area of cognitive science. Conceptual blending theory models aspects of neural co-activation, or in the words of Gilles Fauconnier *the way we think*. For this reason, this volume proposes a shift from the conduit metaphor for human communication to a network model in which interlocutors create a shared cognitive network during the communication process. Since reading text is a mediated form of communication, this volume proposes that originator and reader also participate in creating a shared cognitive network.

Secondly, in order to exhaust the information in the text, the four-fold TD procedure includes a synchronic syntax and semantics analysis, an analysis of the information structure categories of topic and focus, an analysis of cognitive structuring in the text and a discussion of the conceptual blending process used for incorporating extra-textual information (see chapter 1, section B.3). A discussion of the layer feature utilised by many computer programmes contributes to understanding the integrative nature of conceptual blending.

Chapter 2: The Sentence and Beyond

Chapter 2, section A comprises a full explanation of the TD theory and methodology, utilising Jeremiah 3.6-3.11 as a sample text. Section A.1 contains a description of the re-conceptualisation of the relationship between author, text and reader. Subjectivity and objectivity are important to the discussion, as the re-conceptualisation includes a re-alignment of the originator's position. In traditional approaches, the originator is often the object of study, whereas in this model the originator and reader appear together in the subjective position. This re-alignment clarifies the nature of the embodied connection between originator and reader. Section A.2 acknowledges the complexity of the reading process, in which the syntax, semantics and pragmatics of the text combine with extra-textual background knowledge of the world by the seemingly effortless conceptual blending process. The text acts as a *layered blending template* for this process, in which the layers accrue and contribute to a shared conceptual network. Section A.3 provides a full explanation of the network model, which is based upon MST. This theory describes the emergent, multi-dimensional nature of the shared cognitive network, in which mental spaces are opened, structured and linked at the cognitive level, and how the spaces are structured by frames, schemata, and cognitive models. Section A.4 explores how image schemata structure mental spaces by activating background knowledge of the world.

Chapter 2, section B discusses prophetic text and perspective. Perspective is a linguistic construal operation that originates from embodied human experience. This section explains how viewpoint, deixis, and perspective and non-spatial domains affect the construal of prophetic text.

Chapter 2, section C uses Jeremiah 3.6-3.11 as a sample text for a trial run of the TD approach. The main contribution of this section is the introduction the ascendant, recursive TD clause analysis. The discussion also addresses some complexities of clause linkage, and elaborates upon Schneider's differentiation between narrative and discursive text. Research in the area of language typology and universals provides insights into clause linkage that is useful for cross-linguistic research and for understanding the connections between the clauses in the TD analysis.

This chapter elaborates upon the information structure categories of topic and focus, which are integral to the TD approach. MST is also important for the TD approach, and this chapter describes cognitive structuring in Jeremiah 3.6-3.11 by explaining how speech frames open and structure mental spaces. The chapter also provides a preliminary example of how the TD analysis accounts for the recursive blending process involved in reading BH prophetic text.

Chapter 3: Traditional and Cognitive Approaches to BH Grammar

The re-conceptualisation diagram in Figure 1.3 demonstrates that grammar is a significant link between the originator and reader of text. For the originators and readers of BH text, the study of grammar creates and strengthens this connection. Since TD is a cognitive approach, a cognitive approach to BH grammar is desirable. While creating an entire cognitive grammar of BH is beyond the scope of this volume, an initial abbreviated foray into the subject is necessary.

Chapter 3 presents three grammatical theories that explore the connection between syntax and grammatical constructions. Role and Reference Grammar acts as a link between traditional grammar and cognitive grammar. This is due to the RRG assessment of verb-specific semantic roles, which is an assessment that depends upon both syntax and semantics. As its name implies, cognitive grammar explains the cognitive aspects of language processing, such as the relationship between grammar and perception created by the use of the figure-ground distinction in grammatical description. Finally, there is a short introduction to construction grammar.

Chapter 3 describes cognitive approaches to BH terms of perception and cognition. This section describes the RRG assessment of verb-specific semantic roles, thematic relations and semantic macro-roles, such as actor and undergoer, and their relationship to grammatical roles such as subject and object. The section also details the features of prototypical situations and gives an initial assessment of perception and cognition terms in Jeremiah 1.1-6.30.

This section contains a discussion of the BH verbal system. The section consists of an overview, definitions of terms, an examination of the tense versus aspect debate and a proposal for mapping the syntax-semantics interface. The following section introduces cognitive additions to the discussion of space and time in BH text. This includes a description of a cognitive metaphor for time, the TIME IS MOTION metaphor and applies it to the BH verb. The discussion of aspect is elaborated upon by utilising the TIME IS SPACE conceptual metaphor. Finally, the TIME IS SPACE metaphor is brought to bear upon the BH Verb. The TIME IS SPACE metaphor contributes to the discussion of the inherent properties of matter and a sentence-level understanding of BH aspect. A discussion of the inherent properties of matter and BH discourse structure follows.

Chapter 3, section E introduces a discussion of the *binyan* system. Traditional categories provide the basis for an analysis of the conceptual blending operation involved in various grammatical constructions. Chapter 3 outlines the basic categories for cognitive grammar and the BH verb, and provides a starting-point for further research into cognitive grammar and BH.

Chapter 4: Cognitive Structuring in Jeremiah 1.1-6.30

Chapters 4 through 6 contain a full TD analysis of Jeremiah 1.1-6.30. To organise the chapters for this analysis, the text is divided into three sections based upon text-level shifts in text-type. (Section A, Jeremiah 1.1-3.25; Section B, Jeremiah 4.1-4.31 and Section C, Jeremiah 5.1-6.30) Chapters 4 and 5 cover section A, while chapter 6 covers sections B and C. In each chapter a series of diagrams models the viewing arrangement of each section and the emergent cognitive network evident in the text as a whole. Special attention is given to perspective-inducing terms and constructions.

Chapter 4, section A examines the role of Jeremiah 1.1-1.3 in establishing text-level perspective. The narrator's perspective in Jeremiah 1.1-1.3 construes the ground, or base space, for the text-level communication event. Cognitive construction in this section is the result of a series of construct and prepositional phrases that delimit the spatio-temporal boundaries of the reported communication event. These grammatical features indicate that the *containment schema* is used to structure the mental spaces construction, as they evoke the TIME IS A CONTAINER conceptual metaphor.

This chapter discusses space-building terms that occur within Jeremiah 1.4-2.3. Perspective in this section shifts to Jeremiah as first person speaker, which opens a series of embedded mental spaces. The section demonstrates that BH text-deictic terms open primary level spaces, such as the speech domains in Jeremiah 1.4, 1.11, 1.13, and 2.1. Verbs of communication open secondary level speech domains, and verbs of perception and cognition open spaces based upon knowledge, belief and attitude. Various levels of embedding occur, and are modelled in the series of diagrams.

Another key component of this chapter is the introduction of the relationship between conceptual metaphor and literary metaphor, utilising Jeremiah 1.13 as an example. Conceptual metaphor, which is a product of human experience, is not identical to literary metaphor. However, literary metaphor is often an instantiation of conceptual metaphor. (This discussion resumes in chapter 5 section B.)

Cognitive construction in chapter 4 occurs at several levels. Jeremiah 1.1-1.3 forms the base-space for the cognitive network. Jeremiah 1.4-2.1 contains primary level sub-spaces, or speech domains, and secondary level embedded spaces based upon perception and cognition. The LORD is presented as speech-act participant 1, and Jeremiah is presented as speech-act participant 2, setting up a relationship that is important for the following sections of text.

Chapter 5: Cognitive Structuring in Jeremiah 2.1-3.35

Chapter 5 continues the discussion of cognitive structuring in Jeremiah 1.1-6.30 with an examination of the fourth speech domain. Once again, there is a shift in perspective (see Figure 5.2). In this section, Jerusalem emerges as speech-act participant 3, while Jeremiah and the LORD conjoin as a complex speaker – a speaker with one voice, but two perspectives (based upon their respective deictic centres).

Chapter 5 describes the shift in perspective that governs Jeremiah 2.1-3.2. The originator assigns perspective to the various characters in this section. The conceptual scoping that occurs in Jeremiah 1.1-2.2 contributes to achieving human scale, which is a foundational principle in conceptual blending theory This principle helps to explain how the relationship between the disproportionate characters is reconciled by portraying them as human-scale speech act participants. A full TD analysis of Jeremiah 2.1-2.3, including syntax, semantics and information structure, cognitive construction and conceptual metaphor occurs in this section. The difference between literary metaphor and conceptual metaphor is addressed utilising Jeremiah 2.2-2.3 as a sample text.

This leads into a discussion of conceptual metaphor. Chapter 5, section B.5 introduces the addressees and the problem of identity. (This discussion resumes in section G)

Chapter 5 also presents examples of virtual visual scanning in Jeremiah 2.4-2.9 and 2.10. The first example illustrates scoping *from* human scale and the important role of counterfactuals, demonstrating the role of MST in modelling human reasoning. The second example includes an explanation of the path and force image schemata. Chapter 5 proposes a solution to the problem of identity utilising Jeremiah 3.6-3.11/12 as a sample text. The proposed solution highlights the interaction between primary level citation formulae and embedded text, based on cognitive linking of discourse referents. This is useful for modelling the interrelationship between various text originators, such as author and redactor. Additionally, chapter 5 describes space building in poetic text by examining Jeremiah 3.19-3.20. This section concentrates upon verbs of speaking and their cognitive extension by discussing the function of the term אמר, *to speak.*

Chapter 6: Cognitive Structuring in Jeremiah 4.1-6.30

Chapter 6 describes the shift in text-type that occurs in Jeremiah 4.1-6.30, where the text is predominately discursive rather than narrative. Significantly, discursive text differs from narrative text in that it often features first and second person references that draw the reader into the text. This section is a continuation of the fourth speech domain.

Chapter 6, section A uses examples drawn from Jeremiah 4.1-4.31 to explore the relationship between discursive text and perspective. In Jeremiah 4.1-4.2, voice belongs to the complex speaker and perspective is assigned to the LORD. This is a conditional space structured by the path, centre-periphery and containment schemata. In Jeremiah 4.11-4.18 (4.19-4.21), voice belongs to the complex speaker, but at times it is difficult to distinguish whose perspective is being expressed. The centre-periphery schema structures this section. In Jeremiah 4.23-4.26, voice belongs to the complex speaker and perspective is assigned to Jeremiah. This section describes de-creation, un-planting and un-building that occur due to the Lord's response to the unfaithfulness of the people. This section is an instantiation of the ANGER IS A HOT FLUID IN AN ENCLOSED CONTAINER conceptual metaphor.

Chapter 6, section B explains the relationship between embedded quotation and perspective using examples from Jeremiah 5.1-5.14. The embedded quotation spaces are the most deeply nested and draw the reader more fully into the situation at hand. Image schemata and cognitive metaphors proliferate in these examples. The path, centre-periphery, containment and force schemata structure Jeremiah 5.1-5.14. Additionally, the PEOPLE ARE ANIMALS, SOCIAL ORGANISATIONS ARE PLANTS, and ANGER IS A BOILING LIQUID conceptual metaphors structure the examples. This is also the case for the examples drawn from Jeremiah 6.1-6.15. However, a knowledge frame from the area of metallurgy structures Jeremiah 6.27-6.30. These examples highlight the contribution of frames, image schemata and conceptual metaphor to the cognitive network in Jeremiah 5.1-6.30. The chapter concludes with Figure 6.3, a chart that summarises the containment, force, path, and centre-periphery schemata in Jeremiah 1.1-6.30 and a summary of ABSTRACT COMPLEX SYSTEMS METAPHORS and image schemata that appears at the end of the chapter.

Conclusions

The TD approach contributes to the understanding of BH prophetic text in several ways. First, by re-conceptualising the relationship between originator, text and reader it is possible to re-analyse the links between originator and reader. The analogical connection between embodied humans is particularly compelling, as illustrated by the presence of image schemata, frames and cognitive models within the text. By examining the text in light of MST, it is possible to model the cognitive construction underlying the text. Since space building terms and constructions indicate both primary and embedded mental spaces, it is possible to model the various spaces using figure-ground diagrams. Conceptual scoping to (and from) human scale helps to explain the discrepancies between primary speech-act participants within the text – ontologically speaking, the Lord, Jeremiah, and the city of Jerusalem are very different things. However, when the three appear as human-scale speech-act participants, cognitive reorientation allows for a more comprehensive understanding for their interrelationship.

Cognitive linguistics and cognitive grammar are relatively new fields, and discoveries in the field of cognitive science are ongoing, thus opening new avenues of research for the field of biblical studies, particularly in the areas of grammar, linguistics, and conceptual blending. It is hoped that the TD analysis of Jeremiah 1.1-6.30 presented in this volume will open the door a bit wider, allowing further evaluation of the strengths and weaknesses of the cognitive approach to BH text.

Bibliography

Abma, R. *Bonds of Love: Methodic Studies of Prophetic Texts with Marriage Imagery (Isaiah 50: 1-3 and 54:1-10, Hosea 1-3, Jeremiah 2-3)*. Studia Semitica Neerlandica; 40. Assen: Van Gorcum, 1999.

Aejmelaeus, Anneli. "Function and Interpretation of 'Ki' in Biblical Hebrew." *JBL* 105 (1986): 193-209.

Albertz, Rainer. "Jer. 2-6 und die Frühzeitverkündigung Jeremias." *ZAW* 94 (1982): 20-47.

Alter, Robert and Frank Kermode. *The Literary Guide to the Bible*. Cambridge, Mass: Belknap Press of Harvard University Press, 1987.

Andersen, Francis I. *The Hebrew Verbless Clause in the Pentateuch*. JBLMS 14. Nashville: Published for the Society of Biblical Literature by Abingdon Press, 1970.

Arnold, Bill T. and John H. Choi. *A Guide to Biblical Hebrew Syntax*. Cambridge: CUP, 2003.

Bache, Carl. "Aspect and Aktionsart: Towards a Semantic Distinction." *JL* 18 (1982): 57-72.

Bailenson, Jeremy N., Andrew C. Beall and Jim Blascovich. *Gaze and Task Performance in Shared Virtual Environments*. 2002. Accessed. Available from http://www.stanford.edu/~bailenso/papers/VCA%20Gaze.pdf.

Barton, John. *Reading the Old Testament: Method in Biblical Study*. London: Darton Longman & Todd, 1984.

Batistella, Edwin L. *The Logic of Markedness*. New York: OUP, 1996.

Bergen, Robert D. *Biblical Hebrew and Discourse Linguistics*. Dallas: Summer Institute of Linguistics, 1994.

Berlin, Adele. *Poetics and Interpretation of Biblical Narrative*. Bible and Literature Series, 9. Sheffield: Almond Press, 1983.

_____. *The Dynamics of Biblical Parallelism*. Bloomington, Ind: Indiana University Press, 1985.

Bhat, D. N. *The Prominence of Tense, Aspect, and Mood*. Amsterdam: John Benjamins, 1999.

Biddle, Mark. "A Redaction History of Jeremiah 2:1 - 4:2." Doctoral Thesis, University of Zürich 1988, Theologischer Verlag, 1989.

_____. *Polyphony and Symphony in Prophetic Literature: Rereading Jeremiah 7-20.* Macon: Macon University Press, 1996.

Binnick, Robert I. *Time and the Verb: A Guide to Tense and Aspect.* New York and Oxford: OUP, 1991.

_____. *Project on Annotated Bibliography of Contemporary Research in Tense, Grammatical Aspect, Aktionsart, and Related Areas.* 2002. Accessed. Available: http://www.utsc.utoronto.ca/~binnick/TENSE.

Blokland, A. T. den exter. *In Search of Text Syntax: Towards a Syntactic Text-Segmentation Model for Biblical Hebrew.* Amsterdam: VU Press, 1995.

Bodine, Walter Ray. *Linguistics and Biblical Hebrew.* Winona Lake, Ind: Eisenbrauns, 1992.

_____. *Discourse Analysis of Biblical Literature: What It Is and What It Offers.* Semeia Studies. Atlanta: Scholars Press, 1995.

Borowski, Oded. *Daily Life in Biblical Times.* Leiden: Brill, 2003.

Brisard, Frank. *Grounding: The Epistemic Footing of Deixis and Reference.* Cognitive Linguistics Research; 21. Berlin: M. de Gruyter, 2002.

Brockelmann, C. "Die 'Tempora' des Semitischen." *ZP* 3 (1951): 10-154.

Bühler, Karl. "The Deictic Field of Language and Deictic Words." In *Speech, Place, and Action: Studies in Deixis and Related Topics*, eds. R. J. Jarvella and W. Klein, 9-30. Chichester: John Wiley and Sons, 1982.

Bussman, Hadumon. *Routledge Dictionary of Language and Linguistics.* London: Routledge, 1996.

Buth, Randall. "Topic and Focus in Hebrew Poetry: Psalm 51." In *Language in Context: Essays for Robert E. Longacre*, eds. Shin Ja Joo Hwang and William R. Merrifield, 83-96. Arlington: Summer Institute of Linguistics and the University of Texas at Arlington, 1992.

_____. "Word Order in the Verbless Clause: A Functional Approach." In *The Verbless Clause in Biblical Hebrew: Linguistic Approaches*, ed. Cynthia L. Miller, 79-108. Winona Lake, Indiana: Eisenbrauns, 1999.

Bybee, Joan L., Revere Perkins and William Pagliuca. *The Evolution of Grammar: Tense, Aspect, and Modality in the Languages of the World.* Chicago: UCP, 1994.

Carroll, Lewis and Hugh Haughton. *Alice's Adventures in Wonderland.* Centenary ed. Penguin Classics. London: Penguin, 1998.

Carroll, Robert P. *Jeremiah: A Commentary.* Old Testament Library. Philadelphia: Westminster, 1986.

Cloete, Walter Theophilus Woldemar. *Versification and Syntax in Jeremiah 2-25: Syntactical Constraints in Hebrew Colometry.* Atlanta, Ga: Scholars Press, 1989.

Collins, John J. *The Bible after Babel.* Grand Rapids, Michigan: Eerdmans, 2005.

Collins, Terence. *Line-Forms in Hebrew Poetry: A Grammatical Approach to the Stylistic Study of the Hebrew Prophets.* Studia Pohl. Series Maior; 7. Rome: Biblical Institute Press, 1978.

Comrie, Bernard. *Aspect: An Introduction to the Study of Verbal Aspect and Related Problems.* Cambridge Textbooks in Linguistics. Cambridge: Cambridge University Press, 1976.

_____. *Tense.* Cambridge Textbooks in Linguistics. Cambridge: CUP, 1985.

Cook, John A. "The Hebrew Verb: A Grammaticalization Approach." *ZAH* 14 (2001): 117-144.

_____. "The Use of *Wayyiqtol* in Hebrew Poetry." *SBL, Atlanta* (2003).

Cotterell, Peter and Max Turner. *Linguistics and Biblical Interpretation.* London: SPCK, 1989.

Croft, William and D. A. Cruse. *Cognitive Linguistics.* Cambridge Textbooks in Linguistics. Cambridge: Cambridge University Press, 2004.

Cruse, D. A. *Pragmatics.* Oxford: OUP, 2000.

Damasio, Antonio R. *Descartes' Error.* New York: HarperCollins, 2000.

De Beaugrande, Robert and Wolfgang U. Dressler. *Introduction to Text Linguistics.* Longman Linguistics Library 26. London: Longman, 1981.

de Regt, Lenart J. "Domains and Subdomains in Biblical Hebrew." In *Narrative and Comment: Contributions to Discourse Grammar and Biblical Hebrew,* ed. Eep Talstra, 147-161. Amsterdam: Societas Hebraica Amstelodamensis, 1995.

_____. "Macrosyntactic Functions of Nominal Clauses Referring to Participants." In *The Verbless Clause in Biblical Hebrew,* ed. Cynthia L. Miller, 273-296. Winona Lake, Ind: Eisenbrauns, 1999.

Diamond, A. R. and K. M. O'Connor. "Unfaithful Passions: Coding Women Coding Men in Jeremiah 2 - 3 (4.2)." In *Troubling Jeremiah,* eds. A. R. Diamond, K. M. O'Connor, L. Stulman and *SBL.* Composition of the Book of Jeremiah Group, 123-145. Sheffield: Sheffield Academic Press, 1999.

Dobbs-Allsop, F. W. "Biblical Hebrew Statives and Situation Aspect." *JSS* XLV (2000): 21-52.

Douglas, Mary. *Purity and Danger: An Analysis of Concepts of Pollution and Taboo.* London: Routledge, 2003.

Doyle, Brian. *The Apocalypse of Isaiah Metaphorically Speaking: A Study of the Use, Function, and Significance of Metaphors in Isaiah 24-27.* Leuven: Peeters, 2000.

Driver, S. R. and W. Randall Garr. *A Treatise on the Use of the Tenses in Hebrew and Some Other Syntactical Questions.* Grand Rapids, Mich.: William B. Eerdmans, 1998.

Ehlich, Konrad. *Verwendungen der Deixis Beim Sprachlichen Handeln: Linguistisch-Philologische Untersuchungen Zum Hebräischen Deiktischen System.* Frankfurt am Main and Las Vegas: P. Lang, 1979.

_____. "Anaphora and Deixis: Same, Similar, or Different?" In *Speech, Place, and Action,* eds. R. J. Jarvella and Wolfgang Klein, 315-338. Chichester: Wiley, 1982.

Ellinger, K. "Der Sinn des Hebräischen Wortes 'SFY'." *ZAW* 83 (1971): 317-329.

Emerton, J. A. "Samuel Rolles Driver, 1846-1914." In *A Century of British Orientalists 1902-2001,* ed. C. E. Bosworth, 122-138. Oxford: OUP, 2001.

Ewald, Heinrich. *Syntax of the Hebrew Language of the Old Testament.* Translated by James Kennedy. Edinburgh: T and T Clark, 1881. Reprint, Georgias Press, 2005.

Exum, J. Cheryl and David J. A. Clines. *The New Literary Criticism and the Hebrew Bible.* JSOT Sup 143. Sheffield: JSOT Press, 1993.

Fauconnier, Gilles. *Mental Spaces: Aspects of Meaning Construction in Natural Language.* Cambridge: CUP, 1994.

_____. *Mappings in Thought and Language.* Cambridge: Cambridge University Press, 1997.

Fauconnier, Gilles and Eve Sweetser. *Spaces, Worlds, and Grammar.* Chicago: UCP, 1996.

Fauconnier, Gilles and Mark Turner. "Blending as a Central Process of Grammar." In *Conceptual Structure, Discourse and Language,* ed. Adele E. Goldberg, 113-129. Stanford: CSLI, 1996.

_____. *The Way We Think: Conceptual Blending and the Mind's Hidden Complexities.* New York: Basic Books, 2002.

Finch, Geoffrey. *Linguistic Terms and Concepts.* Basingstoke: Palgrave Macmillan, 2000.

Floor, Sebastiaan J. "From Information Structure, Topic, and Focus, to Theme in Biblical Hebrew Narrative." DLit, University of Stellenbosch, 2004.

Follingstad, Carl Martin. "Deictic Viewpoint in Biblical Hebrew Text: A Syntagmatic and Paradigmatic Analysis of the Particle Ki." Doctoral Thesis, Vrije Universiteit te Amsterdam 2001, SIL International, 2001.

Freeman, Margaret H. "Cognitive Mapping in Literary Analysis." *Style* (2002): 1-13.

Geller, Stephen A. *Parallelism in Early Biblical Poetry.* Harvard Semitic Monographs, No. 20. Missoula: Scholars Press, 1979.

_____. "The Dynamics of Parallel Verse." *HTR* 75 (1982): 35-56.

_____. "Through Windows and Mirrors into the Hebrew Bible: History, Literature and Language in the Study of Text." In *A Sense of Text*, 3-40. Winona Lake, Ind: Eisenbrauns, 1982.

Gelston, A. "Some Notes on Second Isaiah." *VT* 21 (1971): 518-521.

Gernsbacher, Morton Ann, and David Hargreaves. "The Privilege of Primacy." In *Pragmatics of Word Order Flexibility*, ed. Doris L. Payne, 83-116. Amsterdam: John Benjamins, 1992.

Gillingham, S. E. *One Bible, Many Voices: Different Approaches to Biblical Studies.* London: SPCK, 1998.

Givon, T. "Beyond Foreground and Background." In *Coherence and Grounding in Discourse*, ed. R. S. Tomlin, 175-188. Amsterdam: John Benjamins, 1987.

Goldfajn, Tal. *Word Order and Time in Biblical Hebrew Narrative.* Oxford Theological Monographs. Oxford: Oxford University Press, 1998.

Greenstein, Edward L. "How Does Parallelism Mean?" In *A Sense of Text*, 41-70. Winona Lake: Eisenbrauns, 1982.

Grimes, Joseph Evans. *The Thread of Discourse.* Janua Linguarum. Series Minor; 207. The Hague: Mouton, 1975.

Grüneberg, Keith. *Abraham, Blessing and the Nations: A Philological and Exegetical Study of Genesis 12:3 in Its Narrative Context.* Berlin: Walter de Gruyter, 2003.

Hardmeier, C. and E. Talstra. "Sprachgestalt und Sinngehalt: Wege Zu Neuen Instrumenten der Computergestützen Textwahrnehmung." *ZAW* 101 (1989): 408-428.

Haspelmath, M., E. König, W. Oesterreicher and W. Raible, eds. *Language Typology and Language Universals: An International Handbook.* Berlin: Walter de Gruyter, 2001.

Hatav, Galia. *The Semantics of Aspect and Modality: Evidence from English and Biblical Hebrew.* Vol. 34 SLCS. Amsterdam: John Benjamins, 1997.

_____. "(Free) Direct Discourse in Biblical Hebrew." *HS* 41 (2000): 7-30.

Hayes, E. R. "Hearing Jeremiah: Perception and Cognition in Jeremiah 1.1-2.2." *HS* 45 (2004): 99-119.

_____. "The Influence of Ezekiel 37 on 2 Corinthians 6:14-7:1." In *The Book of Ezekiel and Its Influence*, 115-118, eds. Johannes Tromp and H. J. De Jonge, Hampshire: Ashgate, 2007.

Heimerdinger, Jean-Marc. *Topic, Focus and Foreground in Ancient Hebrew Narratives.* JSOT Sup 295. Sheffield: Sheffield Academic Press, 1999.

Hendel, Ronald S. "In the Margins of the Hebrew Verbal System: Situation, Tense, Aspect, Mood." *ZAH* 9 (1996): 152-181.

Hoftjitzer, J. "The History of the Database Project." In *Studies in Ancient Hebrew Semantics*, 65-85. Louvain: Peeters, 1985.

Holladay, William L. "Prototype and Copies: A New Approach to the Poetry-Prose Problem in the Book of Jeremiah." *JBL* 79: 351-367.

_____. *The Root Šûbh in the Old Testament with Particular Reference to Its Usages in Covenantal Contexts.* Leiden: E.J. Brill, 1958.

Holmstedt, Robert. "Review of *Focus Structure in Biblical Hebrew: A Study of Word Order and Information Structure*, by Katsuomi Shimasaki." *HS* 44 (2003): 203-215.

_____. "Word Order and Information Structure in Proverbs." *SBL, Atlanta* (2003): 1-20.

Hopper, Paul. "Aspect and Foregrounding in Discourse." In *Syntax and Semantics 12: Discourse and Syntax*, ed. T. Givon, 213-241. New York: Academic Press, 1979.

Horie, Kaoru. "Complement Clauses." In *Language Typology and Language Universals*, ed. M. Haspelmath, 2, 979-993. Berlin: Walter de Gruyter, 2001.

Hospers, J. H. "Some Remarks About the So-Called Imperative Use of the Infinitive Absolute (Infinitivus Pro Imperativo) in Classical Hebrew." In *Studies in Hebrew and Aramaic Syntax*, ed. K. Jongeling, 99-102. Leiden: Brill, 1991.

Jackendoff, Ray. *Languages of the Mind.* Cambridge, Mass: MIT, 1999.

Jakobson, Roman. "Linguistics and Poetics." In *Style and Language*, ed. Thomas Albert Sebeok, 350-377. Bloomington, 1960.

_____. "Poetry of Grammar and Grammar of Poetry." *Lingua* 21 (1968): 597-609.

Janda, Laura A. "A Metaphor in Search of a Source Domain." *CL* 15 (2004): 471-572.

Jenni, Ernst. *Das Hebräische Pi'el: Syntaktisch-Semasiologische Untersuchung Einer Verbalform Im Alten Testament.* Zürich: EVZ-Verlag, 1968.

_____. *Die Hebräischen Präpositionen.* Vol. 1. Stuttgart: Kohlhammer, 1992.

Johnson, Mark. *The Body in the Mind: The Bodily Basis of Meaning, Imagination, and Reason.* Chicago: UCP, 1987.

Jongeling, K. "On the VSO Character of Hebrew ." In *Studies in Hebrew and Aramaic Syntax*, ed. K. Jongeling, 103-111. Leiden: Brill, 1991.

Joosten, Jan. "The Indicative System of the Biblical Hebrew Verb and Its Literary Exploitation." In *Narrative Syntax and the Hebrew Bible*, ed. E. J. Van Wolde, 51-71. Leiden: Brill, 1997.

Joüon, Paul. "Le Sens Du Mot Hébreu 'SFY'." *Journal Asiatique* (1906): 137-142.

Kamp, Albert. "World Building in Job 28." In *Job 28: Cognition in Context*, ed. Ellen Van Wolde, 307-319. Leiden: Brill, 2003.

Kessler, Martin. *Reading the Book of Jeremiah: A Search for Coherence.* Winona Lake, Ind: Eisenbrauns, 2004.

Khan, Geoffrey. *Studies in Semitic Syntax.* London Oriental Series; V. 38. Oxford: OUP, 1988.

King, Philip J. *Jeremiah: An Archeological Companion.* Louisville, Kentucky: Westminster/John Knox Press, 1993.

König, Ekkehard. *The Meaning of Focus Particles: A Comparative Perspective.* Theoretical Linguistics. London: Routledge, 1991.

Kövecses, Zoltan. *Metaphor: A Practical Introduction.* New York and Oxford: OUP, 2002.

Kroeze, J. H. A. "Semantic Relations in Construct Phrases of Biblical Hebrew: A Functional Approach." *ZAH* 11 (1998): 27-41.

Kugel, James L. *The Idea of Biblical Poetry: Parallelism and Its History.* New Haven: Yale University Press, 1981.

Labuschagne, C. J. "The Particles 'hn' and 'hinneh'." In *Syntax and Meaning: Studies in Hebrew Syntax and Biblical Exegesis*, ed. C. J. Labuschagne, 1-14. Leiden: Brill, 1973.

Lakoff, George. *Women, Fire, and Dangerous Things: What Categories Reveal About the Human Mind.* Chicago: UCP, 1987.

Lakoff, George and Mark Johnson. *Metaphors We Live By.* Chicago; London: University of Chicago Press, 1980.

_____. *Philosophy in the Flesh: The Embodied Mind and Its Challenge to Western Thought.* New York: Basic Books, 1999.

Lambrecht, Knud. *Information Structure and Sentence Form: Topic, Focus, and the Mental Representations of Discourse Referents.* Cambridge Studies in Linguistics; 71. Cambridge: Cambridge University Press, 1994.

Langacker, Ronald W. *Foundations of Cognitive Grammar.* Bloomington, Ind: Indiana University Linguistics Club, 1983.

_____. *Foundations of Cognitive Grammar.* Vol. 1. Stanford: SUP, 1987.

_____. *Grammar and Conceptualization.* Cognitive Linguistics Research; 14. Berlin: Mouton de Gruyter, 1999.

_____. "Discourse in Cognitive Grammar." *CL* 12 (2001): 143-188.

_____. *Concept, Image, and Symbol: The Cognitive Basis of Grammar.* 2nd ed. Cognitive Linguistics Research; 1. Berlin: Mouton de Gruyter, 2002.

_____. "Deixis and Subjectivity." In *Grounding: The Epistemic Footing of Deixis and Reference,* ed. Frank Brisard, 21, 1-28. Berlin: Mouton de Gruyter, 2002.

_____. "Context, Cognition, and Semantics: A Unified Dynamic Approach." In *Job 28: Cognition in Context,* ed. E. J. van Wolde, 179-230. Leiden: Brill, 2003.

Lee, David. *Cognitive Linguistics: An Introduction.* Melbourne and Oxford: OUP, 2001.

Lehmann, Christian. "Towards a Typology of Clause Linkage." In *Clause Combining in Grammar and Discourse,* eds. John Haiman and Sandra Thompson, 181-225. Amsterdam: Benjamins, 1988.

Levin, Christoph. *Die Verheissung Des Neuen Bundes : In Ihrem Theologiegeschichtlichen Zusammenhang Ausgelegt.* Göttingen: Vandenhoeck & Ruprecht, 1985.
_____. "The 'Word of Yahweh': A Theological Concept in the Book of Jeremiah." In *Prophets, Prophecy, and Prophetic Texts in Second Temple Judaism,* ed. Michael H. Floyd and Robert D. Haak, 43-62. New York: T&T Clark, 2006.

Levinsohn, Stephen H. "Review of *Topic, Focus and Foreground in Ancient Hebrew Narratives,* by Jean-Marc Heimerdinger." *JTTL* 14 (2002): 126-147.

Lode, Lars. "Postverbal Word Order in Biblical Hebrew: Structure and Function." *Semitics* 9 (1984): 113-164.

_____. "Postverbal Word Order in Biblical Hebrew: Structure and Function: Part Two." *Semitics* 10 (1985): 24-39.

Longacre, Robert E. "The Paragraph as a Grammatical Unit." In *Syntax and Semantics,* ed. Talmy Givon, 12, 115-134. New York: Academic Press, 1979.

_____. *The Grammar of Discourse.* Topics in Language and Linguistics. New York: Plenum, 1983.

_____. *Joseph: A Story of Divine Providence: A Text Theoretical and Textlinguistic Analysis of Genesis 37 and 39-48.* Winona Lake, Ind: Eisenbrauns, 1989.

_____. "Building for the Worship of God: Exodus 25:1-30." In *Discourse Analysis of Biblical Literature: What It Is and What It Offers,* ed. W. R. Bodine, 21-49. Atlanta: Scholars Press, 1995.

Louw, J. P. and E. A. Nida. *Greek-English Lexicon of the New Testament: Based on Semantic Domains*. 2 vols. 2nd ed. New York: United Bible Societies, 1989.

Lowery, Kirk. "Theoretical Foundations of Hebrew Discourse Grammar." In *Discourse Analysis of Biblical Literature: What It Is and What It Offers*, ed. Walter Ray Bodine, 103-130. Atlanta: Scholar's Press, 1995.

————. "Relative Definiteness and the Verbless Clause." In *The Verbless Clause in Biblical Hebrew: Linguistic Approaches*, ed. Cynthia L. Miller, 251-272. Winona Lake, Indiana: Eisenbrauns, 1999.

Lowth, Robert. *Lectures on the Sacred Poetry of the Hebrews*. Vol. 1. London: Routledge/Thoemmes Press, 1995.

Lundbom, Jack R. *Jeremiah 1-20*. Vol. 21A, The Anchor Bible. New York: Doubleday, 1999.

Maimonides, Moses. *The Guide for the Perplexed*. Translated by M. Friedlander. New York: Barnes and Noble, 2004.

Mandelblit, Nili. "The Grammatical Marking of Conceptual Integration: From Syntax to Morphology." *CL* 11 (2000): 197-291.

Marmaridou, Sophia S. A. *Pragmatic Meaning and Cognition*. Pragmatics & Beyond; New Ser. 72. Amsterdam: J. Benjamins Publishing, 2000.

McFall, Leslie. *The Enigma of the Hebrew Verbal System: Solutions from Ewald to the Present Day*. Historic Texts and Interpreters in Biblical Scholarship; 2. Sheffield South Yorkshire: Almond Press, 1982.

McKane, William. "Relations between Poetry and Prose in the Book of Jeremiah with Special Reference to Jeremiah iii 6-11 and xii 14-17." In *A Prophet to the Nations: Essays in Jeremiah Studies*, eds. L. G. Perdue and B. W. Kovacs, 269-284. Winona Lake, Ind: Eisenbrauns, 1984.

————. *A Critical and Exegetical Commentary on Jeremiah*. 2 vols. International Critical Commentary on the Holy Scriptures of the Old and New Testaments. Edinburgh: T. & T. Clark, 1986.

Meier, Samuel A. *Speaking of Speaking: Marking Direct Discourse in the Hebrew Bible*. VT Sup 46. Leiden: Brill, 1992.

Mettinger, Tryggve N. D. "The Hebrew Verb System: A Survey of Recent Research." *ASTI* 9 (1974): 64-84.

Mey, Jacob L. *Pragmatics: An Introduction*. 2d ed. Oxford: Blackwell, 2001.

Michel, Diethelm. *Tempora und Satzstellung in Den Psalmen*. Abhandlungen zur Evangelischen Theologie. Bonn: H. Bouvier, 1960.

Miller, Cynthia L. *The Verbless Clause in Biblical Hebrew: Linguistic Approaches*. Linguistic Studies in Ancient West Semitic. Winona Lake, Ind.: Eisenbrauns, 1999.

_____. *The Representation of Speech in Biblical Hebrew Narrative: A Linguistic Analysis*. HSM. Winona Lake, Ind: Eisenbrauns, 2003.

Moor, J. C. de, ed. *Synchronic or Diachronic? A Debate on Method in Old Testament Exegesis*, Oudtestamentische Studiën 34. Leiden: Brill, 1995.

Moor, Johannes Cornelis de and Wilfred G. E. Watson. *Verse in Ancient near Eastern Prose*. Alter Orient und Altes Testament. Neukirchen-Vluyn: Verlag Butzon und Bercker, 1993.

Morgan, Robert and John Barton. *Biblical Interpretation*. Oxford: Oxford University Press, 1988.

Mulder, M. J. "Die Partikel 'Yaan'." In *Syntax and Meaning: Studies in Hebrew Syntax and Biblical Exegesis*, ed. C. J. Labuschagne, 50-83. Leiden: Brill, 1973.

Muraoka, T. *Studies in Ancient Hebrew Semantics*. Vol. 4 Abr-Nahrain. Supplement Series. Louvain: Peeters Press, 1995.

_____. *Semantics of Ancient Hebrew*. Vol. 6 Abr-Nahrain. Supplement Series. Louvain: Peeters, 1998.

Naudé, J. A. "The Transitions of Biblical Hebrew." In *Biblical Hebrew: Studies in Chronology and Typology*, ed. Ian Young, 369, 189-214. Sheffield: T & T Clark, 2003.

Niccacci, Alviero. "Essential Hebrew Syntax." In *Narrative and Comment*, ed. Eep Talstra, 111-125. Amsterdam: Societas Hebraica Amstelodamensis, 1995.

Niccacci, Alviero and W. G. E. Watson. *The Syntax of the Verb in Classical Hebrew Prose*. JSOT Sup 86. Sheffield: JSOT Press, 1990.

Noonan, Michel. "Complementation." In *Language Typology and Syntactic Description*, ed. Timothy Schopen, 42-140. Cambridge: CUP, 1985.

Nuyts, Jan. *Epistemic Modality, Language, and Conceptualization*. Amsterdam: John Benjamins, 2001.

O'Connor, K. M. "Jeremiah." In *The Oxford Bible Commentary*, eds. John Barton and John Muddiman, 487-528. Oxford: OUP, 2000.

O'Connor, Michael Patrick. *Hebrew Verse Structure*. Winona Lake, Ind: Eisenbrauns, 1980.

Pardee, Dennis. *Ugaritic and Hebrew Poetic Parallelism: A Trial Cut ('Nt I and Proverbs 2)*. VT Sup 39. Leiden: Brill, 1988.

Pardee, Dennis and S. David Sperling. *Handbook of Ancient Hebrew Letters: A Study Edition.* Sources for Biblical Study; No.15. Chico, Calif: Scholars Press, 1982.

Parunak, H. Van Dyke. "Some Discourse Functions of Prophetic Quotation Formulas in Jeremiah." In *Biblical Hebrew and Discourse Linguistics*, ed. Robert D. Bergen, 489-518. Dallas: SIL, 1994.

Petofi, J. S. "Studies in Text Grammar." In *Studies in Text Grammar*, eds. J. S. Petofi and H. Rieser. Dordrecht: Reidel, 1973.

Postma, Ferenc, E. Talstra and M. Vervenne. *Exodus: Materials in Automatic Text Processing.* Instrumenta Biblica 1. Amsterdam: VU Boekhandl, 1983.

Premper, Waldfried. "Universals of the Linguistic Representation of Situations." In *Language Typology and Language Universals: An International Handbook*, ed. M. Haspelmath, 1, 477-495. Berlin: Walter de Gruyter, 2001.

Primus, Beatrice. "Word Order Typology." In *Language Typology and Language Universals: An International Handbook*, ed. M. Haspelmath, 2, 855-898. Berlin: Walter de Gruyter, 2001.

Pröbstle, Martin. "Deixis and the Linear Ordering of Sentence Constituents." *SBL, Denver* (2001): 1-16.

Raible, W. "Language Universals and Language Typology." In *Language Typology and Language Universals: An International Handbook*, eds. M. Haspelmath, E. Konig, W. Oesterreicher and W. Raible, 1, 1-24. Berlin: Walter de Gruyter, 2001.

_____. "Linking Clauses." In *Language Typology and Language Universals: An International Handbook*, eds. M. Haspelmath, E. Konig, W. Oesterreicher and W. Raible, 1, 590-617. Berlin: Walter de Gruyter, 2001.

Rieser, C. F. "On the Development of Text Grammar." In *Current Trends in Text Linguistics*, ed. Wolfgang U. Dressler, 13. Berlin: de Gruyter, 1978.

Rosenbaum, Michael. *Word-Order Variation in Isaiah 40-55: A Functional Perspective.* Assen: Van Gorcum, 1997.

Rubba, Jo. "Alternate Grounds in the Interpretation of Deictic Expressions." In *Spaces, Worlds, and Grammar*, eds. G. Fauconnier and E. Sweetser, 227-261. Chicago: UCP, 1996.

Sailhamer, John. "A Database Approach to the Analysis of Hebrew Narrative." *MAARAV* 5-6 (1990): 319-335.

Sanders, José and Gisela Redeker. "Perspective and the Representation of Speech and Thought in Narrative Discourse." In *Spaces, Worlds, and Grammar*, eds. G. Fauconnier and E. Sweetser, 290-317. Chicago: UCP, 1996.

Sasse, H. J. "Scales between Nouniness and Verbiness." In *Language Typology and Language Universals: An International Handbook,* ed. M. Haspelmath, 1, 495-509. Berlin: Walter de Gruyter, 2001.

Sayers, Dorothy L. *The Unpleasantness at the Bellona Club.* London: Ernest Benn, 1928. Reprint, London: Stoddard and Houghton, 1968.

Schmid, Konrad. *Buchgestalten Des Jeremiabuches: Untersuchungen Zur Redaktions- Und Rezeptionsgeschichte Von Jer 30-33 Im Kontext Des Buches* Wissenschaftliche Monographien Zum Alten Und Neuen Testament. Neukirchen-Vluyn: Neukirchener Verlag, 1996.

Schneider, Wolfgang. *Grammatik des biblischen Hebräisch.* Munich: Claudius Verlag, 1993.

Schweizer, Harald. *Metaphorische Grammatik: Wege zur Integration von Grammatik und Textinterpretation in der Exegese.* St. Ottilien: EOS-Verlag, 1981.

Shimasaki, Katsuomi. *Focus Structure in Biblical Hebrew: A Study of Word Order and Information Structure.* Bethesda, Md: CDL Press, 2002.

Siebsma, P. A. *The Function of the Niph'al in Biblical Hebrew.* Assen, NL: Van Gorcum, 1991.

Spawn, Kevin. *'As It Is Written' and Other Citation Formulae in the Old Testament.* BZAW, ed. Otto Kaiser. Berlin: Walter de Gruyter, 2002.

Steen, Gerard J. "Identifying Metaphor in Language." *Style* (2002): 1-19.

Sternberg, Meir. *The Poetics of Biblical Narrative: Ideological Literature and the Drama of Reading.* Indiana Studies in Biblical Literature. Bloomington, Ind: Indiana University Press, 1987.

Stulman, Louis. *Order Amid Chaos: Jeremiah as Symbolic Tapestry.* Biblical Seminar; 57. Sheffield: Sheffield Academic Press, 1998.

Sweeney, Marvin. "Structure and Redaction in Jeremiah 2-6." In *Troubling Jeremiah,* ed. A. R. Diamond, 200-218. Sheffield: SAP, 1999.

Talstra, E. "Text Grammar and the Hebrew Bible I: Elements of a Theory." *BO* 35 (1978): 169-174.

_____. "Text Grammar and the Hebrew Bible II: Syntax and Semantics." *BO* 39 (1982): 26-38.

_____. "Toward a Distributional Definition of Clauses in Biblical Hebrew." *ETL* 63 (1987): 95-105.

_____. *Computer Assisted Analysis of Biblical Texts: Papers Read at the Workshop on the Occasion of the Tenth Anniversary of the Werkgroep Informatica, Faculty of Theology, Vrije Universiteit, Amsterdam, November 5-6, 1987.* Applicatio 7. Amsterdam: Free University Press, 1989.

_____. "Text Grammar and Biblical Hebrew: The Viewpoint of Wolfgang Schneider." *JTTL* 5 (1992): 269-297.

_____. "Deuteronomy 9 and 10: Synchronic and Diachronic Observations." In *Synchronic or Diachronic: A Debate on Method in Old Testament Exegesis*, ed. J.C. de Moor, 187-210. Leiden: Brill, 1995.

_____. "A Hierarchy of Clauses in Biblical Hebrew Narrative." In *Narrative Syntax and the Hebrew Bible*, ed. E. J. van Wolde, 85-118. Leiden: Brill, 1997.

_____. "A Hierarchy of Clauses in Biblical Hebrew Narrative." In *Narrative Syntax and the Hebrew Bible*, ed. Ellen van Wolde, 85-118. Leiden: Brill, 2002.

_____. "Text Segmentation and Linguistic Levels." (2003): 1-40.

Taylor, John R. *Cognitive Grammar*. Oxford Textbooks in Linguistics. Oxford; New York: Oxford University Press, 2002.

Tov, Emmanuel. "Computer Assisted Research of the Greek and Hebrew Bible." In *Computer Assisted Analysis of Biblical Hebrew Text*, ed. E. Talstra, 87-118. Amsterdam: VU Press, 1989.

van der Merwe, C. H. J. "Recent Trends in the Description of Old Hebrew." *JNSL* 15 (1989): 217-241.

_____. "Explaining Fronting in Biblical Hebrew." *JNSL* 25 (1996): 173-186.

_____. "Reconsidering Biblical Hebrew Temporal Expressions." *ZAH* 10 (1997): 42-59.

_____. "The Elusive Biblical Term *WHYH*: A Perspective in Terms of Its Syntax, Semantics, and Pragmatics in I Samuel." *HS* 15 (1999): 83-114.

_____. "Review of *Topic, Focus and Foreground*, by Jean-Marc Heimerdinger." *Biblica* 81 (1999): 574-578.

_____. "Some Recent Trends in Biblical Hebrew Linguistics: A Few Pointers Towards a More Comprehensive Model of Language Use." *HS* 44 (2003): 7-24.

van der Merwe, C. H. J., J. A. Naudé and J. H. A. Kroeze. *A Biblical Hebrew Reference Grammar*. Sheffield: Sheffield Academic Press, 1999.

van der Merwe, C. H. J. and Eep Talstra. "Biblical Hebrew Word Order: The Interface of Information Structure and Formal Features." *ZAH* 15/16 (2001): 68-108.

van der Wal, A. J. O. "Toward a Synchronic Analysis of the Masoretic Text of the Book of Jeremiah." In *Reading the Book of Jeremiah: A Search for Coherence*, ed. Martin Kessler, 13-23. Winona Lake, Ind: Eisenbrauns, 2004.

van Leeuwen, C. "Die Partikel 'Im'." In *Syntax and Meaning: Studies in Hebrew Syntax and Biblical Exegesis*, ed. C. J. Labuschagne, 15-48. Leiden: Brill, 1973.

Van Valin, Robert D. *An Introduction to Syntax*. Cambridge: CUP, 2001.

Verheij, A. J. C. *Basisgrammatica Van Het Bijbels Hebreeuws*. Delft: Eburon, 2002.

_____. *Bits, Bytes, and Binyanim: A Quantitative Study of Verbal Lexeme Formations in the Hebrew Bible*. Orientalia Lovaniensia Analecta; 93. Leuven: Peeters: Departement Oosterse Studies, 2000.

Viberg, Åke. "Verbs of Perception." In *Language Typology and Universals: An International Handbook*, ed. M. Haspelmath, 2, 1294-1309. Berlin: Walter de Gruyter, 2001.

Wallace, Stephen. "Figure and Ground: The Interrelationship of Linguistic Categories." In *Tense-Aspect: Between Semantics and Pragmatics*, ed. Paul J. Hopper, 201-219. Amsterdam: John Benjamins, 1982.

Waltke, Bruce and M. O'Connor. *An Introduction to Biblical Hebrew Syntax*. Winona Lake, Ind: Eisenbrauns, 1990.

Watson, Wilfred G. E. *Classical Hebrew Poetry: A Guide to Its Techniques*. 2nd ed. JSOT Sup 26. Sheffield: JSOT Press, 1986.

_____. *Traditional Techniques in Classical Hebrew Verse*. JSOT Sup 170. Sheffield: Sheffield Academic Press, 1994.

Weinrich, Harald. *Tempus: Besprochene und Erzählte Welt*. 2 ed. Stuttgart: Kohlhammer, 1971.

Wendland, Ernst R. *The Discourse Analysis of Hebrew Prophetic Literature*. Vol. 40, Mellen Biblical Press Series. Lewiston, New York: Mellen Biblical Press, 1994.

Werth, Paul. "How to Build a World (in a Lot Less Than Six Days, Using Only What's in Your Head)." In *New Essays on Deixis: Discourse, Narrative, Literature*, ed. Keith Green, 49-80. Amsterdam: Rodopi, 1995.

_____. *Text Worlds: Representing Conceptual Space in Discourse*. London: Longman, 1999.

Wolde, E. J. van. "Who Guides Whom? Embeddedness and Perspective in Biblical Hebrew Narrative and in I Kings 3.16-28." *JBL* 114 (1995): 623-642.

_____. "Linguistic Motivation and Biblical Exegesis." In *Narrative Syntax and the Hebrew Bible*, ed. E. J. van Wolde, 21-50. Leiden: Brill, 1997.

_____. *Ruth and Naomi*. London: SCM Press, 1997.

_____. "The Verbless Clause and Its Textual Function." In *The Verbless Clause in Biblical Hebrew*, 321-335. Winona Lake, Ind: Eisenbrauns, 1999.

Zewi, Tamar. "Review of *Word Order and Time,* by Tal Goldfajn." *JSS* 46: 143-146.

Index of Biblical References

Index of Authors

Index of Subjects